THE SATURDAY EVENING POST

FIBER & BRAN BETTER HEALTH COOKBOOK

William Mason Brown
RASPBERRIES

THE SATURDAY EVENING POST

FIBER & BRAN BETTER HEALTH COOKBOOK

Cory SerVaas, M.D.

Charlotte Turgeon & Frederic Birmingham

THE CURTIS PUBLISHING COMPANY • INDIANAPOLIS, INDIANA

The Saturday Evening Post
Fiber & Bran Better Health Cookbook

Jean White, Managing Editor
Jack Merritt, President, Book Division
David M. Price, Production Manager
Astrid Henkels, Louise Fortson, Louis Harm, Marie Caldwell,
Lynn Troup, Geri Watson, Steve Miller, Gary Moore, Dwight Lamb, Jon Cashen

*Special thanks to Judy Weber, who tested many of the recipes
included in this collection, and to the following individuals
and institutions for their assistance: Mary Alice Butz,
Trudi Dendurent, Anne Means, Julie Moore, Alvin Robinson, and
Jan Stetina; The Bread Shop Kitchen, Earth Gardens, and Wildflower restaurants:
Elam's Milling Company, Hodgson Mill, Kansas Wheat Institute,
The Kellogg Company, Kretschmer's Wheat Germ Products,
The Rice Council, and South Dakota State University.*

Contents

Foreword

If wire-netting enclosing fruit trees has a neglected hole in it, the birds will soon discover it and the value of the netting will be to a large extent lost. It is the aim of prisoners of war to detect and make use of any weak spot in the defenses prepared to prevent their escape. In either case no elaborate reinforcement of that which is sound and reliable can compensate for a neglected weakness, an overlooked defect, an omitted necessity.

A diet designed to safeguard health is analogous to a barrier erected to safeguard the occupants of a building from invasion from without or to prevent inmates of a prison from escaping from within. Even though highly commendable, the most elaborate precautions taken to ensure an adequate intake of known nutritional requirements and to guard against noxious impurities, together with efforts to balance dietary components in correct quantities, may not be sufficient to ward off diet-related disease.

The significant word in the previous sentence is "known." Before vitamins were discovered, carefully planned diets which were assumed to be in every way adequate could in certain circumstances result in scurvy, pellagra or beri-beri. It is only relatively recently that the roles and importance of potassium and iodine have become adequately appreciated and, as a result, the supply of iodine in cooking salt in regions where iodine is deficient has done more for populations concerned than the construction of huge hospitals staffed with skilled surgeons to operate on thyroid disease.

To return to our initial analogy, it is possible to laboriously scrutinize the minutest weaknesses in the defense system and yet overlook a glaring and unnoticed defect. Current research is suggesting that this is exactly what has been happening in the realm of diet. Lone voices over several decades have been pointing unheeded fingers at fiber as a dietary requirement, but those playing the arc-lights on protein, vitamin and calorie needs, and on the disadvantageous changes in the quality of our fats and cooking oils, for the most part considered fiber as an inert, valueless and disposable component of foods and consequently tended to discard it as a virtual contaminant.

Just as the unsuspected lack of certain vitamins and minerals allowed certain diseases to emerge in communities in which these deficiencies occurred, so it now appears that a far larger hole in our dietary defenses may be represented by the man-created deficiency of fiber in our modern Western diets.

Circumstantial evidence, much of it in the form of epidemiological studies, suggests that many of our commonest diseases may be due in part to fiber-depleted diets. That these diseases are causally related to a lack of fiber must with few exceptions be considered as well-supported hypotheses which require testing before speculation can be replaced by attested fact; nevertheless, if even half of the diseases under suspicion and at present being actively investigated prove to be even partly preventable by increasing our fiber intake, the possibility of disease prevention would be enormous.

The diseases in question are not obscurities of minor significance, but some of the commonest ailments afflicting Western man. They include coronary heart disease, the commonest cause of death; diverticular disease of the colon, the commonest large-bowel disorder; appendicitis, the commonest indication for an emergency abdominal operation; colo-rectal cancer, second only to lung tumors as a cause of cancer death; varicose veins and hemorrhoids, the commonest vascular disorders; diabetes and obesity, respectively the commonest endocrine and nutritional disorders; and gallstones, the commonest indication for abdominal surgery. And finally, constipation, an almost ubiquitous complaint in Western countries.

Until recently the word "fiber" was used as a blanket term to include a variety of polysaccharides together with lignin, undigested in the human small intestine. The position has been analogous to that of vitamin B in the 1930's. Just as this is now recognized to include a group of substances with differing physiological properties, so the components of fiber are now being subdivided and the specific action of each investigated. Prevalences of the diseases listed may soon be in part related to specific components of fiber, possibly from particular plants.

With our present admittedly deficient knowledge, one thing can be said categorically: Increasing fiber intake prevents constipation by increasing the size and softness of stools passed.

Epidemiologically high prevalences of all these diseases of affluence are associated with the passage of small firm stools, whereas low prevalences are associated with large soft stools. People are prepared to go to endless lengths, usually with limited success, to alter the "milieu intérieur" of their blood to that associated with low prevalences of coronary heart disease, i.e. low cholesterol and triglyceride levels. Yet the relationship between prevalences of these Western diseases and bowel behavior is more consistent than that between heart disease and blood lipids, and the "milieu intérieur" of the bowel can be easily changed to that desired merely by adding sufficient fiber.

The critic will reply that the case is not yet proved or the mechanisms adequately understood, and will consequently advocate postponing action. In St. Mark's Gospel, chapter 44, verse 27 we read, "A man scatters seed on the land. . . . The seed sprouts and grows . . . how, he does not know." The farmer here acted on time-honored associations between seed time and harvest. Had he claimed scientific status that inhibited action until the intricacies of seed germination were intellectually grasped, he and his family would soon have starved.

This book has been written by those who fully appreciate the potential benefits of fiber-rich diets and it is presented as a practical manual to enable ordinary people to apply personally the measures which, if adopted, could go far to ward off much unnecessary illness.

As in the matter of smoking, so in the realm of diet, scientifically discovered means of minimizing disease confer no benefit until personally and practically applied. This book will serve as a bridge between theory and practice, and when a sufficient number of people have increased their fiber intake over a long enough period of time, the proverbial saying "the proof of the pudding is in the eating" may be particularly applicable.

DENIS BURKITT, M.D.

Introduction

You can have it both ways! You can enjoy frivolous dinner parties with tasty, attractive dishes every day and still avoid the pitfalls of the Westernized fiber-depleted diets so incriminated recently by many medical researchers. The recipes we bring you are designed to make it easy for you to put more fiber in your food.

My collaborators on this book won't let me preach to you about the evils of the "normal balanced diet" which many Americans complacently feel they eat.

"No one likes a reformer," admonished my husband. "Hold back," he bade me.

But I'd like to shout from the housetops—*it's hard to cure the diseases we're getting from years of wrong eating.* It's much cheaper and easier to *prevent* diseases by drastically changing our eating habits and by becoming less sedentary as a people.

This book is about cooking for better health without losing the fun of eating.

Could it be that a change in our food habits as simple as adding high-fiber bran to our diet would give protection against a whole battery of Westernized man's diseases? Hope springs eternal in the human breast and optimists always stand ready to believe. Others among us, including our most learned nutritionists, may feel immediately offended at the thought that experts could have overlooked something so basic—and be first inclined to cast doubt and disparage the whole subject.

But the history of medicine proves repeatedly that we medics have erred in the past in our reluctance to change accepted doctrine. To carefully investigate *any* new proposition with an open mind is still the best method of furthering scientific discovery, and so it was with an open mind—not too much optimism and not too much skepticism, but an "I'm from Missouri, show me" attitude—that *SatEvePost* editors embarked on a high-fiber diet fact-finding mission to South Africa to authenticate this book. The Republic of South Africa is recognized as a haven for physicians and epidemiologists wishing to compare diseases of large numbers of people who have, for their entire lives, never tasted of our Westernized refined carbohydrates, who rather have eaten their own "unsophisticated" diet containing surprisingly large quantities of unrefined carbohydrates and indigestible fiber, often in the form of coarsely ground maize, millet or other grains.

The other condition which makes South Africa an exceptionally unique area for observing diet and disease is its interface with the still-primitive tribes being treated with sophisticated medical care, brought to the hinterlands by missionaries, volunteers and the South African government. Huge native populations now have available to them the latest medical examinations and treatments. Volunteer medical specialists are dispatched into remote areas by helicopters, and some mission records are available dating back for many generations.

We wanted to interview clinicians in the hospitals, many of whom have never published any papers or done research at all, but who have treated the illnesses of primitive Africans by the thousands. We wanted to query the everyday pathologists who never publish in medical journals, but who have performed hundreds of autopsies on primitive Africans. These experienced clinicians would know whether vessels from these primitive subjects showed as much atherosclerosis (cholesterol plaques causing "hardening of the arteries") as ours.

The story we heard from involved medical personnel all over South Africa came through loud and clear. In a nutshell, appendicitis, diverticulitis, hiatal hernia, varicose veins, cancer of the colon, diabetes, myocardial infarctions, rheumatoid arthritis, obesity, gallstones, kidney stones and hemorrhoids are *far less prevalent* in the primitive *tribal* populations and become slightly *more prevalent* in populations described as *rural* where the diet habits are only slightly Westernized. In *urbanized populations* such as Soweto, a black township outside Johannesburg, where traditional "mealie meal" is scorned in favor of white bread with cola drinks, the Bantus' diseases *begin in an orderly progression to parallel* those of our own Westernized population.

No self-respecting person of scientific inclination would dare say that just because these people don't have our diseases until they eat our foods, it then follows that eating our foods gives them our diseases. However, it *is* enough to make one sit up and take notice.

And this is what the scientific community in South Africa is doing. Baboons in a large Pretoria research center are being fed a diet of whole meal dark brown bread. An exact number of their counterparts are getting white bread. Blood samples from both groups are being tested. Researchers there, branching out from the fiber thesis, point out that the magnesium in the maize is felt to be protection from kidney stones, which are almost unheard of in tribal villages where maize is the staple diet. We were shown rat kidneys filled with multitudinous stones which resulted when the rats were fed magnesium-free diets. (White populations have kidney stones ninety times more frequently than people from primitive Bantu tribes.)

No investigation of diet-correlated disease in South Africa could be undertaken without an interview with Dr. Alexander R.P. Walker of Johannesburg, a prolific contributor to the medical journals of most countries of the world. There is a relationship between the length of time food remains in the digestive tract and cancer of the colon. Short transit time is equated with less diverticular disease as well. We have Dr. Walker to thank for giving us his source for transit time markers. These are harmless capsules made of completely inert vegetable dye which colors the stool a bright red. After swallowing a capsule, the time it takes to find a red stool is one's transit time, and there are very interesting statistics to prove that long transit times are associated with cancer of the colon, diverticulitis, hemorrhoids and many other unpleasant diseases.

Through his good offices, we were able to buy a supply of the red capsules and to leave a trail of transit time participants in some of the most interesting social circles of Cape Town, Pretoria and Johannesburg. A few competitive sports, believing their fast transit times might set a new record, have sent cables and telegrams asking to be entered into the records. Bantu youngsters, however, are almost always the winners, with average times as short as eight to twelve hours. (Studies show that the average fiber intake of an African Bantu is about twenty-five grams a day, which is a far cry from the average three grams consumed by most Americans.)

Our best White African transit time has been eighteen hours, and in North America the winner has been a New York attorney who telegramed a fourteen-hour result.

Another runner-up is an alleged sixteen hours claimed by a house guest from Paris. A gourmet food editor, after a visit to Indianapolis, sent a postcard in red ink announcing, "The red messenger arrived after forty-four hours, . . ." but she protested it wasn't a fair test since subsequent travel by air to her home in New England must surely have altered her regular schedule. She demanded a retrial.

In case you're thinking this talk about transit time is too indelicate a conversation to be included in a book about food, then neither is a colostomy a very pleasant subject anywhere, especially unpleasant if it belongs to you or someone you love.

"Don't be misled just because you have a bowel movement daily," Dr. Walker cautioned us; "the train could be five days late every day." In other words, testing transit time is important. (Should you or your physician wish to order a supply of transit markers, we got ours from Saphron Laboratories, 50 Commando Road, Johannesburg and from Fred Ingram Pharmacy, 56 Kotze Street, Hillbrow, Johannesburg.)

The facts were more convincing than we had hoped. Dr. Walker's sincerity and honest dedication made everything he had published seem more relevant. He told about 100,000 black African workers having had only twenty-two cases of appendicitis when their diet had consisted of large amounts of mealie meal, legumes and vegetables, whereas 850 such operations would be expected in a corresponding group of whites on their Westernized diets.

In the tribal villages, my African host, an internist, told me patients with a "painful abdomen" are not operated on for appendicitis without being asked these questions: "Do you have any money?" "Can you write?" "Do you own a wristwatch?" If the victim answers "No" to all of the above, he is presumed not to have been subjected to our Westernized food long enough to be a candidate for appendicitis, and an appendectomy would not be undertaken.

Although as yet no one seems to know why, in Africa where whole cereal intake is high, there seems to be much less osteoporosis in the elderly than in Westernized populations. Elderly Africans have only one-tenth the number of hip fractures that our elderly Westernized diet population have, according to a researcher in Pretoria. "Studies on bone densities of elderly Africans have shown much less attrition of bone in these people than in the Westernized diet population," he reported as a result of his research.

A psychiatric nurse, trained in Dallas, and now head of the government's nurse training programs for all of the South African homelands, said tribal royalty were usually obese because they would be accustomed to having Western diet delicacies brought to them. Any tribal African patient, she said, who arrived claiming he was royalty but was not obese would be suspected by the native black medical personnel of being an impostor.

In all of the clinics and research centers we visited, we found friends of Dr. Denis Burkitt. There are everywhere those who subscribe to his theories of high-fiber diet lessening degenerative diseases—some more rigidly than others, but always his work received the highest respect and acclaim, even from his medical colleagues who might not personally underwrite every one of his theories. For example, a prominent nutritionist in Cape Town believes from a strictly pragmatic point of view that white sugar is an economically efficient food to give energy to the hungry in a continent where there are still some starving populations. He believes that if a diet contains not more than 15 percent unrefined carbohydrates, the sugar can be metabolized without doing harm.

The editors of this book are of the opinion that the world will owe Dr. Denis Burkitt more of a debt than it is presently aware, as we become increasingly conscious of both our own peril as an overcivilized community and the astonishingly simple remedy for which he has crusaded. After a distinguished career including thirty-three years as a surgeon in Africa and numerous honors for his discovery of Burkitt's lymphoma, his current field is in what the British call "geographic pathology" and what is termed "epidemiology" in this country. It is a study of diseases as they exist within groups of people, and comparisons with other contrasting groups. It is this work, with special reference to the nutrition field, which led to the following Burkitt observations on the varying diets of people in Africa and Western nations, and how this affects their health.

"Let me compare our Western way of life and that of rural Africa. The commonest cause of death among Americans is coronary heart disease: There's practically none in Africa. The commonest American abdominal operation is gallstones: There's none in Africa. The commonest emergency operation in the United States is appendicitis: There's virtually none of that in rural Africa. Last year a surgeon friend of mine in a rural African hospital said that after thirty-three years he's still waiting for his first case of appendicitis. The commonest disease of the bowel in America is diverticular disease: There's none among Africans who eat a primitive diet.

"Perhaps as many as a fifth of our population have hiatal hernia: There's none in

Africa. Obesity is a national concern in America. No African community, living traditionally, has an obesity problem. The problem of varicose veins is rare in Africa. Nearly half of our population over age fifty are affected by hemorrhoids. Not so in Africa. The same applies to cancer of the bowel, the second most common cause of cancer death after lung cancer.

"These largely Western diseases are related to diet. Race has nothing to do with it. It's the way we live and the food we eat. Look at what happens when the Japanese go to live in Hawaii. These diseases are rare in Japan but become common when the people take on the American diet in Hawaii.

"We eat more fat, not a lot more. We eat a little more protein, but what we have totally changed is the nature of our carbohydrate food. We've removed the unabsorbable roughage of fiber which we considered unnecessary because it provides few or no nutrients. We take it out of our food and give it to our livestock to keep them healthy and we are just now advocating putting donkeys' food back on the breakfast table. We remove this fiber, for instance, in the making of white flour and sugar. White flour and sugar are fiber-stripped calories. Obesity becomes a problem if you eat calories without fiber. You can live on carbohydrates and not become fat if they are unrefined carbohydrates. People in Ireland can eat potatoes and still lose weight. That's because the fiber in the diet, the roughage, the unabsorbable part, regulates the behavior of the gastrointestinal canal more than anything else.

"Nutritionally speaking, the removal of these natural fibers in our food is causing many of our common diseases. Compared to world standards, America and England are, you might say, constipated nations. Americans today pass only about 110 grams of stool whereas a village African will pass between 300 and 500 grams. An Asian is somewhere between the African and American but closer to the African. That may sound strange but we believe there's enough evidence to indicate a correlation between the amount of stool passed each day and the contracting of these Western diseases. By taking the fiber out of our food we have slowed the passage of waste through our intestines. For example, in an African village, on a high-fiber diet, 80 percent of swallowed markers will pass through the bowel in about thirty to thirty-five hours. In England, in young people, it takes three days. In older people, a fortnight! That's what I mean when I say we are a constipated nation and we need to get more natural fiber back into our food. Unfortunately, too many doctors still treat the commonest disease of the bowel, diverticular disease, by giving people food free of roughage. This complicates the problem because we are feeding people with the cause of the disease, a fiber-depleted diet.

"Coronary heart disease and diverticular disease are often associated in patients. In an article written by Dr. Hugh Trowell, a well-known British physician; Dr. Neil Painter, the world authority on diverticular disease; and myself with some knowledge of epidemiology, we argued that because coronary heart disease and diverticular disease are so closely associated they must have common causative factors. The article was published in the *American Journal of Digestive Diseases*. We believe that the removal of the unabsorbable fiber from our diets is a much more important factor in coronary heart disease than either the consumption of fats or the eating of cholesterol. If you do eat cholesterol, you don't absorb all of it if you have a high-fiber diet. And every community in the world on a high-fiber diet has a low prevalence of coronary heart disease and diverticular disease.

"I'm not the only one who feels that within the next few years, after further testing and cross-checking, fiber-depleted diets will be recognized as one of the major factors behind coronary heart disease and diverticular disease. Also gallstones. Dr. K. W. Heaton has published a book in England in which he argues that the most important single cause of gallstones in the Western world today is eating carbohydrates depleted of their fiber.

"This food fiber is comprised of heavy celluloses and lignin material, varying in different plants according to type and age. Basically, it passes through the small intestine undigested by our enzymes. A kind of natural and necessary laxative. Probably the most practical way to restore the fiber to our foods would be to replace white flour with whole-grain flour. Whole-grain bread is very coarse, very dense. Eating whole-grain bread might do as much for the health of Americans as giving up smoking, and I'm a very strong anti-smoker. Now there are some good high-fiber cereals, bran cereals. The fiber is palatable enough and easy to obtain that way. A good bran cereal for breakfast can do a lot of good. Simply bran. So I suppose the easiest thing for Americans, and a good beginning, is a breakfast of one of the good bran cereals.

"I've been asked the question often—Does stringy meat have these natural fibers? The answer is no. You see, when we talk about fiber we mean the long complicated carbohydrate molecules which are the structure of all plant material. It is the skeleton of every plant, in the wall of every cell. In primitive times man generally had eaten his starch inside this cell envelope. Now, with modern processing, we've taken it out and literally disposed of these enveloping fibers by feeding them to our horses and donkeys. It's not the way nature intended.

"Less than an ounce of bran a day will revolutionize your gastrointestinal behavior. That would be equivalent to maybe one or two dessert spoons.

"People can actually lose weight eating starches and sugar in the natural state, that is with their fibers intact. In certain parts of Ireland, for instance, where they practically live on potatoes, they don't have the history of diseases common to North Americans. They conducted an experiment involving several pairs of brothers born in western Ireland. One brother would stay in Ireland while the other came to America and records were kept because the brothers had the same genetic background. The ones in America ate fewer starches and fats but, oddly enough, had far more coronary disease and higher serum cholesterol levels. This surprised a lot of people. Dr. Trowell interpreted this as having to do with the fact that the brothers remaining in Ireland were eating 30 to 40 percent more fiber than their American counterparts because of the Irish whole meal bread and potatoes. It seems that as long as you have enough fiber in your food, whether or not you are eating the fat and the cholesterol, you virtually needn't worry much about it. The old idea that you can avoid a coronary by eating steak and salad every day just isn't true. You ought to be eating more potatoes and less steak; the salad doesn't matter. At any rate, we feel you might avoid that coronary by eating more bran, or foods within their natural fibers."

The dramatic impact of Dr. Burkitt's discoveries, when reduced to a chart, conveys an imperious message which is the basic word of this cookbook. For the facts of his observations on the correlation of certain diseases in the United States, where the natural fibers are milled out of our bread, as compared to the African areas he mentions, where these fibers are normally eaten and the disease absent or rare, see the chart at the end of this chapter.

Americans have nearly the highest rate of colon cancer in the world. It strikes about 42 out of every 100,000 American men, usually between the ages of thirty-five and sixty-four. The rate is higher in New York State, at 46 per; in

Connecticut it jumps to 52 per. Americans have 900 percent more cancer of the colon than Nigerians and 1,300 percent more than the people of Uganda. Item: The Africans eat a high-fiber diet, while our fiber intake is about the lowest of any nation in the world.

Dr. Burkitt's answer is a simple high-fiber diet. Glance for a moment, if you will, at the list of foods at the end of this chapter, and find the ones which are highest in fiber content. They could change your life.

A report released by the Senate Select Committee on Nutrition and Human Needs, titled "Dietary Goals for the United States," recommends that Americans must drastically change their eating habits if they want to live longer.

Dr. Mark Hegsted, professor of nutrition at Harvard University and one of the nutritionists who helped write the report, said: "There will undoubtedly be many people who will say we have not proven our point; we have not demonstrated that the dietary modifications we recommend will yield the dividends expected.

"The question to be asked is not why should we change our diet, but why not. What are the risks associated with eating less meat, less fat, less saturated fat, less cholesterol, less sugar, less salt and more fruits, vegetables, unsaturated fat—and cereal products—especially whole-grain cereals? There are none that can be identified and important benefits can be expected."

The recommended changes in the American diet include:

1. Increase consumption of complex carbohydrates (grain products, vegetables and fruits) to account for 55 to 60 percent of the energy (caloric) intake.

2. Reduce overall fat consumption from approximately 40 to 30 percent of energy intake.

3. Reduce saturated fat consumption to account for about 10 percent of total energy intake; and balance that with poly-unsaturated and mono-unsaturated fats, which should account for about 10 percent of energy intake each.

4. Reduce cholesterol consumption to about 300 mg. a day.

5. Reduce sugar consumption by about 40 percent to account for about 15 percent of total energy intake.

6. Reduce salt consumption by about 50 to 85 percent to approximately 3 grams a day.

In addition to leaving the salt shaker off the table, the report suggests leaving the potato chips and pretzels in the store. Specifically, the report recommends the following changes in food selection and preparation:

1. Increase consumption of fruits and vegetables and whole grains.
2. Decrease consumption of meat and increase consumption of poultry and fish.
3. Decrease consumption of foods high in fat and partially substitute poly-unsaturated fat for saturated fat.
4. Substitute nonfat milk for whole milk.
5. Decrease consumption of butterfat, eggs and other high cholesterol sources.
6. Decrease consumption of sugar and foods high in sugar content.
7. Decrease consumption of salt and foods high in salt content.

By following their recommended dietary goals, the committee contends, not only is there likely to be an increase in the life span and a decrease in illness, but there can be a "significant reduction in food costs. Savings can be achieved through reduction of and substitution of fats, sugar and expensive, fatty protein sources." In other words, beans are a cheaper (and now it would appear healthier) source of protein than marbled steak.

Dr. Hegsted believes that Americans developed their unhealthy eating habits by happenstance related to our affluence, the productivity of our farmers and the activities of our food industry. "The diet we eat today," he states, "was not planned or developed for a particular purpose."

One study quoted in the report says: "Television is the primary source of information for the American public today and TV advertisements for 'empty calorie' foods have a tremendous impact on what Americans eat. Positive nutrition education from other sources is comparatively minuscule in this country."

Our reason for writing this book is to help large numbers of people enjoy the immediate health benefits to be gained from adding bran to their diet, since this is the easiest and quickest way to remedy a lifestyle of eating which has become fiber-depleted.

After bran, we should begin to include other foods just down the scale from bran in fiber content. We have listed these major fiber-containing foods for your easy reference at the end of this chapter.

It is with great enthusiasm that *The Saturday Evening Post* editors have set about to make this the most enticing cookbook of fiber and bran recipes that has ever been assembled. No matter how effective in disease prevention the high-fiber diet will turn out to be when all the results are in, many years from now, those who have had the fun of following Charlotte Turgeon's superb and infallibly tasty recipes and Fred Birmingham's merriment will be the winners. Most of our recipes do not require more than supermarket shopping. For example, in a high-fiber kitchen, you would never be caught without a box of bran cereal on your shelf ready to be used for breakfast, for baking, for desserts, etc. Bran is one of the easiest ways to change to a high-fiber diet overnight. You'd have to eat a peck of tossed salad to give you fiber equivalent to a serving of bran cereal.

CORY SERVAAS, M.D.

FOODS HIGH IN FIBER

Fiber in grams per 100-gram serving.
One gram equals 0.035 ounces.

	Grams		Grams
Unprocessed wheat bran	9.1	Whole wheat crackers	2.4
Wheat bran cereals	7.8	Currants	2.4
Dried figs	5.6	Artichokes	2.4
Guavas	5.6	Shredded wheat cereal	2.3
Black raspberries	5.1	Pecans	2.3
Blackberries	4.1	Dates	2.3
Dried apricots	3.8	Popcorn	2.2
Sunflower seeds	3.8	Rye crackers	2.2
40% bran flakes cereal	3.6	English walnuts	2.1
Millet, cooked	3.2	Puffed wheat cereal	2.0
Brazil nuts	3.1	Peas, green	2.0
Raisin bran flakes	3.0	Parsnips	2.0
Filberts (hazelnuts)	3.0	Peanut butter	1.9
Loganberries	3.0	Black-eyed peas	1.8
Red raspberries	3.0	Bran muffins	1.8
Peanuts	2.7	Brussels sprouts	1.6
Almonds	2.6	Broccoli	1.5
Wheat germ	2.5	Dry beans, cooked	1.5
Macadamia nuts	2.5	Winter squash	1.4
Sesame seeds	2.4	Green peppers	1.4

For a longer list of foods in alphabetical order, with calorie counts as well as fiber content for each, see the chart at the end of the Reference Chapter.

PERCENTAGE OF CALORIES FROM FAT IN FOODS

Over 50%	Cream Cheese	Ground beef—regular
	Weiners	Salmon, tuna (canned in oil)
	Peanuts and peanut butter	Pork—loin and butt
	Pork lunch meats	Granola
	Most cheese and cheese spreads	
	Tongue	
50%	Eggs	
	Chicken—roasted, flesh & skin	Ice cream
	Beef—porterhouse, T-bone, round	Cream cheese sandwich
	rump, lean ground, kidney	Peanut butter sandwich
	Pork—fresh & cured ham & shoulder	
	Lamb—shoulder, rib	
	Salmon—red sockeye, canned	
40%	Whole milk	
	Beef—sirloin, arm, flank, heart	Lunch meat or
	Turkey—flesh & skin, dark meat	Cheese spread sandwich
	Lamb—leg, loin	
	Pork—heart, kidney	
	Chicken—dark meat, roasted flesh	
30%	Creamed cottage cheese	
	Beef—heel of round, pot roast	
	Liver—pork, chicken, lamb, beef	
	Fish—bass, ciscoe, oysters, salmon (pink)	
20%	Chicken—roasted, light meat broilers—no skin	
Under 20%	Fish—haddock, cod, tuna (water pack),	Skim milk cheese
	ocean perch, halibut, smelt, sole	Uncreamed cottage cheese
	Shellfish—most	Skim milk
	Porridge (cooked cereal grains)	Most breakfast cereals
	Bread	(other than Granola type)
	Most peas, beans and lentils	

Source: "NutriScore," Fremes, Sabry, 1976.

Nutritionists everywhere are recommending that fat consumption be reduced. Foods near the bottom of the chart shown here contain the lowest percentage of fat—for better health include more of these in your diet. Included in this cookbook are many recipes for using cereal grain products, dried peas and beans, low fat milk and cheeses made from skim milk. These foods, along with whole grain bread and fish, and most shellfish, are sources of protein that are not high in fat.

PREVALENCE OF NONINFECTIOUS DISEASES

CONDITION	IN THE UNITED STATES	IN AFRICA
Ischemic heart disease	Responsible for a third of all deaths	Virtually unknown. Incidence just beginning to increase slowly in large cities
Appendicitis	The most frequent of abdominal emergencies	Virtually unknown in rural areas. Incidence starting to rise in more Westernized communities
Diverticular disease	The most common disease of the colon	Almost unknown
Gallstones	Present in some 10% of the adult population	Exceedingly rare
Varicose veins	Present in over 10% of the adult population	Present in probably under 0.1% of those living in a traditional manner. Increasing with adoption of Western customs
Deep vein thrombosis and resultant pulmonary embolism	These make hospital life increasingly hazardous	Very rare
Hiatus hernia	Demonstrable in nearly half the population over the age of 50 years	Almost unknown
Hemorrhoids	Demonstrable in nearly half the population over the age of 50 years	Rare or very rare according to degree of Westernization
Cancer of the colon and rectum	Second only to lung cancer as a cause of death from neoplasms	Rare
Obesity	Nearly half the adult population is markedly overweight	Rare among those living wholly on traditional diets. Becomes common with urbanization and adoption of Western foods

The diseases listed in this chart based on Dr. Burkitt's observations are all much more common among Americans, who eat a low-fiber diet, than among Africans whose diet is high in fiber.

FOOD
FOR THOUGHT

More Than Lip Service

Knowledge indeed is a desirable, a lovely possession,
but I do not scruple to say that health is more so.
It is of little consequence to store the mind with
science if the body be permitted to become debilitated.

—*Thomas Jefferson*

With a welcoming flourish of whisk and skillet, we beg your leave at the very outset of this sturdy volume—firmly, delightedly, thoughtfully, and perhaps even a bit proudly—to pronounce that this is a Cookbook.

As such, we are therefore heir to those two prerequisites of gracious and artful cuisine which the subtle and knowing Chinese have decreed for centuries as the beckoning gifts of happy and healthy dining—*hsien* ("flavor") and *hsiang* ("aroma"), said by twentieth-century scholars Hsiang Julin and Tsuifeng Lin to be "to food what soul is to man." This secret was, alas, already commonplace in their sophisticated civilization thousands of years ago while our own benighted ancestors were still daubing themselves blue and munching bark and earthworms as they danced around trees in celebration of their advanced culture.

We say *alas* because even in our own time, while men walk on the moon, we often unblinkingly give way to mad fads distilled by gurus, food nuts and gustatory ginks via a myriad of so-called diets (not excepting that most astonishing non sequitur of them all, that of non-eating) which divert us from our proper quest toward good health, nature's highest achievement, with every imaginable and sometimes unimaginable dietary experiment, both grisly and unnatural.

To them we say NO . . . and also fiddle-faddle, tommyrot and poppycock. We are concerned here only with the health and happiness which intelligently selective dining enjoyment can bring the sometimes puzzled human being. To that end, the recipes offered here contain only natural and homey elements available to us all. The accent in their preparation has been on the *delicious*, which the sage Chinese knew all along was the signpost to the eternal verities of long and rewarding existence.

2

But let us tarry for a moment by chopping block and blender. This is a *high-fiber* cooking book.

Why?

Your health is your greatest treasure. But let us suppose that you are given a choice right now of deciding whether all of the money you make for the rest of your life were to be the real thing, or a substantial part of it counterfeit. Obviously, if you were to opt for the counterfeit, you could look forward to untold difficulties, harassment, unhappiness, and even severe penalties if everything inherent in such a decision were to back up on you suddenly or over the long run and clout you when you least expected it. No one with any sense at all would hesitate to decide for the real thing; the better course rather than counterfeit.

Yet, when it comes to food, we have—yes, *we* have—not only accepted in many ways the counterfeit, but reached out for it in a seeming lunge for self-destruction as mindless as the lemmings' suicidal rush for the deep-sea waters which ultimately engulf them.

How can this be, we may ask ourselves in all good faith, when dedication to progress is part of our way of life, most particularly when it concerns our own survival? The ways of discovery and social enlightenment, of medicine and science, of the humanities and philosophy are ours for the asking. Surely *we* have advanced beyond the Middle Ages in embracing knowledge personally more rewarding than plumbing and transportation.

The answer is, of course, yes, although not in every facet of our lives. Curiously enough, in that important category of food we have actually zigged and zagged ourselves back into a kind of dark age ignorance.

Let us look at this body of ours, this temple of the spirit, this incredible achievement of nature. And let us start out with the reflection that good health, the very rudder of our life journey, is not a right, but a job it is up to each of us to perform. There is no escape. Do it well, and live happily; do it unwell, and live—if at all—in anguish. Once more, the Chinese outdo us in terse eloquence. Lu Yu writing in *Ch'a Ching* or *The Classic of Tea,* almost a millennium before that soothing beverage became known in the West: "Born to this earth are three kinds of creatures. Some are winged and fly. Some are furred and run. Still others stretch their mouths and talk. All of them must eat and drink to survive."

The biological record of our own human race is not so glittering in our mores of eating that it entitles us to look down too patronizingly on our fellow animals. Well enough could Brillat-Savarin grump in the early nineteenth century: "Animals feed themselves, men eat; but only wise men know the art of eating. . . . The destiny of nations depends upon how they nourish themselves." But mankind had not previously, nor has since, achieved any epochal understanding of his own feeding problems. We are mighty slow even today in recognizing the significance of some life-or-death fact when it is placed before us. That is why this book came into being.

In reviewing the enemies of mankind, if we were to appoint a commission to isolate the wretches who have caused the most suffering and pain, high on its list for immediate execution—if possible, in some excruciating manner in which the "punishment suits the crime"—would be some embarrassingly familiar culprits.

In a word—ourselves.

The world has indeed progressed since the days when handicapped people were considered to be objects of hilarity, subjects for gargoyle statuary on the façades of cathedrals. It is now generally accepted that old ladies with cracked voices and a high level of irritability do not ride around on broomsticks but in taxicabs and might rather be assisted than burned at the stake. We have advanced to a state of ethnic harmony where we can at least be ashamed of the open warfare we wage upon our fellow human beings, and the excellence of our plumbing has rocketed to levels of perfection far exceeding that of our children's ability to spell.

This is progress. But what would you call a society which by pursuing a false myth of palatability and sales appeal of food packaging has wished upon itself—and mind you, this is precisely what we have done—a Pandora's box of some of the most horrible diseases known to man?

This is not to suggest that we are a nation of fools. Far from it. But we must remember that gastronomically we came from nowhere to the electronic age in 300 years. If our Indians were Stone Age people in the way they lived off the land, our first colonists were worse. They were dreamers and idealists and men of action—except when it came to feeding themselves. Some of our early colonies simply succumbed to starvation. Our Pilgrims might have been nibbling on the Plymouth Rock itself shortly after their landing had they not learned from the Indians how to live off the land of that barren coast, a life-and-death struggle which was won only after a year of agrarian struggle under Indian tutelage, a triumph we celebrate annually with a fete called Thanksgiving.

As our nation progressed from an agricultural to an industrial economy in the nineteenth century and the hunter or farmer turned in his gun or plow in exchange for the sedentary life of the factory or office worker, eating became less a matter of fueling up for prodigious physical exertions than for the mere provision of brain and nervous energy. We stopped stoking in the food for sheer "man" power, and turned more to eating for enjoyment as a thing in itself. That's when we did it to ourselves.

Not that we were not warned. There were mighty prophets of doom abroad in the land such as—to mention one who has been immortalized by the Graham cracker—a self-styled physician, clergyman and bunco artist yclept Sylvester Graham (1794-1851) who based his dietary theories equally upon Scriptural authority and his own dreams. The Reverend Graham was dead set against baker's white bread as the starvation diet of a declining nation. But since he was also dead set against drinking, unchastity, eating of meat, phrenology, condiments, tea, chicken pie and "excessive lewdness," it was only by his extraordinary and unrelenting lecturing abilities that he was able to gather true believers about him in New England, and particularly in Boston, where there have always been easy pickings for cultists with a bent for religious fundamentalism, or its opposite, atheism.

This Boston of which the *Northampton Hampshire Gazette* editorialized: "The Bostonians are a dyspeptic variety of the human family, and the man who professes to cure or prevent that direful disease takes them on the weakest side. The surest way of approaching most men is said to be through a dinner, but you must secure a Bostonian by telling him how to digest one. No doubt Mr. Graham can do it scientifically."

Perhaps we should not be too cavalier in our attitude toward the good but occasionally somewhat goofy Sylvester Graham, since it was he who inspired a far more capable individual to enter into the nutrition field, a man whose last name is a household word in the entire world today . . . John Harvey Kellogg. (The famous breakfast food packages bearing the name of W.K. Kellogg celebrate John Harvey's younger brother Will, the man who developed the business into the giant it is today after the brothers jointly revolutionized the breakfasts of a nation with their creation of highly palatable, handy and nutritious foods from grain. John carried on as a doctor in the nutrition field, making the town of Battle Creek, Michigan, the mecca of breakfast food believers as well as competing manufacturers who did their best to imitate the brothers or even to hijack their secrets by any known trick of commercial sabotage. However, Will Kellogg was a business genius who developed late in life to become a match for the best and the worst of his rivals and who drove the name and fame of Kellogg and Battle Creek into the history books and menus of nations all over the globe.)

John was influenced by Dr. Graham while attending the Bellevue Medical School, New York City, in 1874. The frugal young student stashed a barrel of apples and a barrel of Graham crackers in his rented room, and lived on a diet of this duo. Once a week he treated himself to a coconut and a side dish of potatoes or oatmeal to complete his menu. At a time when the usual breakfast in this country, whether you needed a stoking like this or not, consisted of meat and/or fried eggs, fried potatoes, lots of boiled coffee and bread topped with molasses, with a side dish of fried mush or cornmeal, topped off with a whopping triangle of pie for dessert, John was regularly breakfasting on seven Graham crackers and two apples. After a year of this diet plus an exercise regimen he was feeling fine. It also set him to thinking about foods and their relation to health.

The Kellogg story, including both brothers and their triumphs in medicine and industry, is a classic of Americana which makes inspiring reading; but the full story can only be written in book length, as many volumes of their eventful careers dramatically attest. Suffice it to say here that when Dr. Kellogg's stars led him to Battle Creek, Michigan, to take over as director of what was to be the most famous "sanatorium" in the world, which numbered among its devotees royalty, scientists, industrialists, political personages, Hollywood stars and just plain folks giving their all in an effort to help the doctor find out what was ailing 'em and to cure it, he became the greatest exponent that this country had ever known, even until today, of a medical program built around proper diet rather than drugs. Many of his patients were invalids suffering from digestive disturbances and Dr. Kellogg dreamed and labored to devise vegetarian foods which would be highly digestible, attractive in taste, and beneficial to these captive but amenable "guinea pigs."

He featured "Granula"—leftover bread which had been dried in an oven and then ground up, and also zwieback (literally "twice-baked" in German), a raised bread which was sliced and then oven baked. He also devised "Caramel Coffee," a cereal coffee substitute made of burned bread crusts, bran and molasses.

After one patient broke her false teeth on the zwieback, which had a faint family resemblance to the Rosetta Stone, Dr. Kellogg replaced the teeth and also set out to find something a little easier on the choppers than zwieback. In the late 1870's he tried mixing wheat, which contains practically no fat, with oatmeal and cornmeal, which have a higher fat content. The grains were formed into biscuits and baked until the starch was thoroughly dextrinized and then ground into granular form. He called it "Granola"—his patients, led by those with false teeth, cheering him to the echo. Out of that beginning before the turn of the century evolved experiments in the preparation of grain foods which created the form of "flakes" of wheat, barley, oats, corn and other grains.

All told, it was not surprising in view of his other accomplishments that Doctor Kellogg was far ahead of his time in advocating the kind of food we are only now beginning to appreciate. He put meat and butter substitutes composed mostly of nuts and grains on the sanatorium menu in the last quarter of the nineteenth century. He made up these simplicities into "steaks" and "roasts" for sweet palatability's sake. Coffee and tea were taboo on his sanatorium menu, and pie or cake was mighty scarce. Alcohol in any form was out.

Not all of Dr. Kellogg's enthusiasms have withstood the test of time, but he was a man of many parts, and on the whole he was a full two generations ahead of his time in an astonishing understanding of health. A former secretary of the doctor wrote back in 1956:

"Some of the things John Harvey Kellogg talked about fifty years ago are again being seriously considered today. For instance, he discussed lung cancer from smoking more than a half century ago . . . . Before the turn of the century the 'san' commanded its patients to follow a practice which again has become fashionable: the counting of calories. The dining room menu listed opposite each dish the number of units of proteins, fats or carbohydrates therein. I can remember Dr. John begging employees to drink yogurt buttermilk and to use molasses. A member heard Dr. Kellogg tell his guests that the day would come when there would be so many people mentally ill that there would not be half enough facilities to take care of them."

Nor was Dr. Kellogg less prophetic in other fields. Before 1900 he wrote an article entitled "Fresh Air and Sunshine in the Treatment of Tuberculosis," which was (Oh, the thorny path of the innovator!) branded as "heresy" by the Boston Medical Society. He was an innovator as well in surgical techniques, and in the evolution of health theories including "Biologic Living." A prophet far ahead of his time. But Dr. Kellogg was also a man possessed of such gargantuan energies in his rather diminutive frame that he was able to project the thrust of his ideas around the globe, illuminated by his great flair for personal showmanship, and supported by the corporate empire his brother Will erected around their joint efforts. Their name, Kellogg, became synonymous with the idea of an intelligently selected diet which is also enjoyable to eat.

In the overall sense, however, the voices of Graham and Kellogg, hampered as they were by the limited communications facilities of their time, were merely the cries of prophets keening in the wilderness of apathy. They were interesting especially to sufferers who found in them a surcease or actually a cure from the pain of disease, and they were intriguing to thinkers in every field of endeavor, who had the intelligence to link other branches of science and human experience with the findings of these lonely and frequently belittled pioneers. Would that they could have foreseen how their theories have climbed into the spotlight of scientific regard in our own time, albeit almost a full century after the Battle Creek impulse had its first stirrings.

We might have listened to these prophets a little more carefully at that, if only to understand our often pointless wanderings in a world of plenty.

This planet, after all, is indeed a huge place, even though cartographers and politicians would have us adopt the viewpoint that all has already been seen and said. By no means. The worlds of our sustenance have scarcely been discovered, much less explored. We are fortunate in many ways—when we stumbled upon the Americas in the fifteenth and sixteenth centuries, the human race was enriched by an incredible variety of marvelous foods which had been previously unknown on the small parts of Europe, Asia and Africa which made up the then-existing world. Not only were there the indigenous animals and fowl—deer, turkeys, bison, bear and fish of wondrous diversity—but 80 percent of the plant foods familiar to us today were unknown to Europeans when Columbus first put mailed foot on the strand of Santo Domingo in

1492. Corn, potatoes, squash, tapioca, cocoa, pineapples, avocados, tomatoes, vanilla beans and different members of the capsicum family (wild pepper) were newly discovered gifts of the New World. Broad beans and limas had been known in Europe for a long time, but all of the others we rely upon so affectionately—green beans, the navy beans immortalized in bean soup and baked beans, the red kidney beans so welcome in chili and bean salad, and the pinto bean—are all-American through and through.

That is no reason to leave us smug and content over our plenty. We have reached out and taken what was easiest for the grasping, for we are essentially as lazy as a chimp dozing on a branch of a banana tree. But that great student and authority of hunger and food supply as the moving force behind world politics, Josue de Castro, of the Instituto de Nutricao, Universidade do Brasil, Rio de Janeiro, Brasil, points out that while primitive man had a vast number of native plants and animals at his disposal, civilized man has scarcely advanced beyond the slingshot stage in his utilization of such abundance. There are some 2 million known species of animals; we have domesticated only about fifty for our food supply. Of the world's 350,000 vegetable species, only 600 are cultivated by man. We have even lagged far behind the ancients in our resourcefulness for our own well-being. One small community on the Gold Coast of Africa, when living in the primitive state, included in their diet some 114 species of fruit, 46 species of leguminous seeds and 47 species of greens!

"The reduced number of food elements used by civilized groups is a direct consequence of the impossibility of supplying great demographic concentrations with a wide variety of products. Little by little, down through the ages, mankind has sacrificed variety to quantity, limiting the regular food supply to those substances of the most concentrated food value which are relatively easy to produce and to preserve. In thus limiting his diet civilized man has increased the likelihood of chronic shortages of certain essential nutritional factors, a situation that a widely varied diet would tend to correct. When many different foods are eaten, specific deficiencies that may develop one day are made up the next, while on a monotonous never-changing diet the deficiencies are consolidated, and grow worse as time goes on."

There you have it. We are eating more and more of what we need less and less. This cookbook does not suggest that you throw out everything in your kitchen larder and subsist exclusively on the bran (which is sometimes whimsically termed "donkey food"). Nor can you in any likelihood take to the bush for your own vast improvement in health, since it is not at all our premise that you have to be primitive to be healthy. We only suggest that you ponder the wisdom—or the lack of it—of our ways having to do with regular diet and take steps to sidestep the dangerous existing hazards to your health and even to your life.

To such sentiments we must add our own heartfelt wish that you find, in the culinary adventures which follow, a measure of innovation in your diet which is just plain fun and enjoyment as well as a shibboleth to a healthier life in the future.

It is time, more than ever, to heed the oft-quoted aphorism of Professor Brillat-Savarin: "Tell me what you eat and I shall tell you what you are."

That is why your most important duty in this world is to eat for a living. That is one way, at least, to earn our fondest wish for you: "May you live all the days of your life."

MORNING GLORIES

Pancakes, Waffles and Coffeecakes

Health and good estate of body are
above all gold, and a strong body
above infinite wealth ...

—Ecclesiastes

Each day has a new beginning—breakfast—and that is the logical place to begin improving the diet by adding fiber and eliminating saturated fats. The rules are simple: Down with bacon and eggs (if you can't bear to give them up entirely, serve them once in a while as a luncheon or dinner entree). Down with sugary doughnuts and pastries.

Up with whole-grain breads and cereals, skimmed or low-fat milk, and fresh fruit. *Eat* the fruit, don't just drink the juice.

Here and on the following pages are more suggestions for adding fiber—and adding variety—to the breakfast menu:

Try new kinds of cooked cereals. Try bulgur, bulgur combined with soy grits, steel-cut oats, millet and buckwheat. To increase protein and calcium, stir in dry milk powder near the end of the cooking time. For added flavor, stir in granola, raisins, chopped figs or dates. Serve with yogurt, applesauce or maple syrup, as a change from the usual milk.

Try all the ready-to-eat cereals that are good sources of fiber. For new flavor, mix several kinds together and add such extras as flaked coconut, uncooked oatmeal or wheat germ.

Make speckled pancakes—use any of the recipes given here or one of your own. As soon as the batter is poured out on the griddle, sprinkle over it any or all of the following: bran cereal, granola, chopped nuts, blueberries or raspberries. Turn and cook the second side as usual. Pancakes like these don't need to be drowned in syrup, as tasteless white pancakes do. Top these with applesauce, cottage cheese, or with just a wee dribbling of honey. . . . Proof that a "good" breakfast doesn't have to be boring!

12

Breakfast Brancakes with Orange Syrup

YIELD: 12 TO 14 5-INCH PANCAKES

SYRUP:

1 cup sugar

Dash of salt

1 teaspoon grated orange peel

2 teaspoons cornstarch

½ cup orange juice

¼ cup butter or margarine

1 orange, peeled and divided into sections

BRANCAKE BATTER:

1½ cups unbleached white flour

3 teaspoons baking powder

¾ teaspoon salt

2 tablespoons sugar

1 egg

2 cups milk

1 teaspoon grated orange peel

1 cup wheat bran cereal*

Prepare the syrup: In a saucepan combine the sugar, salt, grated orange peel and cornstarch. Gradually add the orange juice, stirring constantly. Add the margarine and bring to a boil. Cook the syrup until it is thickened and clear, stirring constantly; then remove from the heat and stir in the orange sections. Serve warm or cooled.

Prepare the batter: Stir together the flour, baking powder, salt and sugar. Set aside.

In a large mixing bowl, beat the egg until foamy. Stir in the milk, orange peel and bran cereal. Let stand 1 or 2 minutes, until the cereal is softened.

Add the dry ingredients to the cereal mixture and stir just until all the dry ingredients are moistened.

Cook the pancakes on a lightly oiled preheated griddle, turning once to brown both sides. Serve immediately, with butter and the orange syrup.

*Throughout this book wheat bran cereal refers to such products as Kellogg's All-Bran, Bran Buds and Nabisco 100% Bran.

Granola Pancakes

YIELD: 8 SMALL PANCAKES

1 egg

1 cup plus 2 tablespoons sour milk *

1 tablespoon vegetable oil

½ cup unbleached white flour

½ cup whole wheat flour

½ teaspoon baking soda

1 teaspoon baking powder

½ teaspoon salt

1/3 cup granola (without raisins)

1 tablespoon grated coconut

Beat the egg until foamy.

Stir in the sour milk and vegetable oil.

In another bowl stir together the flours, baking soda, baking powder and salt. Mix in the granola and coconut.

Combine the liquid and dry ingredients and stir just until combined.

Drop the batter, ¼ cup at a time, on a lightly oiled griddle or an electric skillet heated to 375 degrees F. When the edges are dry and the surface bubbly, turn the pancakes and brown the second side.

Serve immediately, with butter and honey.

*To make sour milk, measure 1 cup plus 1 tablespoon milk and add 1 tablespoon vinegar or lemon juice. Stir and let stand 3 minutes.

Wheat Germ Pancakes

YIELD: 16 5½-INCH PANCAKES

1 cup whole wheat flour

1 cup unbleached white flour

2/3 cup wheat germ

¼ cup sugar

4 teaspoons baking powder

1 teaspoon salt

2½ cups milk

½ cup vegetable oil

2 eggs

In a large mixing bowl combine the flour, wheat germ, sugar, baking powder and salt. Stir to blend.

In another bowl beat together the milk, oil and eggs.

Pour the liquid ingredients into the dry ingredients and stir just until all are moistened.

Pour the batter, 1/3 cup at a time, onto a hot, lightly oiled griddle. Bake first side until the edges are dry and bubbles appear near the center. Turn and bake the second side. Serve hot with butter and honey.

Sourdough Buckwheat Pancakes

YIELD: ABOUT 10 5-INCH PANCAKES

1 teaspoon active dry yeast
½ cup lukewarm water
1 tablespoon honey
1 tablespoon vegetable oil

½ teaspoon salt
1½ cups water
1½ cups buckwheat flour
½ cup whole wheat flour

Prepare the batter the evening before the pancakes are to be served for breakfast. Dissolve the yeast in the ½ cup lukewarm water. Add the honey and let stand until bubbly (about 5 minutes).

Add the oil, salt, the additional 1½ cups water and the flour. Beat until blended; then cover and let rise overnight.

In the morning, stir down the batter and bake, 1/3 cup at a time, on a hot oiled griddle.

Old-Fashioned Buckwheat Cakes

YIELD: 12 TO 16 PANCAKES

½ cup unbleached white flour   *1 egg*
1 cup buckwheat flour   *1½ cups sour milk * or buttermilk*
1 teaspoon baking powder   *1 tablespoon vegetable oil*
½ teaspoon salt   *2 tablespoons molasses*

Combine the flours, baking powder and salt. Stir and set aside.

In another bowl beat the egg. Add the sour milk or buttermilk, oil and molasses and blend well.

Combine the liquid and dry ingredients and stir just until all the dry ingredients are moistened.

Heat an electric skillet to 375 degrees F., or a griddle until a few drops of water sizzle when dropped on the surface. Brush with a little vegetable oil; then pour on the batter, ¼ cup at a time, and bake until bubbles appear all over the top. Turn and brown the other side. Serve immediately with butter and honey or syrup.

*To make sour milk, measure 1½ cups milk and stir in 1½ tablespoons lemon juice or vinegar.

Wheat Germ-Banana Pancakes

YIELD: 10 TO 12 5-INCH PANCAKES

1 cup unbleached white flour   *2 eggs*
½ cup wheat germ   *1½ cups milk*
1 teaspoon baking powder   *½ cup mashed banana (1 large banana)*
½ teaspoon salt

Combine the flour, wheat germ, baking powder and salt. Stir until well mixed together.

In another bowl, beat the eggs; then beat in the milk and the banana.

Combine the moist and dry mixtures and stir just until blended.

For each pancake, pour 1/3 cup of the batter onto a hot, lightly oiled griddle. Sprinkle additional wheat grem on the uncooked surface, if desired. Cook until the edges are browned and the top bubbly; then turn and cook the other side until browned. Serve immediately with melted butter.

Cornmeal Waffles

YIELD: 4 LARGE WAFFLES

1½ cups boiling water   *1 cup unbleached white flour*
½ cup yellow cornmeal   *½ teaspoon baking soda*
3 tablespoons butter or margarine   *2 teaspoons baking powder*
3 eggs, separated   *1 tablespoon sugar*
¾ cup buttermilk or sour milk   *½ teaspoon salt*

Bring the water to a boil and gradually add the cornmeal, stirring continually until smooth. Add the butter, stir until melted, and set aside to cool.

When the cornmeal mixture is lukewarm, beat in the yolks of the 3 eggs. Add the buttermilk or sour milk and beat well.

In another bowl, stir together the flour, baking soda, baking powder, sugar and salt.

Combine the moist and dry ingredients and stir just until all the dry ingredients are moistened.

Beat the egg whites until they stand in stiff points. Add to the batter and gently fold in, stirring only until barely blended.

Preheat the waffle iron. Pour about ½ cup of batter onto the grids, close immediately and cook about 5 minutes. Serve with butter and syrup or, for luncheon, with creamed chicken or cheese sauce.

Health Waffles with Orange Molasses

YIELD: 4 LARGE OR 6 SMALL WAFFLES

*Three different grains and fresh orange juice go into these waffles,
intended for a hearty breakfast. Topped with cottage cheese,
they make a substantial luncheon dish.*

1½ cups unbleached white flour

¼ cup wheat germ

½ cup yellow cornmeal

1 cup uncooked oatmeal (rolled oats)

2 tablespoons baking powder

½ teaspoon salt

1 teaspoon grated orange rind

½ cup butter or margarine, melted

3 eggs

2 cups buttermilk

1 cup orange juice

Cottage cheese (optional)

ORANGE MOLASSES SYRUP:

1 cup orange juice

1 tablespoon cornstarch

½ cup molasses

¼ cup sugar

2 tablespoons butter or margarine

In a large mixing bowl combine the flour, wheat germ, cornmeal, oatmeal, baking powder, salt and orange rind. Stir until blended.

In another bowl stir together the melted butter or margarine, eggs, buttermilk and orange juice.

Combine the liquid and dry ingredients and stir just until all are moistened. Let the batter stand 30 minutes.

Make the syrup: In a small saucepan stir together the orange juice and cornstarch; then add the molasses, sugar and butter. Cook, stirring constantly, until the syrup thickens and comes to a boil.

Bake the waffles in a preheated waffle iron 5 minutes or until lightly browned.

Top each waffle with a spoonful of cottage cheese, if desired, and serve with the warm syrup.

Bran Cereal Waffles

YIELD: 4 SERVINGS

¾ cup unbleached white flour (or ½
    cup white and ¼ cup whole wheat
    flour)
1 teaspoon baking powder
½ teaspoon baking soda
¼ teaspoon salt

¼ cup sugar or honey
1 cup wheat bran cereal
2 eggs, separated
1 cup milk or buttermilk
6 tablespoons butter or margarine,
    melted

Stir together the flour, baking powder, baking soda, salt, sugar and bran cereal.

In another bowl, combine the egg yolks, milk and melted butter. (If using honey, add it to this mixture rather than to the dry ingredients.) Beat well.

Beat the egg whites until they stand in soft points.

Add the egg-milk mixture to the dry ingredients and stir just until all are moistened. Gently fold in the egg whites.

Bake in a preheated waffle iron 5 minutes or until golden brown. (The batter should make 8 waffle squares or 4 round waffles.)

Leftover waffles may be frozen and reheated in toaster or oven for serving at a later time.

Prune Coffeecake

YIELD: 9 SERVINGS

1 cup unbleached white flour
¾ teaspoon baking powder
¾ teaspoon baking soda
½ teaspoon salt
½ teaspoon cinnamon
1 cup wheat bran cereal
½ cup butter or margarine, softened
2/3 cup sugar
2 eggs
1 cup sour cream

½ cup finely chopped pitted prunes

TOPPING:
3 tablespoons unbleached white flour
½ cup (packed) brown sugar
2 teaspoons cinnamon
½ cup wheat bran cereal
3 tablespoons butter or margarine,
    softened

Preheat the oven to 350 degrees F. Oil a 9-inch square baking pan.

Combine the flour, baking powder, baking soda, salt, cinnamon and bran cereal. Stir until blended.

In another bowl, cream together the butter or margarine and sugar.

Beat in the eggs.

Stir in the sour cream.

Add the dry ingredients and stir just until all the dry ingredients are moistened.

Prepare the topping: Combine all the ingredients in a small bowl and mix until evenly crumbly.

Spread half of the batter in the prepared pan. Sprinkle half the prunes and half the topping mixture over the batter. Spoon the remaining half of the batter on top, then sprinkle with the remaining prunes and topping.

Bake 40 minutes or until a wooden pick inserted near the center comes out clean. Cut into squares and serve warm.

Wheat Germ Coffeecake

YIELD: 6 TO 8 SERVINGS

1½ cups unbleached white flour
3 teaspoons baking powder
½ teaspoon salt
½ cup brown sugar
½ cup wheat germ
1 cup milk
*½ cup corn or safflower oil or
  melted margarine*
1 egg
1 teaspoon vanilla extract

*1 11-ounce can mandarin oranges,
  drained, or 4 slices of canned
  pineapple*

TOPPING:
¼ cup wheat germ
*¼ cup whole wheat or unbleached white
  flour*
¼ cup (packed) brown sugar
¼ teaspoon cinnamon
¼ cup butter or margarine

Preheat the oven to 375 degrees F. Oil an 8-inch square baking pan.

In a large mixing bowl combine the flour, baking powder, salt, brown sugar and wheat germ. Stir until blended.

In another bowl beat together the milk, oil or melted margarine, egg and vanilla extract.

Add the liquid ingredients to the dry mixture and stir just until all the dry ingredients are moistened.

Prepare the topping: In a small bowl stir together the wheat germ, flour, brown sugar and cinnamon. Cut in the butter or margarine and stir until the mixture is crumbly.

Pour the batter into the prepared pan. Arrange the fruit on top and sprinkle the topping mixture over all.

Bake 40 to 45 minutes. Serve warm, with butter.

Whole Wheat Maple Ring

YIELD: 2 COFFEECAKES

3 to 3½ cups unbleached white flour

2 packages dry yeast

½ teaspoon nutmeg

¾ cup milk

½ cup water

¼ cup oil

½ cup honey

2 teaspoons salt

2 eggs, room temperature

2 cups whole wheat flour

2 tablespoons butter, melted

½ cup packed light brown sugar

½ cup chopped pecans

1 tablespoon cinnamon

1 teaspoon maple flavoring

Icing (optional)

In a large mixing bowl stir together 2 cups of the unbleached white flour, the yeast and nutmeg.

Heat the milk, water, oil, honey and salt until warm (120 degrees F.), stirring to blend.

Slowly add the warm liquid to the flour-yeast mixture and beat 3 minutes with an electric mixer on medium speed, or 200 strokes by hand.

Add the eggs and beat until smooth.

Blend in 1 cup of the whole wheat flour and beat 1 minute more. Let rest 5 minutes.

Stir in the rest of the whole wheat flour and enough additional unbleached white flour to make a soft dough. Turn out onto a lightly floured surface and knead until smooth and satiny, about 8 to 10 minutes.

Put the dough into a lightly oiled bowl, turning so that all sides are coated. Cover with a clean cloth and let rise in a warm place (80 to 90 degrees F.) 1 hour or longer.

Punch the dough down and let it rest for 10 minutes.

Divide the dough in half. Shape each half into a rectangle about 8 by 15 inches. Brush the tops with melted butter.

Stir together the brown sugar, nuts, cinnamon and maple flavoring. Sprinkle over the dough.

Roll each rectangle of dough lengthwise jelly roll fashion, sealing the edges. Form into rings by joining the ends and place on an oiled baking sheet. With scissors or a knife, cut through the rings from the outside almost to the center, in 1-inch slices. Turn each slice down slightly.

Cover with a clean cloth and let rise in a warm place 30 to 45 minutes.

Preheat oven to 350 degrees F. Bake rings 25 to 30 minutes.

Cool. Drizzle or spread with frosting (see Reference chapter), if desired.

Peachy Bran Coffee Cake

YIELD: 9 SERVINGS

1 1-pound can sliced peaches
1 cup wheat bran cereal
1 egg
¼ cup butter or margarine, softened
1 cup unbleached white flour

2½ teaspoons baking powder
½ teaspoon salt
¾ teaspoon cinnamon
¼ cup sugar

Preheat the oven to 400 degrees F. Oil a 9-inch square baking pan.

Drain the peaches, reserving the syrup.

Combine the bran cereal and 2/3 cup of the syrup from the peaches in a large mixing bowl. Stir and let stand until the moisture is absorbed.

Add the egg and soft butter or margarine and beat well.

In another bowl, stir together the flour, baking powder, salt and ¼ teaspoon of the cinnamon.

Add the dry ingredients to the other mixture and stir just until all the dry ingredients are moistened.

Pour the batter into the prepared pan. With a floured spoon make grooves in the batter diagonally across the pan about 1½ inches apart, forming a lattice. Place the drained peach slices in the grooves. Sprinkle the remaining cinnamon and the sugar over all.

Bake 30 minutes. Serve warm, with butter if desired.

Breakfast Bars

YIELD: 8 LARGE BARS

These are good for breakfast and equally good to take on a hike or to eat as a very satisfying snack.

6 tablespoons frozen orange juice
  concentrate, thawed
¼ cup chopped dried apricots
½ cup chopped dates
¼ teaspoon salt
1/3 cup chopped walnuts
½ cup butter or margarine, softened
1 cup (packed) brown sugar

1 egg
¾ cup unbleached white flour
¾ cup whole wheat flour
1 cup uncooked oatmeal (rolled oats)
2 tablespoons sesame seeds
1 teaspoon baking powder
¼ teaspoon baking soda
1 teaspoon grated orange rind

Preheat the oven to 350 degrees F. Oil a 9-inch square baking pan.

In a saucepan combine the orange juice concentrate, the apricots, dates and salt. Cook over low heat, stirring occasionally for 5 minutes or until the mixture thickens. Remove from the heat, stir in the walnuts and set aside.

In a large mixing bowl cream together the butter or margarine and the brown sugar. Beat in the egg.

In another bowl, stir together the flour, oatmeal, sesame seeds, baking powder, baking soda and orange rind.

Add the dry ingredients to the creamed mixture, half at a time, blending well after each addition. The dough will be dry and crumbly.

Press half the dough in the bottom of the prepared pan. Spread the fruit mixture over the dough, then sprinkle the remaining dough mixture on top. Bake 35 minutes. Serve warm or cold.

Breakfast Muesli

YIELD: 3 TO 4 SERVINGS

We can thank the Swiss for this nourishing and tasty one-dish meal. Serve it to children who say they are tired of cereal, or to adults on hot summer mornings. It can also become a light luncheon or a dessert.

½ cup uncooked oatmeal (rolled oats)
2 apples, chopped but not peeled
2 tablespoons raisins
2 tablespoons pecans or walnuts,
   finely chopped or ground

1 tablespoon wheat germ
1-2 tablespoons honey
1-2 tablespoons lemon juice
Yogurt or milk

Mix together the oatmeal, apples, raisins, nuts, wheat germ, honey and lemon juice. Add just enough yogurt or milk to moisten the oatmeal and serve.

If a softer texture is desired, pour a little boiling water over the oats in the evening and let stand overnight. Stir in the other ingredients just before serving.

Millet and Fruit Breakfast

YIELD: 4 TO 6 SERVINGS

4 cups water
1 teaspoon salt
1 cup hulled millet

¾ cup raisins
¾ cup chopped apples, unpeeled

Bring the water to a boil in a large saucepan.

Stir in the salt and millet, reduce the heat and simmer, covered, 40 minutes or until the millet is soft and most of the water is absorbed.

Stir in the raisins and the chopped apples. Cook 12 minutes longer or until the apples are heated through but still a little crisp. Serve with honey and milk.

Cinnamon Apple Patties

YIELD: 8 TO 10 SMALL PANCAKES

2 eggs
3 tablespoons sugar
1 teaspoon salt
½ teaspoon cinnamon
½ cup water

½ cup whole wheat flour
1 teaspoon grated lemon peel
3 cups finely chopped apples (unpeeled)
Vegetable oil for frying

Beat the eggs until foamy.

Add the sugar, salt, cinnamon and water. Beat well.

Stir in the flour, grated lemon peel and apples.

Generously oil a griddle or an electric skillet heated to 375 degrees F. For each pattie drop about ¼ cup of the apple mixture and flatten it slightly with a spatula. Cook the patties about 2 minutes on each side, adding more oil as needed.

Serve the patties hot, with honey or with a mixture of cinnamon and sugar.

Breakfast Nog

YIELD: ABOUT 3½ CUPS

2 cups low-fat milk
3 ripe bananas

½ cup wheat germ
2 tablespoons honey

Place all ingredients in the blender and spin at high speed 1 minute. Serve in tall glasses with straws.

RISE AND SHINE

Breads, Quickbreads and Muffins

"A loaf of bread," the Walrus said,
"Is what we chiefly need:
Pepper and vinegar besides
Are very good indeed."

—*Lewis Carroll in* "Through the Looking Glass"

What could be a more tantalizing and wonderful smell than the pervasive aroma of fresh bread baking in the ovens? Or the nose-tickling scents of banana bread and bran muffins? What more soul-satisfying than the nourishment of loaves made from the true grains of the earth?

Alas, in all too few homes does this happy olfactory love affair take place. We herewith enter a plea to bring back those loving, loaf-ing days when bread was a treat.

Once bread was highly esteemed as a nutritious and wholesome food—"the staff of life," poets called it. "Lady" became a title of respect among the Anglo-Saxons because it meant "giver of the loaf." The Egyptians were proud to be known in the Eastern world as "bread-eaters"—they devised more than fifty different kinds; they offered it to their gods in tribute, placed it in their tombs as sustenance in the hereafter, and they paid the workers who built the eternal pyramids a daily wage of three loaves of bread plus two jugs of the beer they called "liquid bread." For thousands of years, whole grain bread was the staple food of humble people throughout Europe—and there is good reason to believe they were healthier than the nobles who dined on richer fare.

To appreciate how it came about that bread lost its importance in our lives, we must consider two things—first, the structure of wheat itself, and, second, the history of flour milling.

In structure, the grain of wheat consists of concentric layers somewhat like the growth rings in a tree. Outside are the brown layers containing much indigestible but valuable fiber—the bran. In the center is the white endosperm which makes up 85 percent of the weight of the grain and contains most of the starch along with the less concentrated protein. At the base of the kernel, barely visible to the naked eye, is the tiny wheat germ or embryo from which a new wheat plant can grow. The wheat germ makes up only about 3 percent of the total weight of the grain but it is extremely rich in concentrated protein, fat and several of the B vitamins.

In ancient times the milling of wheat meant merely crushing the grains coarsely between rough-textured stones. Flour made in this way was coarse-textured and brownish, but it contained all parts of the grain—the bran and the vitamin-rich wheat germ along with the starchy white endosperm. Today we would call it 100 percent extraction flour; no part of it was discarded or lost in processing.

In the eighteenth century, industrial developments enabled the millers to introduce many technical *"improvements"*—grinding the grain into finer particles, sifting it, bleaching it to make it whiter. Around 1870 mills began to be equipped with powerful steel rollers and sieves of finely woven silk cloth that could separate out all of the bran and also the wheat germ. For the first time it was possible to produce cheaply a highly refined white flour consisting solely of the endosperm. Some was 70 percent extraction, meaning that it contained only 70 percent, by weight, of the original grain.

This pleased the millers, who could sell the sifted-out bran at a profit as feed for livestock. Also, because the oil-rich wheat germ had been removed from it, the refined flour could be kept longer without becoming rancid. The flour was less subject to infestation by insects and rodents—simply because it was less nutritious.

The millers' customers were pleased because they could now place on their tables a fine-textured, snow-white bread they regarded as a superior product.

But was it? Compared to coarse-textured brown bread made from 100 percent extraction flour it contained less protein, less of the B vitamins, less calcium and iron, and less of several different trace minerals. Also, it contained much less of the fiber with which we are particularly concerned in this book.

Here, then, is a plea for return to the kind of bread that can support life! Crunchy, brown, full-bodied bread that is satisfying and nutritious. We include here recipes for all kinds—quickbreads made with baking powder or soda, sourdough breads, even special breads to bake in crockpot and microwave oven. We challenge you to make your own—your family will smile and salaam to the yeast!

Whole Wheat Bread

YIELD: 3 LOAVES

3 cups lukewarm water
2 packages active dry yeast
4 tablespoons honey, molasses or barley
   malt

Whole wheat flour
4 tablespoons vegetable oil
1 tablespoon salt

Put the lukewarm water into a large bowl.

Stir in the yeast until it dissolves.

Add the sweetener of your choice.

Add 3 cups of whole wheat flour and beat 100 times by hand or for about 2½ minutes with an electric beater. Cover with a towel and let rise 20 minutes.

Add the oil and salt and 3 to 4 cups more of flour. The mixture when stirred should come away from the sides of the bowl.

Turn all the mixture onto a lightly floured working surface and knead vigorously for 5 to 10 minutes, adding more flour as needed until the dough is smooth, shiny and elastic.

Wash out the mixing bowl. Dry well and grease the bowl lightly with oil. Put in the ball of dough and turn it around so that the surface is coated. Cover and let rise for 1 hour or until doubled in size.

Oil 3 loaf tins.

Punch down the risen dough and divide into 3 equal parts. Shape into loaves and place in the tins. Cover and let rise 30 minutes.

Preheat the oven to 350 degrees F.

Bake 50 minutes. Turn out the loaves immediately and cool on a wire rack.

Buttermilk Raisin Bread

YIELD: 2 LOAVES

*Buttermilk Raisin Bread tastes like a Christmas stollen, but it
is an even more substantial and nourishing specialty
bread. The method given here is quick and easy.*

3 cups unbleached white flour
2 cups whole wheat flour
2 packages active dry yeast
¼ cup sugar
2 teaspoons ground cinnamon
1 teaspoon salt

¾ cup water
1/3 cup butter
½ cup buttermilk*
2 eggs, at room temperature
1½ cups golden raisins

Stir together the flours.

In a large mixing bowl place 1¾ cups of the flour mixture. Add the yeast, sugar, cinnamon and salt and stir until blended.

In a saucepan, heat the water and butter to warm (120 to 130 degrees F.). Remove from the heat and stir in the buttermilk. (*If buttermilk is not available, substitute ½ cup milk and 1½ teaspoons vinegar, blended and allowed to stand 5 minutes at room temperature.)

Add the combined liquids to the flour mixture and beat 2 minutes at medium speed in an electric mixer.

Add the eggs and beat 2 more minutes. Stir in the raisins. Add enough additional flour to make a stiff dough. Let the dough rest 5 minutes.

On a floured board knead the dough 5 to 8 minutes. Cover the dough with the mixing bowl and let rise for 30 minutes.

Divide the dough into halves and shape each into an oblong loaf. Place on baking sheet. Brush the tops with oil. Let rise for 30 minutes.

Preheat oven to 375 degrees F. Bake loaves 25 minutes. Remove from oven and cool. Drizzle frosting over top crust, if desired.

Oatmeal Molasses Bread

YIELD: 2 LOAVES

3 cups whole wheat flour   *½ cup powdered milk*
3 or 4 cups unbleached white flour   *¼ cup wheat germ*
1 cup oatmeal (rolled oats)   *4 tablespoons soft butter or margarine*
2½ teaspoons salt   *2 cups very warm water*
2 packages active dry yeast   *½ cup unsulfured molasses*

Grease 2 medium-size (8½-inch by 4½-inch) bread tins.

Combine 3 cups of whole wheat flour with 3 cups of white flour in a bowl.

Put 2 cups of the flour mixture into a large electric mixer bowl with the oatmeal, salt, yeast, powdered milk, wheat germ and shortening.

Mix the water and molasses and add it to the dry ingredients, beating at medium speed for 2 minutes.

Add ½ cup of the flour mixture and beat at high speed for 2 minutes. Continue adding the flour mixture, until the dough is soft and workable. When the dough becomes too heavy for your particular mixer, stir in the flour with a wooden spoon.

Turn the dough onto a floured surface and knead for 10 minutes until the dough is smooth and elastic, adding more flour if necessary.

Place in a greased bowl, turning the bread so that it is coated on all sides. Cover and let rise in a warm (80 to 85 degrees F.) place for 1 hour.

Knead down and cut in half. Shape each half and put into loaf tins. Cover and let rise 45 minutes or until doubled.

Preheat the oven to 350 degrees F. Bake 40 minutes.

Remove from pan. Paint crust with a little butter or margarine. Cover with a clean cloth until cool.

"Best Bread in the World"

YIELD: 2 LOAVES

*This bread freezes well and is especially good served
warm as an accompaniment for homemade soups
and salads.*

2 cups boiling water

1 cup uncooked oatmeal (rolled oats)

2 packages active dry yeast

1/3 cup lukewarm water

1 tablespoon salt

½ cup honey

2 tablespoons butter, melted

2½-3 cups unbleached white flour

1½-2 cups whole wheat flour

1 egg yolk

Sesame seeds

Pour the boiling water over the old-fashioned rolled oats. Let stand until thoroughly softened.

Soak the yeast in lukewarm water. It must not be hot. You can test it by dropping a little on your wrist.

Add the salt, honey and melted butter, cooled to lukewarm, to the oats.

Making sure that the oats are just lukewarm, add the yeast and mix well.

Gradually add the flours and knead with your hands until the dough is smooth and elastic. This should take approximately 10 minutes.

Put into a lightly oiled bowl, turning it around to coat the dough on all sides. Cover with a cloth and let rise for 1 hour or until doubled in bulk.

Oil 2 bread tins.

Punch down the risen bread dough and cut in half. Knead each half briefly and shape into loaves. Place them in the bread tins. Cover and let rise until the pans are full. Preheat the oven to 350 degrees F.

Beat the egg yolk lightly with a teaspoon of water. Brush the surface of each loaf with the egg mixture and sprinkle with sesame seeds. Bake 35 to 40 minutes.

Turn the loaves out on a rack and let cool.

Whole Wheat Pita Pouches

YIELD: 18 POUCHES

*These pouches, which have been used since Biblical times, can
be stuffed with meat, cheese and vegetables to serve as
dripless sandwiches. They can also be split, buttered
and toasted like English muffins.*

6 cups warm water	*2 tablespoons salt*
4 packages active dry yeast	*½ cup vegetable oil*
½ cup honey	*2 cups cornmeal*
Whole wheat flour	*2 cups sesame seeds*

Combine the water and the yeast in a large bowl and, when they are blended, add the honey and 6 cups of whole wheat flour. Beat vigorously for 100 strokes or 2½ minutes with an electric beater. Cover and let stand for 30 minutes.

Toast the sesame seeds under the broiler until golden brown.

Stir in the salt, vegetable oil, cornmeal, toasted sesame seeds and enough addition-al flour so that the dough does not stick to the sides of the bowl. Cover and let rise in a warm place until doubled in volume.

Punch the dough down and divide in half. Roll out on a lightly floured surface to a thickness of ½ inch. Cut into circles with a 3-inch cookie cutter. Working with the palms of your hands, flatten each circle out to measure 7 inches. A rolling pin can be used if preferred but it is not traditional.

Place 4 circles on a baking sheet which has been lightly oiled. Bake 15 minutes at 350 degrees F. Repeat the process until all the dough has been used.

To serve, cut the circles in half. Each half can be opened from the cut edge to form a crescent-shaped pouch.

Rye Bread

YIELD: 3 LOAVES

3 cups lukewarm water	*4 tablespoons vegetable oil*
2 packages active dry yeast	*1 tablespoon salt*
4 tablespoons honey, molasses or barley	*2½ cups rye flour*
* malt*	*2 teaspoons caraway seeds*
Whole wheat flour	

Place the water in a bowl and stir in the yeast until well blended. Add the sweetener of your choice and 3 cups of whole wheat flour. Beat 100 times or 2½ minutes with an electric beater. Cover and let rise for 15 minutes.

Add the oil, salt, rye flour and caraway seeds. Mix well and add enough of the whole wheat flour (3 to 4 cups) so that the dough no longer sticks to the side of the bowl.

Turn the dough out on a floured working surface and knead for 10 minutes.

Wash out the mixing bowl and dry thoroughly. Grease the interior of the bowl with vegetable oil. Put in the dough and turn it around so that all the surfaces of the dough are coated. Cover with a towel and let rise at room temperature for 1 hour or until doubled in bulk.

Grease 3 loaf tins with vegetable oil.

Punch down the dough and divide it into 3 parts. Knead each part, slightly shaping it into a loaf. Fill the tins. Cover with a towel and let rise 30 minutes.

Preheat the oven to 350 degrees F.

Bake 50 minutes. Turn out the loaves immediately onto a wire rack to cool.

Sour Starter

Sour starter may be bought in health stores and mixed with water, but it can easily be made at home and stored in the refrigerator for continued use. Put 2 cups of milk in a quart jar. Cover with a double thickness of cheesecloth and secure it with an elastic band. Let stand at room temperature for 24 hours. Blend in 2 cups of whole wheat or unbleached white flour, mix well, replace the cheesecloth and let stand, preferably outdoors, in a protected place for 12 hours. Bring indoors and keep in a warm place until the mixture is very bubbly. Water can be substituted for the milk, thus eliminating the first 24 hours of this process but milk gives the mixture a special flavor. Put the mixture into a container that allows room for expansion. Keep covered in the refrigerator. When the starter is used it should be replenished with equal amounts of milk or water and flour. This mixture should be used and replenished every week. If you do not bake regularly pour out half the starter and replenish it with fresh water or milk and flour every week.

Sour Rye Bread

YIELD: 2 OR 3 LOAVES

2 cups starter made with whole wheat flour
2½ cups rye flour
2½ cups lukewarm water
4 tablespoons vegetable oil
1 tablespoon salt
Whole wheat flour

Combine the starter with the rye flour, lukewarm water, oil and salt. Mix well and add enough whole wheat flour to make a soft dough that no longer sticks to the sides of the bowl. Beat well.

Turn onto a lightly floured working surface and knead until smooth and elastic, or for 10 minutes, adding more whole wheat flour as necessary.

Place in a lightly oiled bowl, turning it around to coat all sides. Cover with a damp towel and let rise until doubled.

Lightly oil a baking sheet.

Punch down the dough and divide it into 2 or 3 parts. Shape into oval loaves and place on the baking sheet. Cover with a damp towel and let rise for 30 to 40 minutes or until almost doubled.

Preheat the oven to 350 degrees F.

Bake 45 to 50 minutes.

High Fiber Onion-Rye Buns

YIELD: 12 TO 18 BUNS

1 cup milk

2 tablespoons honey

1 teaspoon salt

3 tablespoons butter or margarine

1 package active dry yeast

½ cup lukewarm (110 degrees F.)
  water

3 cups unbleached white flour

2 tablespoons caraway seeds

6 tablespoons minced onion

½ cup wheat germ

1-1¼ cups rye flour

1 egg

2 teaspoons water

Scald the milk and combine it in a mixing bowl with the honey, salt and butter or margarine. Stir well and cool to lukewarm.

Dissolve the yeast in the warm water and combine with the milk mixture.

Add the white flour and beat vigorously for 1 minute or until the batter is very smooth.

Add the caraway seeds, onion, wheat germ and enough rye flour so that the dough is firm enough to knead.

Turn the dough out onto a floured surface and knead for 8 minutes.

Wash out the mixing bowl. Dry it well and coat it with oil, butter or margarine. Place the dough in the bowl and turn it around so that the dough is coated on all sides. Cover and let rise in a warm place for 1 hour or until doubled.

Punch the dough down and roll it out with your hands into a long rope about 1½ inches thick. Cut into 1½-inch pieces and shape into buns. Place in oiled muffin tins or on an oiled baking sheet, placing them 2 inches apart. Cover with a towel and let rise until doubled.

Preheat the oven to 400 degrees F. Beat the egg with the water and brush the tops of the buns.

Bake 12 to 15 minutes or until nicely browned.

Pumpernickel Bread

YIELD: 3 LOAVES

3 cups lukewarm water

4 packages active dry yeast

1¾ cups molasses

3 cups whole wheat flour

½ cup sour starter

4 tablespoons vegetable oil

1 tablespoon salt

2½ cups buckwheat flour

2½ cups rye flour

Put the lukewarm water into a large bowl.

Stir in 2 packages of yeast until it dissolves.

Add 4 tablespoons of the molasses.

Add 3 cups of whole wheat flour and beat 100 times by hand or for 2½ minutes with an electric beater. Cover with a towel and let rise 15 minutes.

Dissolve the remaining yeast in 4 tablespoons of lukewarm water and mix with the rest of the molasses which should be at room temperature.

Add the yeast mixture, the homemade sour culture, the vegetable oil and salt to the contents of the large bowl. Stir until blended.

Add the buckwheat and rye flour and enough additional whole wheat flour to form a soft ball that no longer sticks to the side of the bowl.

Turn the mixture onto a lightly floured working surface and knead vigorously until the dough is smooth (8 to 10 minutes). Add more whole wheat flour as necessary.

Put the dough into a lightly oiled bowl, turning it around to coat the entire surface. Cover with a towel and let rise in a warm place until doubled or about 2 hours.

Dust a large baking sheet with poppy seeds, cornmeal or whole wheat flour.

Punch down the dough and cut in 3 parts. Knead the bread into balls and place on baking sheet. Cover with a towel and let rise 30 to 40 minutes.

Preheat the oven to 450 degrees F.

Brush the tops with a little milk or water. Bake 10 minutes. Reduce the heat to 350 and bake 25 to 30 minutes longer.

Shredded Wheat Bread

YIELD: 6 LOAVES

Mary Emma Butz, wife of the former Secretary of Agriculture, contributes this recipe for an unusual bread that makes especially good toast.

2 packages active dry yeast

1/3 cup lukewarm water

3 tablespoons sugar

3 large shredded wheat cereal biscuits

3 tablespoons vegetable oil or
   margarine

½ cup sugar

½ cup molasses

1 tablespoon salt

2 cups boiling water

2 cups lukewarm water

9-12 cups whole wheat or unbleached
   white flour

In a small bowl dissolve the yeast in the 1/3 cup of lukewarm water and stir in the 3 tablespoons sugar. Set aside.

Crumble the shredded wheat biscuits into a large mixing bowl. Add the shortening, ½ cup sugar, molasses and salt. Pour in the 2 cups of boiling water and stir until the cereal is softened and the other ingredients blended. Stir in the lukewarm water and let stand to cool.

Combine the two mixtures.

Stir in flour enough to make a stiff dough that pulls away from the sides of the bowl. Turn out onto a lightly floured board and knead until smooth and elastic. Wash the mixing bowl and oil it generously. Put the dough in and turn it, so all sides are coated with oil. Cover and let stand in a warm place 1½ hours or until doubled.

Punch down the dough and shape into 6 loaves. Place in oiled bread pans and let rise 1 hour. Bake at 375 degrees F. for 45 minutes. Brush the top crusts with melted butter. Remove from the pans and cool thoroughly on a wire rack before slicing.

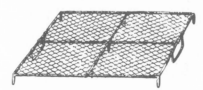

Wheat Germ Refrigerator Buns

YIELD: 20 BUNS

2 packages active dry yeast

3 tablespoons brown sugar

1 tablespoon salt

3½ cups unbleached white flour

4 tablespoons butter or margarine, cut
  in small pieces

2 cups milk

3 eggs

1 cup wheat germ

2 to 2½ cups whole wheat flour

Vegetable oil

In a large mixing bowl stir together the dry yeast, sugar, salt and 2 cups of the unbleached white flour. Add the butter.

Heat the milk until warm to the touch (do not scald). Add the warm milk to the flour-yeast mixture and beat with an electric mixer on medium speed 2 minutes, scraping the sides of the bowl occasionally.

Add the remaining 1½ cups of unbleached white flour and stir until blended. Add 2 eggs and beat at high speed 1 minute, or until the mixture is thick and elastic.

Stir in the wheat germ.

Gradually stir in just enough whole wheat flour (about 2 cups) to make a soft dough that pulls away from the sides of the bowl.

Turn the dough onto a lightly floured surface and knead 5 to 8 minutes or until the dough is smooth and elastic. Cover the dough with plastic wrap, then with a towel, and let it rest 20 minutes.

Punch down the dough. Divide it in half. Divide each half into 10 equal portions, and form each into a smooth ball.

Arrange 10 balls in each of 2 oiled 9-inch round pans. Brush tops with a little vegetable oil. Cover loosely with plastic wrap and refrigerate overnight.

Remove the buns from the refrigerator 1 hour before serving time. Uncover the pans and let stand at room temperature 30 minutes. Preheat oven to 400 degrees F.

Brush the tops of the buns with the remaining egg, beaten, and sprinkle with a little more wheat germ. Bake 25 to 30 minutes.

Salvador Dali
THE BASKET OF BREAD

Whole Wheat-Potato Bread

YIELD: 2 LOAVES

1¾ cups unbleached white flour

2 packages active dry yeast

1 cup milk

½ cup water

2 tablespoons butter

2 tablespoons honey

1 tablespoon salt

1½ cups seasoned mashed potatoes

½ cup dairy sour cream

½ cup minced onion

2 teaspoons chopped tarragon

1 teaspoon garlic powder

5-6 cups whole wheat flour

Spoon white flour into dry measuring cup; level.

Stir together the white flour and yeast.

Heat milk, water, butter, honey and salt over low heat until warm (120 degrees), stirring to blend.

Add the liquid ingredients to flour-yeast mixture and beat until smooth or about 3 minutes.

Add the potatoes, sour cream, onion, tarragon and garlic powder. Beat until smooth.

Stir in enough of the whole wheat flour to make a moderately stiff dough. Turn out onto a floured surface; let rest 4 minutes. Knead until smooth or for about 5 minutes.

Cover and let rise in a warm place until doubled or about 45 to 50 minutes.

Punch down. Divide the dough in half; shape into two loaves.

Place in two greased 8½-inch by 4½-inch or 9-inch by 5-inch pans. Let the dough rise again until almost doubled in volume, about 30 minutes.

Preheat oven to 350 degrees F.

Bake 35 to 40 minutes. Remove the loaves from the tins to a wire rack. Brush the tops with vegetable oil while the bread is hot.

Raisin Whole Wheat Bread

YIELD: 3 LOAVES

3 cups lukewarm water   *4 tablespoons vegetable oil*
3 packages dry active yeast   *1 tablespoon salt*
¾ cup honey   *1½ cups raisins*
Whole wheat flour   *3 tablespoons cinnamon*

Put the water into a large bowl. Add the yeast and stir until dissolved.

Add 4 tablespoons of the honey and 3 cups of flour. Beat 100 strokes by hand or for about 2½ minutes with an electric beater. Cover and set aside for 20 minutes.

Stir in the oil, salt, raisins, cinnamon, the rest of the honey and enough additional flour (3 to 4 cups) so that the dough forms a soft mass that no longer sticks to the bowl. Turn onto a lightly floured surface and knead for 8 minutes, adding more flour as needed.

Put the dough into a lightly oiled bowl, turning it so that all sides are coated. Cover and let rise for 1 hour or until doubled in size.

Lightly oil 3 bread tins.

Punch down the dough and divide into 3 parts. Knead each part slightly, shaping it into a loaf. Place the loaves in the tins. Cover and let rise 30 minutes.

Preheat the oven to 350 degrees F.

Bake 50 minutes. Turn out the breads immediately and cool on a wire rack.

Whole Wheat Corn Bread

YIELD: 3 LOAVES

3 cups warm water   *2½ cups cornmeal*
2 packages dry active yeast   *4 tablespoons vegetable oil*
Honey   *1 tablespoon salt*
6-7 cups whole wheat flour

Combine the water and yeast and stir until blended. Add 4 tablespoons of the honey and 3 cups of the whole wheat flour. Beat 2½ minutes with the electric beater or 100 strokes by hand. Cover with a towel and let rise about 20 minutes.

Add the cornmeal, 1/3 cup of honey, the oil, and the salt. Mix well. Stir in enough whole wheat flour so that the dough no longer sticks to the sides of the bowl.

Turn the dough onto a lightly floured working surface and knead the dough for 8 to 10 minutes or until the dough is smooth, adding whatever whole wheat flour is necessary.

Put the dough in a lightly oiled bowl, turning it so that all the sides are coated. Cover with a towel and let rise in a warm place until doubled.

Grease 3 loaf tins with vegetable oil.

Punch down the dough and divide it into 3 parts. Shape each part into a loaf and place in a tin. Cover with a towel and let rise 30 minutes or until doubled.

Preheat the oven to 350 degrees F.

Bake 50 minutes. Turn out of the tins onto a rack to cool.

Whole Wheat Cheese Bread

YIELD: 3 LOAVES

3 cups warm water

2 packages active dry yeast

4 tablespoons barley malt, honey
  or molasses

Whole wheat flour

4 tablespoons vegetable oil

1 tablespoon salt

¾ pound medium Cheddar cheese,
  grated

1½ teaspoons freshly ground black
  pepper

1½ teaspoons caraway seeds

¾ to 1 teaspoon minced garlic or
  1 tablespoon garlic powder

Mix the water and yeast until blended. Add the sweetener of your choice and 3 cups of whole wheat flour. Beat for 100 strokes or for 2 to 3 minutes with an electric beater. Cover and let stand 20 to 30 minutes.

Add the oil, salt, grated cheese, pepper, caraway seeds and garlic. Mix well.

Stir in enough whole wheat flour so that the dough no longer sticks to the sides of the bowl.

Turn the dough onto a floured surface and knead for 8 to 10 minutes, adding whole wheat flour as necessary until the dough forms a smooth shiny ball.

Put the dough into a lightly oiled bowl, turning it so that all the sides are coated. Cover and let rise for 1 hour or until doubled.

Oil 3 bread tins.

Punch down the dough and divide into 3 parts. Lightly knead and shape each part into a loaf and place the loaves in the tins. Cover with a towel and let rise 30 minutes or until doubled.

Preheat the oven to 350 degrees F.

Bake the bread for 45 to 50 minutes. Turn loaves out onto a wire rack to cool.

Whole Wheat Apple-nut Rolls

YIELD: 18 ROLLS

2 cups whole wheat flour
1½ cups unbleached white flour
1¼ cups milk
¼ cup margarine
¼ cup honey
¼ cup brown sugar

2 teaspoons salt
2 packages active dry yeast
½ cup warm water
½ cup finely chopped apple
½ cup chopped pecans or walnuts

In a large mixing bowl, stir together the whole wheat and unbleached flours.

Heat the milk until it almost boils, then stir into it the margarine, honey, brown sugar and salt. Cool to lukewarm.

Add the yeast to the warm water and stir until dissolved; then add it to the warm milk mixture.

Stir the liquid into the flour mixture, adding a little more flour if it is needed to make a thick, smooth batter. Cover and let stand in a warm place until doubled in bulk (about 45 minutes).

Stir the batter down and mix in the apple and nuts. Spoon equal quantities of the batter into 18 oiled muffin cups. Cover and let stand in a warm place 30 minutes.

Preheat oven to 400 degrees F.

Bake rolls 20 minutes or until nicely browned on top.

Hot Roll Bran Bread

YIELD: 1 LOAF

This recipe is a good one for people who think making yeast bread is difficult. Success with a package mix will show them how easy it is.

1 cup wheat bran cereal	*½ cup boiling water*
¼ cup wheat germ	*1 package hot roll mix*
½ teaspoon salt	*¾ cup very warm water (130 degrees F.)*
1 tablespoon butter or margarine	*2 eggs*
1 tablespoon honey	

In a large bowl, combine the bran cereal, wheat germ, salt, butter, honey and boiling water. Set aside to cool to lukewarm.

Dissolve the yeast from the hot roll mix package in the very warm water.

Add the yeast, the flour mixture from the hot roll mix package and the eggs to the cereal mixture. Stir until well blended.

Cover the bowl with a clean towel and set it in a warm place until the dough is light and doubled in size (30 to 45 minutes).

Generously grease a 9-inch by 5-inch or 8-inch by 4-inch loaf pan. Spoon the dough into the greased pan, cover, and set it in a warm place until dough is light and doubled in size (30 to 40 minutes).

Preheat the oven to 375 degrees F.

Bake the bread 40 to 50 minutes or until crust is a deep golden brown. (If the bread becomes too brown before the baking time is up, cover the pan with foil.) Remove from the pan immediately and cool on a wire rack.

Seven Grain Bread

YIELD: 3 LOAVES

3 cups warm water

2 packages active dry yeast

4 tablespoons barley malt, honey or
   molasses

Whole wheat flour

4 tablespoons vegetable oil

1 tablespoon salt

½ cup buckwheat flour

½ cup soy flour

½ cup cornmeal

½ cup uncooked oatmeal (rolled oats)

½ cup rye flour

½ cup millet, cracked if desired

Combine the water and yeast and mix until blended. Add the sweetening of your choice and 3 cups of whole wheat flour. Beat 100 strokes or for 2½ minutes with an electric beater.

Stir in the oil, salt, the buckwheat flour, soy flour, cornmeal, rolled oats, rye flour, millet and enough whole wheat flour so that the dough no longer sticks to the sides of the bowl.

Turn the dough onto a floured surface and knead 8 to 10 minutes or until the dough is firm and elastic.

Grease a bowl with vegetable oil and put in the dough, turning it so that all sides are coated. Cover with a towel and let rise in a warm place until doubled.

Lightly oil 3 bread tins.

Punch down the dough and divide it into 3 parts. Knead lightly and shape into loaves. Place the loaves in the tins. Cover and let rise for 30 minutes or until doubled.

Preheat the oven to 350 degrees F.

Bake 50 minutes and turn out immediately onto a rack to cool.

Soy Sunflower Bread

YIELD: 3 LOAVES

3 cups warm water
2 packages active dry yeast
4 tablespoons barley malt or honey
Whole wheat flour

½ cup chopped sunflower seeds
¾ cup soy flour
4 tablespoons vegetable oil
1 tablespoon salt

Combine the water and yeast and stir until blended. Add the barley malt or honey and 3 cups of whole wheat flour. Beat 100 strokes by hand or for 2½ minutes with an electric beater. Cover and let stand for 20 to 30 minutes.

Stir in the sunflower seeds, soy flour, vegetable oil and salt. Mix well and add enough whole wheat flour so that the dough no longer sticks to the bowl.

Turn the dough onto a floured working surface and knead for 8 to 10 minutes, adding whole wheat flour as necessary, until you have a smooth, shiny ball.

Oil a bowl and put in the dough, turning it so that the entire surface is coated. Cover and let rise in a warm place for 1 hour or until doubled.

Grease 3 loaf tins with vegetable oil.

Punch the dough down and divide it into 3 parts. Knead and shape each part into a loaf and place it in a tin. Cover with a towel and let rise until doubled.

Preheat the oven to 350 degrees F.

Bake the bread 45 to 50 minutes. Turn out on a rack to cool.

Quick Whole Wheat-Banana Bread

YIELD: 9 TO 12 SERVINGS

2½ cups whole wheat flour
½ cup honey
3½ teaspoons baking powder
¾ cup milk

3 tablespoons oil
1 egg, slightly beaten
1 cup mashed bananas (2 or 3 ripe bananas)

Preheat the oven to 350 degrees F.

Oil a 9-inch by 9-inch baking dish.

Combine in a bowl the flour, honey, baking powder, milk, vegetable oil, egg and mashed bananas. Mix just long enough to blend.

Bake 55 minutes.

Variation: This same recipe can be used for making muffins.

Pumpkin Nut Bread

YIELD: 1 LOAF

1½ cups unbleached white flour	*¼ cup margarine or butter*
2 teaspoons baking powder	*½ cup sugar*
½ teaspoon baking soda	*1 egg*
½ teaspoon salt	*½ cup milk*
1 teaspoon cinnamon	*1 teaspoon vanilla extract*
½ teaspoon ground cloves	*1 cup pumpkin*
¼ teaspoon ginger	*1 cup wheat bran cereal*
¼ teaspoon allspice	*½ cup chopped nuts*

Preheat the oven to 350 degrees F. Oil a 9-inch by 5-inch loaf pan.

In a small mixing bowl, stir together the flour, baking powder, soda, salt and spices. Set aside.

Measure the margarine and sugar into large mixing bowl. Beat until well combined. Add the egg, milk and vanilla. Beat well.

Mix in the pumpkin, bran cereal and nuts. Add the dry ingredients to the contents of the large bowl and mix thoroughly.

Spread the batter in the prepared pan and bake about 50 minutes or until a wooden pick inserted near center comes out clean. Cool completely before slicing.

Serve half slices sandwich-style with softened cream cheese as the filling.

Caraway Onion Quickbread

YIELD: 1 LOAF

¼ cup butter or margarine

1/3 cup minced onion

1 cup wheat bran cereal

1 cup buttermilk or sour milk

1 egg

1½ cups unbleached white flour

1 teaspoon baking powder

1 teaspoon baking soda

1 teaspoon salt

2 teaspoons caraway seeds

Preheat the oven to 350 degrees F. Oil a 9-inch by 5-inch loaf pan.

Melt the butter or margarine in a heavy saucepan. Add the minced onion and cook over low heat, stirring occasionally, until the onion is tender. Remove from the heat. Stir in the bran cereal and buttermilk and let stand for 2 minutes or until the cereal is softened and most of the liquid absorbed. Beat in the egg.

In a large mixing bowl combine the flour, baking powder, baking soda, salt and caraway seeds. Stir until well mixed.

Add the onion-cereal mixture to the dry ingredients and stir just until all are moistened.

Pour the batter into the prepared pan and bake 30 to 35 minutes or until a wooden pick inserted near the center comes out dry. Cool 10 minutes in the pan, then turn out onto a wire rack.

Apricot Oatmeal Bread

YIELD: 1 LOAF

1 cup wheat bran cereal

½ cup uncooked oatmeal (rolled oats)

2 eggs

1 1/3 cups milk

¼ cup vegetable oil

½ cup honey

1 cup chopped dried apricots

½ cup chopped nuts

2 cups whole wheat flour

1 tablespoon baking powder

2 teaspoons ground cinnamon

1 teaspoon salt

Preheat the oven to 350 degrees F.

Combine the bran cereal and oatmeal in a mixing bowl.

In another mixing bowl beat together the eggs, milk, vegetable oil and honey.

Add the egg-milk mixture to the cereal and stir together.

Stir in the apricots and nuts.

In another bowl stir together the flour, baking powder, cinnamon and salt.

Add the cereal mixture all at once to the dry ingredients and stir only until all of the dry ingredients are moistened.

Pour the batter into an oiled 9-inch by 5-inch loaf pan and bake 55 minutes to 1 hour, or until done. Remove from the pan and cool completely on a wire rack before slicing.

Steamed Boston Brown Bread

YIELD: 8 TO 10 SERVINGS (3 LOAVES)

2 cups whole wheat flour

1 cup yellow cornmeal

1½ teaspoons baking soda

1 teaspoon baking powder

1 teaspoon salt

1 cup seedless raisins

½ cup chopped nuts (pecans or walnuts)

¼ cup unbleached white flour

2 cups buttermilk or sour milk *

½ cup molasses

Wash carefully and dry 3 No. 2-size cans (about 2½-cup capacity). Coat the insides generously with vegetable oil or soft margarine and set aside.

In a large mixing bowl, stir together the whole wheat flour, cornmeal, baking soda, baking powder and salt.

Stir in the raisins, nuts and white flour.

Add the buttermilk or sour milk and the molasses and stir just until all the dry ingredients are moistened.

Spoon the batter into the cans. Cover the tops with a double thickness of waxed paper and tie securely with string.

Place the cans on a rack in a large kettle and add boiling water to a level within 2 inches of the tops of the cans. Cover the kettle tightly and steam 2½ hours or until done. (Check several times during cooking period and add more water if needed.)

Lift cans from the hot water, remove paper and string and place on a rack to cool for 10 minutes. Then remove the bread from the cans (use a knife to loosen around the edges, if needed) and finish cooling the loaves on the rack. Serve warm or cold.

* For a substitute, combine 2 scant cups of milk with 2 tablespoons of vinegar and let stand 5 minutes at room temperature.

Banana Date Bread

YIELD: 1 LOAF

2 cups unbleached white flour
1 teaspoon baking powder
½ teaspoon baking soda
½ teaspoon salt
¾ cup cut, pitted dates
1/3 cup boiling water

1½ cups mashed, fully ripe bananas
1½ cups wheat bran cereal
½ cup margarine or butter, softened
¾ cup sugar
2 eggs
½ cup coarsely chopped nuts (optional)

Preheat the oven to 350 degrees F. Oil a 9-inch by 5-inch loaf pan.

Stir together the flour, baking powder, soda and salt. Set aside.

In a small mixing bowl stir together the dates and water. Cover, let stand 10 minutes. Add the mashed bananas and cereal. Let stand 2 to 3 minutes or until cereal is softened.

Meanwhile, in a large mixing bowl beat the margarine and sugar until well blended. Add the eggs. Mix well.

Stir in the cereal mixture, the dry ingredients and the nuts.

Spread the batter in the prepared pan and bake 1 hour or until a wooden pick inserted near the center comes out clean. Let cool 10 minutes before removing from pan. Cool completely. For easier slicing, wrap tightly and store overnight.

Carrot Bread

YIELD: 2 LOAVES

2½ cups whole wheat flour

2/3 cup sugar or honey

1 teaspoon baking powder

1 teaspoon baking soda

1 teaspoon ground cinnamon

½ teaspoon salt

3 eggs, beaten

½ cup vegetable oil

½ cup milk

2 cups shredded carrots

½ cup chopped pecans

Preheat the oven to 350 degrees F.

In a large mixing bowl, stir together the whole wheat flour, sugar, baking powder, baking soda, cinnamon and salt.

In another bowl combine and beat well the eggs, vegetable oil and milk. If using honey rather than sugar, add it at this time.

Add the liquids to the dry ingredients and stir just until all are moistened.

Fold in the shredded carrots and pecans.

Pour the batter into 2 oiled loaf pans and bake 1 hour. Cool; then store the bread in the refrigerator. It will slice more easily and taste even better the next day.

Banana Honey Bread

YIELD: 1 LOAF

2 cups unbleached white flour

1 teaspoon baking powder

½ teaspoon baking soda

½ teaspoon salt

1½ cups mashed, fully ripe bananas

1½ cups wheat bran cereal

½ cup margarine or butter, softened

2/3 cup honey

2 eggs

½ cup coarsely chopped nuts (optional)

Preheat the oven to 350 degrees F. Oil a 9-inch by 5-inch loaf pan.

Stir together the flour, baking powder, soda and salt. Set aside.

In a small mixing bowl, stir together the mashed bananas and cereal. Let stand 2 to 3 minutes or until the cereal is softened.

Meanwhile, in a large mixing bowl beat the margarine and honey until well blended. Add eggs. Mix well.

Stir in the cereal mixture, the dry ingredients and the nuts.

Spread the batter in the prepared pan and bake 1 hour or until a wooden pick inserted near the center comes out clean. Let cool 10 minutes before removing from the pan. Cool completely before slicing.

Always Ready Bran Muffins

YIELD: 2 DOZEN

These muffins are made, stored in the refrigerator and baked whenever they are wanted. About 25 minutes before serving, preheat the oven to 400 degrees F. Spoon the batter into Teflon-lined or buttered muffin tins, filling them 2/3 full. Bake 18 minutes and serve. You can make 2 muffins or enough for a large group.

3 cups wheat bran cereal
1 cup boiling water
1 cup sugar
½ cup margarine
2 eggs

2½ cups unbleached white flour
2½ teaspoons baking soda
1 teaspoon salt
1 pint buttermilk

Put 1 cup of bran in a small bowl. Add the water, stir once and let stand to soften.

Cream the margarine and sugar in a mixing bowl.

Beat the eggs slightly.

Combine the flour, soda and salt.

Combine the softened bran, the remaining bran, the eggs, flour mixture and buttermilk with the margarine and sugar and stir until thoroughly mixed. Pour into a plastic container. Cover tightly and store in the refrigerator for a minimum of 12 hours and a maximum of 6 weeks.

Best Bran Muffins

YIELD: 12 MUFFINS

1½ cups wheat bran cereal
1 cup milk
1 egg
1/3 cup soft shortening

1½ cups sifted all-purpose flour
½ cup sugar
3 teaspoons baking powder
1 teaspoon salt

Preheat the oven to 400 degrees F.

Combine the bran cereal and milk in a mixing bowl. Let stand 2 minutes or until most of the moisture is absorbed.

Add the egg and shortening. Beat until well blended.

Sift together the flour, sugar, baking powder and salt.

Add the dry ingredients to the cereal mixture and stir just until all are moistened.

Spoon the batter into oiled muffin cups (3/4 full) and bake 25 minutes or until lightly browned. Serve hot.

Wheat Cereal Muffins

YIELD: 2 DOZEN

3 cups quick-cooking wheat cereal
1 cup boiling water
½ cup vegetable oil
1½ cups brown sugar or 1 cup honey
2 eggs, beaten

2 cups buttermilk
2½ cups whole wheat flour
2½ teaspoons baking soda
1 teaspoon salt

Preheat the oven to 400 degrees F.

Pour the boiling water over the wheat cereal and stir. Let stand until well soaked.

In another bowl, combine the vegetable oil, brown sugar or honey, eggs and buttermilk. Beat until well blended; then stir the mixture into the wheat cereal.

Sift together the flour, soda and salt. Add to the batter and stir just until all the dry ingredients are moistened.

Spoon the batter into oiled muffin cups, filling each just 2/3 full. Bake 15 to 20 minutes or until a wooden pick inserted near the center of a muffin comes out clean.

Applesauce Cornmeal Muffins

YIELD: 12 MUFFINS

1 cup yellow cornmeal

1/3 cup unbleached white flour

3 tablespoons brown sugar

2 teaspoons baking powder

½ teaspoon salt

½ cup milk

1 egg

3 tablespoons vegetable oil

1 cup canned applesauce

Preheat the oven to 425 degrees F.

In a large mixing bowl, stir together the cornmeal, white flour, brown sugar, baking powder and salt.

In another bowl beat together the milk, egg and vegetable oil. When they are well blended, stir in the applesauce.

Add the liquid mixture to the dry ingredients and stir just until all the dry ingredients are moistened.

Spoon the batter into oiled muffin cups, which should be about ¾ full. Bake about 25 minutes, or until lightly browned.

Bran Pineapple Muffins

YIELD: 12 MUFFINS

1 cup wheat bran cereal

½ cup milk

1 cup crushed pineapple, drained

½ cup raisins

1 egg, beaten

¼ cup vegetable oil, melted margarine
   or butter

1 cup whole wheat flour

2 teaspoons baking powder

½ teaspoon salt

¼ teaspoon baking soda

½ cup brown sugar or 1/3 cup molasses

Preheat the oven to 400 degrees F.

Stir together the bran, milk, pineapple and raisins and set aside.

In a large mixing bowl stir together the oil or melted shortening and the egg. Mix well.

Stir together the flour, baking powder, salt, baking soda and brown sugar. (If you are using molasses, stir it into the egg-oil mixture.)

Add the dry ingredients to the egg-oil mixture and stir.

Add the bran-pineapple mixture and stir just until blended.

Spoon the batter into 12 oiled muffin cups (the cups should be about 2/3 full) and bake 25 to 30 minutes.

Molasses Bran Muffins

YIELD: 12 MUFFINS

1 cup whole wheat flour
1 teaspoon baking soda
2 teaspoons baking powder
¾ cup buttermilk
½ cup molasses

2 tablespoons vegetable oil, melted
  margarine or butter
1 egg, beaten
1½ cups wheat bran cereal
½ cup raisins

Preheat the oven to 400 degrees F.

Stir together the flour, baking soda and baking powder. Set aside.

In another bowl, blend together the milk, molasses, oil or melted shortening, egg, cereal and raisins. Let stand 2 minutes or until the cereal is softened.

Combine the dry and liquid ingredients and stir just until all are moistened.

Spoon the batter into 12 oiled muffin cups (cups should be approximately 2/3 full) and bake 15 to 20 minutes.

Bran Bread with Raisins

YIELD: 1 LOAF

1½ cups sifted all-purpose flour

½ cup sugar

1 teaspoon baking powder

1 teaspoon baking soda

1 teaspoon salt

1½ cups wheat bran cereal

1½ cups seedless raisins

¼ cup soft shortening

1½ cups hot water

1 egg

1 teaspoon vanilla flavoring

¾ cup chopped nuts

Preheat the oven to 350 degrees F.

Sift together the flour, baking powder, soda and salt.

In another bowl combine the bran cereal, raisins, shortening and hot water. Stir until the shortening is melted.

Add the egg and vanilla. Beat well.

Add the sifted dry ingredients and stir just until all the dry ingredients are moistened.

Spread the batter in a well-oiled loaf pan and bake about 1 hour. Cool thoroughly before slicing.

Zucchini Bread

YIELD: 2 LOAVES

3 cups whole wheat or unbleached
   white flour

1¼ cups wheat germ

3 teaspoons baking powder

1 teaspoon salt

2 teaspoons cinnamon

1 cup chopped nuts

2 eggs

1¾ cups brown sugar or honey

2 teaspoons vanilla extract

2/3 cup vegetable oil

3 cups grated zucchini

Preheat the oven to 350 degrees F.

Mix together the flour, wheat germ, baking powder, salt, cinnamon and nuts.

In another bowl beat the eggs until they are light-colored and fluffy. Beat in the sugar or honey, vanilla extract and vegetable oil. Stir in the grated zucchini.

Add gradually the flour mixture, stirring until blended.

Turn the batter into 2 oiled and floured 8½-inch by 4½-inch loaf pans and bake 1 hour or until a wooden pick inserted near the center comes out clean. (If using glass pans, bake at 325 degrees F.) Cool 5 to 10 minutes in the pan; then remove to a wire rack.

Cranberry Wheat Germ Bread

YIELD: 1 LOAF

2 cups unbleached white flour

1 cup sugar

½ cup wheat germ

2 teaspoons baking powder

½ teaspoon baking soda

1½ teaspoons salt

1 cup chopped raw cranberries

½ cup chopped pecans

3 tablespoons grated orange rind

½ cup orange juice

¼ cup warm water

1 egg

2 tablespoons vegetable oil

Preheat the oven to 350 degrees F.

In a large mixing bowl, combine the flour, sugar, wheat germ, baking powder, baking soda and salt. Stir until well blended.

Stir in the cranberries, nuts and orange rind.

In a small bowl combine the orange juice, water, egg and oil. Stir until well blended.

Add the liquid mixture to the dry ingredients, all at once, and stir just until all ingredients are moistened.

Spread the batter in a well-oiled loaf pan and bake 50 to 60 minutes or until a wooden pick inserted near the center comes out clean. Remove from pan and cool on a wire rack.

Peanut Butter Bread

YIELD: 1 LOAF

1½ cups unbleached white flour
3 teaspoons baking powder
½ teaspoon salt
1 1/3 cups milk
2 cups wheat bran flakes with raisins

1/3 cup peanut butter
½ cup sugar
1 egg, slightly beaten
¼ cup chopped peanuts

Preheat the oven to 350 degrees F.

Stir together flour, baking powder and salt.

In a small mixing bowl, stir together the milk and bran cereal.

Beat the peanut butter and sugar until well blended. Add the egg. Mix well.

Stir in the cereal mixture, the dry ingredients and the peanuts.

Spread the batter in an oiled loaf pan and bake about 1 hour or until a wooden pick inserted near the center comes out clean. Remove from the pan. Cool completely before slicing.

Bran Nut Bread

YIELD: 1 LOAF

1 cup whole wheat flour
1½ cups unbleached white flour
2 teaspoons baking powder
½ teaspoon baking soda
½ teaspoon salt
¼ cup vegetable oil

¾ cup sugar
1 egg, slightly beaten
1¼ cups milk
1 cup wheat bran cereal
1 cup pecans or walnuts, chopped

Preheat oven to 350 degrees F.

Stir together the flour, baking powder, baking soda and salt.

In a large mixing bowl, combine the vegetable oil, sugar, egg, milk and bran cereal. Stir until blended. Let stand 2 minutes or until the cereal is softened.

Add the dry ingredients to the liquid mixture. Mix only until combined.

Fold in the nuts and pour the batter into an oiled loaf pan. Bake 50 minutes.

Variation: Add 2 tablespoons grated orange peel along with the last of the dry ingredients.

Orange Pecan Wheat Germ Bread

YIELD: 1 LOAF

1 cup sugar
½ cup soft butter or margarine
1 tablespoon grated orange rind
2 eggs
2¾ cups unbleached white flour
½ cup wheat germ

3 teaspoons baking powder
½ teaspoon baking soda
1 teaspoon salt
1 cup orange juice
½ cup chopped pecans

Preheat the oven to 350 degrees F.

Combine the sugar, butter or margarine and the orange rind in a mixing bowl and cream together.

Add the eggs, 1 at a time, beating well after each addition.

In another bowl combine the flour, wheat germ, baking powder, baking soda and salt. Stir until well mixed together.

Add the dry ingredients and the orange juice alternately to the creamed mixture, stirring just until all ingredients are moistened.

Fold in the chopped nuts.

Pour the batter into a well-oiled loaf pan and bake 55 to 60 minutes or until a wooden pick inserted near the center comes out clean. Remove the bread from the pan and cool it on a wire rack.

Old-Fashioned Corn Bread

YIELD: 12 TO 16 SERVINGS

1 cup sifted unbleached white flour
3 teaspoons baking powder
½ teaspoon salt
1 cup yellow cornmeal

1 cup milk
2 eggs, beaten
¼ cup honey or maple syrup
¼ cup melted butter or bacon drippings

Preheat the oven to 425 degrees F.

Sift together the flour, baking powder and salt. Add the cornmeal and stir until well mixed.

In another bowl combine the milk, eggs, honey or maple syrup and the melted butter or bacon drippings.

Add the liquids to the dry ingredients and stir just until all are moistened.

Pour the batter into an oiled 8-inch square baking pan and bake about 20 minutes or until done in the center and lightly browned. To test for doneness insert a toothpick or cake tester in the center. If it comes out dry the corn bread is done.

Three-Layer Corn Bread (Unleavened)

YIELD: 12 TO 16 SQUARES

1 cup cornmeal
1 cup whole wheat pastry flour
½ teaspoon salt
1 egg, beaten

½ cup honey
¼ cup vegetable oil
3 cups milk or buttermilk

Preheat the oven to 350 degrees F.

Combine and stir together the cornmeal, whole wheat flour and salt.

In another bowl beat together the egg, honey, vegetable oil and milk.

Add the liquids to the dry ingredients and stir just until all are moistened.

Pour the batter into an oiled or buttered 8-inch square pan and bake 50 minutes. Serve warm with butter and honey.

Pumpkin Muffins

YIELD: 12 MUFFINS

1½ cups unbleached white flour
2½ teaspoons baking powder
1 teaspoon salt
1 teaspoon ground cinnamon
½ teaspoon ground nutmeg
1¼ cups wheat bran cereal
2/3 cup milk

¾ cup seedless raisins
1 cup canned pumpkin
½ cup sugar
1 egg
½ cup soft shortening
1½ teaspoons sugar

Preheat the oven to 400 degrees F.

Stir together flour, baking powder, salt, cinnamon and nutmeg. Set aside.

Measure the cereal, milk, raisins, pumpkin and the ½ cup sugar into a large mixing bowl. Stir to combine. Let stand about 2 minutes or until the cereal is softened.

Add the egg and shortening. Beat well.

Add the dry ingredients, stirring only until combined.

Portion the batter evenly into 12 greased 2½-inch muffin-pan cups. Sprinkle with the 1½ teaspoons sugar. Bake about 35 minutes or until the muffins are golden brown. Serve warm.

Pineapple Corn Muffins

YIELD: 15 MUFFINS

1 cup whole wheat flour
1/3 cup soy flour
3 teaspoons baking powder
1 teaspoon salt
1 cup yellow cornmeal
½ cup nonfat dry milk powder

2 eggs, beaten
1 cup drained crushed pineapple
1 cup liquid (juice from the pineapple
    plus water)
½ stick (2 ounces) margarine, melted
2 tablespoons honey

Preheat the oven to 400 degrees F.

Combine the whole wheat flour, soy flour, baking powder, salt, cornmeal and dry milk powder. Stir until mixed together well.

In another bowl combine the eggs, pineapple, liquid, melted margarine and honey. Stir but do not overmix.

Add the pineapple mixture to the dry ingredients and stir just until all the dry ingredients are moistened.

Spoon the batter into oiled muffin cups, filling them almost to the top. Drizzle a little honey over the top of each muffin and bake 15 to 20 minutes, or until just done. Do not overbake.

High Protein Muffins

YIELD: 12 TO 18 MUFFINS

2 cups soy flour	3 slightly beaten eggs
1 cup nonfat dry milk powder	3 tablespoons vegetable oil, melted
¼-1 teaspoon salt	butter or margarine
1 tablespoon baking powder	Grated rind of 1 orange
1 cup chopped nuts	¾ cup orange juice
1 cup chopped dates or raisins	3 tablespoons honey

Preheat the oven to 350 degrees F.

Sift together, into a large mixing bowl, the soy flour, dry milk powder, salt and baking powder.

Stir the nuts and dates or raisins into the dry ingredients.

In another bowl beat together the eggs, shortening, orange rind, orange juice and honey.

Add the egg-orange juice mixture to the dry ingredients and stir just until all the dry ingredients are moistened.

Spoon the batter into oiled or buttered muffin cups (2/3 full) and bake 25 minutes or until lightly browned.

Wheat Germ-Banana Muffins

YIELD: 12 MUFFINS

1½ cups whole wheat or unbleached
  white flour
1 cup wheat germ
½ cup brown sugar
3 teaspoons baking powder
½ teaspoon salt

1 cup mashed ripe banana (2 or 3
  bananas)
½ cup milk
¼ cup vegetable oil, melted butter or
  margarine
2 eggs, beaten

Preheat the oven to 400 degrees F.

Combine and stir together the flour, wheat germ, brown sugar, baking powder and salt.

In another bowl combine the bananas, milk, oil and eggs. Stir just until mixed together.

Add the banana mixture to the dry ingredients and stir just until all the dry ingredients are moistened.

Spoon the batter into 12 oiled or paper-lined muffin cups and bake 20 to 25 minutes. Serve warm.

Cheese Spoon Bread

YIELD: 6 SERVINGS

1 cup yellow cornmeal
¼ cup whole wheat flour
1 teaspoon salt
3 cups milk

3 eggs, beaten
1 cup Cheddar cheese, shredded
  (¼ pound)
1 teaspoon baking powder

About 1 hour before serving time preheat the oven to 350 degrees F. and begin preparation, as the spoon bread should be served the minute it is done. Spoon breads, like soufflés, fall quickly, so advance planning is important.

Combine and mix together the cornmeal, flour and salt.

Scald the milk in a large heavy saucepan.

Add the dry ingredients to the hot milk, pouring in a thin, steady stream and stirring constantly until the mixture comes to a full boil. Remove from the heat.

Beat the eggs. Pour a little of the hot cornmeal mixture into the eggs and beat well; then stir the eggs and the cheese into the hot mixture. Stir until the cheese melts.

Sprinkle the baking powder over the mixture and stir it in.

Pour the batter into a well-oiled round 1½-quart baking dish or soufflé dish and bake 45 minutes or until puffed and browned. Serve immediately, with butter.

Bran Crepes

YIELD: 12 TO 16 CREPES

2 cups milk
¼ cup wheat bran cereal
2 eggs, beaten
¾ cup unbleached white flour

¼ teaspoon salt
2 teaspoons sugar
2 tablespoons vegetable oil

Pour the milk over the bran and let stand 10 minutes.

Add the eggs and beat well.

Combine the flour, salt and sugar and stir into the liquids.

Add the oil, blend well and let the batter rest 30 or, better yet, 60 minutes.

Heat and lightly oil a 6-inch skillet or crepe pan. Pour in a large spoonful of the batter and tilt the pan to coat the bottom with a thin film. Cook just until lightly browned on the underside; then flip and cook the other side for about 30 seconds.

Whole Wheat Baking Powder Biscuits

YIELD: 15 TO 20 BISCUITS

1 cup sifted unbleached white flour
1 cup whole wheat flour
3 teaspoons baking powder
¾ teaspoon salt

½ cup soft shortening, butter or
*   margarine*
¾ cup milk

Preheat the oven to 450 degrees F.

Sift together the flours, baking powder and salt into a mixing bowl.

Cut in the shortening using a pastry blender or 2 knives, until the mixture resembles coarse meal.

Add the milk and mix lightly and quickly with a fork, just until all the dry ingredients are moistened.

Turn the dough onto a lightly floured board and knead gently 6 to 8 times.

Roll the dough ½ to ¾ inch thick for fluffy biscuits or ½ inch thick for crisp, crusty biscuits. Cut with a 2-inch floured round cutter.

Bake on an ungreased baking sheet 10 to 15 minutes, depending on thickness, or until done and lightly browned.

Slow Cooker Steamed Rye Bread

YIELD: 1 LOAF

*One of the most successful new appliances to appear in recent years
is the slow cooker or crock pot that does the job back-of-the-stove
cooking did in great-grandmother's day. This bread and the
following one are designed for "baking" in
this kind of slow cooker.*

1 cup rye flour	1 teaspoon baking soda
1 cup whole wheat flour	¾ cup molasses
1 cup cornmeal	2 cups water
1 teaspoon salt	½ cup raisins
1 teaspoon baking powder	

Combine the flours, cornmeal, salt, baking powder and soda in a large mixing bowl. Stir until blended.

Stir in the molasses and water. Mix well. Stir in the raisins.

Pour the batter into a well-oiled baking pan intended for use in the slow cooker or into a well-oiled 2-pound coffee can. Cover with the lid provided, or with foil punctured in several places to let the steam escape.

Pour 1½ cups of water into the slow cooker and set the pan in. Cook 2½ to 4 hours with the cooker set on High.

Slow Cooker Brown Bread

YIELD: 1 LOAF

¼ cup very warm (not hot) water	*2 tablespoons sugar*
1 package active dry yeast	*2 tablespoons brown sugar*
½ teaspoon sugar	*2 tablespoons molasses*
½ cup milk	*1 cup whole wheat flour*
1 tablespoon butter or margarine	*½ cup water*
1½ teaspoons salt	*2-2½ cups unbleached white flour*

Stir together the warm water, yeast and ½ teaspoon sugar. Set aside.

Combine in a small saucepan the milk, butter or margarine, salt and sugar. Heat until the butter melts, then pour into a large mixing bowl.

Stir in the brown sugar, molasses, whole wheat flour and water. Stir in the dissolved yeast.

Add gradually 1 cup of the white flour while beating with an electric mixer. Beat for 2 minutes.

Stir in enough additional flour to make a dough that pulls away from the sides of the bowl.

Place the dough in a well-oiled baking pan intended for use in the slow cooker or in a well-oiled 2-pound coffee can. Cover with the lid provided, or with foil punctured in several places to let the steam escape. Bake 2 to 3 hours with the cooker set on High.

Microwave Casserole Bread

YIELD: 1 LOAF

1½ cups water	*2 tablespoons butter or margarine*
1/3 cup cornmeal	*¼ cup very warm (not hot) water*
1 teaspoon salt	*1 package active dry yeast*
1/3 cup molasses	*3¼ cups unbleached white flour*

Combine the water, cornmeal and salt in a saucepan. Cook, stirring frequently, until the mixture comes to a boil and begins to thicken.

Remove from the heat. Stir in the molasses and butter or margarine and set aside to cool to lukewarm.

Stir the yeast into the warm water and add to the cornmeal mixture.

Add the flour, half at a time, blending well after each addition.

Spread the dough evenly in a 2-quart casserole or loaf pan. Brush the top with vegetable oil or softened butter or margarine. Cover the casserole and refrigerate overnight.

Uncover the casserole and bake in the microwave oven 10 minutes, or until no doughy spots remain. There will be no brown crust.

Note: Yeast doughs rise extra-high in a microwave oven, so the casserole or loaf pan should be only half full when it goes into the oven.

STIRRING
EXPERIENCES

Soups and Chowders

Health is a precious thing,
and the only one, in truth, which deserves that
we employ in its pursuit not only time,
sweat, trouble, and worldly goods, but even life.

—*Michel de Montaigne*

S oup may be as old as civilization, and there is perhaps some lingering tribal instinct that bids us boil and bubble combinations of meat and vegetables to create a satisfying luncheon dish or the appetizing prelude to a more elaborate meal.

We know that the good word *soup* dates back to *sop* or *sup*, born in the days before the invention of the spoon permitted a genteel ladling of liquid from bowl to mouth, when a crust of bread served as utensil, to be itself consumed when no longer useful.

Home-style, made-from-scratch soups are the best soups. Preparing them is easy, though time-consuming. One good trick is to start the soup the day before you intend to serve it; it will taste even better because the flavors will have had time to mingle in the refrigerator overnight.

The soups made from lentils, dry peas and beans are the ones richest in fiber. To add fiber to other soups, stir in bran (either unprocessed bran or bran cereal) and serve them with whole-grain bread.

You will find in this collection recipes for unusual soups. You will also find old favorite soups with new seasonings and garnishes to give them fresh appeal—caraway seeds and tamari in the Split Pea Soup, guacamole on the Mexican Carrot Soup, miso paste in the Onion Soup, dill in the Cabbage Soup. Gazpacho is particularly nutritious because its ingredients lose no minerals or vitamins in cooking. Cucumber Yogurt Soup, refreshingly original in its main ingredients, also rejoices in snippets of onion, green pepper, celery seed, parsley and a passel of other tasty herbs. *Voilà! Fibroso et formidable!*

Claude Monet
STILL LIFE

Vichyssoise à la Santé

YIELD: APPROXIMATELY 8 SERVINGS

1 large onion
1½ bunches scallions (green onions)
3-4 medium-size new potatoes
1 small bunch fresh parsley
2 tablespoons vegetable oil
3 cups vegetable broth
¼ teaspoon mace

1/8 teaspoon kelp powder
1 teaspoon tamari
5 cups milk (cashew milk—see Reference Chapter—may be used)
1 teaspoon salt
1 potato, boiled and diced
½ cup chopped chives

Peel the onion and slice very thin.

Wash the green onions and cut into 1-inch lengths, both green and white parts.

Peel the potatoes and slice thin.

Chop the parsley.

Heat the oil in a deep skillet and sauté the onions until soft. Add the potatoes, parsley, 2 cups of the vegetable broth, mace and kelp powder. Cook until the potatoes are just tender and remove from the heat.

Add the remaining vegetable broth and pour the mixture into a blender.

Add the tamari and spin until smooth.

Refrigerate until very cold. The soup thickens as it chills.

Add the milk and salt and mix well.

Serve in a soup tureen garnished with the cold boiled, diced potato and chopped chives.

Curried Zucchini Soup

YIELD: 4 SERVINGS

2 pounds (3 small) zucchini
2 large yellow onions
½ pound (2-3) tomatoes
1 quart vegetable stock or water
3 tablespoons butter, margarine or
  vegetable oil

1 teaspoon whole wheat flour
4 tablespoons water
1 teaspoon curry powder
1/8 teaspoon ginger
½ teaspoon salt
Dash of cayenne pepper

Wash the zucchini and dice coarsely. Peel and slice the onions.

Heat 2 tablespoons of butter, margarine or oil in a kettle and sauté the zucchini and onions until the onions are soft.

Add the vegetable stock or water and cook 20 minutes.

Slice the tomatoes and sauté them briefly in the remaining butter, margarine or oil. Add to the other vegetables and bring to a boil.

Mix the flour, water, curry powder, ginger, salt and cayenne. When they are blended, add them to the soup. Simmer 6 minutes.

Force the mixture through a strainer or food mill or spin in a blender. Season to taste with salt and pepper.

Onion Soup

YIELD: 1 GALLON

Make this soup a day or two in advance. It improves with age.

7 large onions
4 tablespoons vegetable oil
1 gallon vegetable stock (see Reference
  Chapter), beef stock or water

4 tablespoons tamari (soy sauce)
4 tablespoons miso (soybean paste)
Whole wheat bread
Shredded mozzarella or Cheddar cheese

Peel and slice the onions. Heat the oil in a soup kettle and sauté the onions over moderate heat until soft. Stir frequently.

Add the stock or water and bring to a boil. Add the tamari. Cover and simmer 25 minutes.

Put the miso in a small bowl and whisk in 1 cup of the soup until blended. Add the mixture gradually to the soup, whisking constantly. Simmer 5 minutes longer. Taste and add more tamari if necessary. Cool before placing in the refrigerator.

Croutons: Cut 3-inch rounds of thickly sliced whole wheat bread. Place the bread on a baking sheet. Toast lightly on one side. Turn and spread the toast lightly with butter (optional). Sprinkle liberally with shredded cheese and broil until the cheese melts.

To serve: Place a crouton in an onion soup ramekin or in a soup plate. Pour the hot soup over the crouton and serve immediately.

Corn and Cheddar Cheese Chowder

YIELD: 8 SERVINGS

1 1/3 cups potatoes, diced	*1 2/3 cups buttermilk*
2 2/3 cups boiling salted water	*Corn kernels from 4 ears, or 2 cups*
1 bay leaf	*canned corn*
1/3 teaspoon sage	*1 tablespoon brewer's yeast (optional)*
2/3 teaspoon ground cumin seeds	*5 green onions (scallions), chopped*
4 tablespoons margarine	*1/3 teaspoon each nutmeg, salt, cayenne*
1 onion, chopped	*1 1/3 cups grated Cheddar cheese*
4 tablespoons whole wheat flour	*2 tablespoons chopped parsley*

Boil the potatoes in salted water with bay leaf, sage and cumin in a covered saucepan for 15 minutes.

Heat the margarine and sauté the onion just until tender. Add the flour and mix until blended. Add the buttermilk and whisk until the mixture thickens, keeping the heat very low.

Pour the mixture into the potato mixture gradually, stirring constantly.

Add the corn, yeast, green onions, nutmeg, salt and cayenne and simmer for 10 minutes, adding water if too thick.

Add the cheese, mix well and heat until melted, being careful not to let the soup boil.

Serve in soup bowls garnished with chopped parsley.

Sweet and Sour Cabbage Soup

YIELD: 8 TO 12 SERVINGS

*Make this soup a day ahead. It improves with
24 hours or more of aging.*

2 pounds head cabbage	8 gingersnaps, crumbled
1½ cups finely diced onions	2 teaspoons salt
½ cup finely diced carrots	Pepper to taste
¼ cup finely diced celery	¾ cup honey
1 can (28 ounces) tomatoes	¼ cup brown sugar
9 cups water	1 teaspoon sour salt, or powdered
½ teaspoon celery salt	vitamin C
½ teaspoon crumbled dill weed	

Cut cabbage into quarters, remove the core and any limp outer leaves and shred.

Bring the water to a boil. Add the cabbage, onions, carrots, celery and tomatoes and let the mixture boil again.

Add the celery salt, dill weed, gingersnaps, salt and pepper. Cover and simmer for 2¼ hours.

Add the honey, brown sugar, sour salt or powdered vitamin C. Bring to a boil and cook over medium heat for 15 minutes.

Taste for seasoning, making sure that there is enough pepper.

Serve very hot and accompany it with onion, dill or rye bread spread with butter or margarine.

Gazpacho

YIELD: 6 SERVINGS

1 1-pound loaf French or Italian bread	*½ teaspoon paprika*
5 large tomatoes	*¼ teaspoon black pepper*
1 medium cucumber	
2 onions	*GARNISH:*
3 cloves garlic	*3 hard-cooked eggs*
1 green pepper	*1 small cucumber, diced*
½ cup olive oil	*1 small red pepper, minced*
1/3 cup red wine vinegar	*Green scallions, chopped*
2 cups tomato juice	*Chopped parsley*
1½ teaspoons salt	*Croutons*

Slice the bread into thick chunks and cover with cold water. Let stand 5 minutes.

Peel the tomatoes, cucumber, onions and garlic. Cut them in chunks into the blender and add half the green pepper, seeded and cut into pieces. Squeeze the water out of the bread and add it to the mixture in the blender.

Spin in the blender until well mixed. Remove the top and add the oil gradually while spinning, as when making mayonnaise. (If you do not have a blender, chop the vegetables very fine and mix well by hand.)

Transfer the mixture to a soup tureen. Thin with the vinegar and tomato juice, then stir in the salt, pepper and paprika. Chill 2 hours or longer.

Serve the garnish in separate bowls around the tureen. The rest of the green pepper is minced and combined with the red pepper as one of the garnishes.

Lentil Soup

YIELD: 8 SERVINGS

2 cups lentils

Cold water

1 1/3 tablespoons butter

3 tablespoons sesame or soy oil

4 cloves garlic, finely chopped

3 onions, chopped

1 large bunch celery, chopped

1/3 cup celery leaves, chopped

3 carrots, thickly sliced

½ cup brown rice

6 tablespoons chopped parsley

2 quarts water or vegetable stock (see
    Reference Chapter)

2 teaspoons salt and ½ teaspoon pepper

4 tablespoons brewer's yeast (optional)

2 tablespoons miso (soybean paste)

Lemon slices

Place lentils in bowl, cover with cold water and let soak while preparing the vegetables.

In a heavy kettle, heat the butter and oil and sauté the garlic, onions, celery, celery leaves, carrots, brown rice and half the chopped parsley for about 3 minutes.

When the onions have wilted, drain the lentils and add to the other vegetables.

Add the water or stock, salt, pepper and yeast. Bring to a boil, cover and simmer until vegetables are tender (about 1½ hours).

Remove 2/3 cup of the broth and mix with the miso until smooth. Return to kettle and cook 20 minutes.

Serve in individual soup bowls garnished with lemon slices and the remaining parsley.

Variation: Barley or millet can be used in place of brown rice.

Roman Bean Soup

YIELD: 7 CUPS

½ pound beans (pinto, cranberry,
  kidney or any red bean)
3 quarts water or vegetable stock
  (see Reference Chapter)
3 stalks celery
3 carrots
1 onion
3 tablespoons chopped parsley
2 cloves garlic, crushed

3 tablespoons oil (safflower, peanut
  or corn)
1 cup canned tomatoes
4 teaspoons salt
1/8 teaspoon dry basil or ¼ teaspoon
  chopped fresh basil
½ cup brown rice, or small seashells
Grated Parmesan cheese

Carefully pick over the beans to remove any foreign particles. Place in large saucepan.

Cover with water or stock. Add celery, carrots and onion. Cover and simmer 1½ hours or until beans are almost tender.

Sauté the parsley and garlic in oil for 2 minutes and add to the soup.

Add the tomatoes. Season with salt, pepper and basil. Cover and simmer 30 minutes longer.

Remove 2 cups of the whole beans to save for later use. Put the remaining ingredients through a food mill or process in a blender or food processor.

Put the soup back in the soup kettle, adding water or vegetable stock if the soup seems too thick. Taste for seasoning.

Add the rice or seashells to the soup and simmer until they are tender. The rice will take longer than the seashells.

Add the whole beans to the soup. Taste again for seasoning.

Serve the soup very hot garnished with Parmesan cheese.

Corn Chowder

YIELD: 6 TO 8 SERVINGS

½ cup butter, margarine or vegetable oil
4 tablespoons chopped onion
½ cup chopped celery
4 tablespoons chopped green pepper
1 cup diced potatoes
2 cups water
2 teaspoons turmeric
½ bay leaf

1 teaspoon salt
¼ teaspoon white pepper
2 cups milk
3 tablespoons whole wheat flour
4 ears corn kernels or 2 cups canned
  corn kernels
2 tablespoons chopped parsley
2 tablespoons diced pimientos

Heat the butter, margarine or oil in a deep pan.

Add the onion, celery and pepper and sauté just until the onion is tender.

Add the potatoes, water, turmeric, bay leaf, salt and pepper. Cover and simmer for 20 minutes.

Combine the milk and flour and, when they are blended, add them to the soup.

Add the corn, parsley and pimientos. Stir and cook until the soup thickens. Serve soup hot.

Cold Russian Borscht

YIELD: 6 SERVINGS

5 cups beet broth from cooking beets or
  mixture of beet broth and other
  vegetable broth
1½ cups cooked beets
1 cup chopped onion
1 cup shredded green cabbage
Juice of 1 lemon

½ teaspoon ground caraway seeds
1 tablespoon chopped parsley
1½ teaspoons chopped tarragon
  (optional)
Salt
Yogurt

Slip the skins off 4 to 6 beets, depending on the size. Chop enough to make 1½ cups.

Steam the chopped onion in ¼ cup of water in a covered saucepan for 5 minutes or until tender.

Steam the shredded cabbage in ¼ cup of water in another covered saucepan for 6 to 8 minutes.

Add the vegetables to the beet broth. Mix well and add the lemon juice, caraway seeds, parsley and tarragon, if desired. Salt to taste. Chill several hours in the refrigerator.

Serve in individual soup bowls topped with a tablespoon of yogurt.

Note: Beet broth is made by scrubbing small fresh beets very thoroughly and cooking them about 45 minutes in lightly salted water to cover. For 5 cups of beet broth you will need 2 pounds of beets. Vegetable broth can be mixed half and half with beet broth. If fresh beets are not available, canned beets and canned juice may be used.

Sunflower Soup

YIELD: 8 SERVINGS

1/3 cup oil (safflower, peanut or corn)	*3 quarts vegetable stock (see*
1 onion	*Reference Chapter)*
2 cups sunflower seeds	*2 teaspoons savory*
1 tablespoon salt	*4-5 cups fresh spinach*

Heat the oil in a 4-quart pan.

Chop the onion and sauté it in the oil just until tender. Do not brown.

Add the sunflower seeds and salt. Stir briefly and add the vegetable stock. Cover and simmer 40 minutes.

Wash the spinach carefully. Drain well and shred quite fine. Add the spinach and the savory to the soup. Cover and simmer 8 minutes.

Puree the soup in a blender or food processor. Taste for seasoning.

Serve in preheated soup bowls, garnished with a few shreds of spinach.

Best Barley Soup

YIELD: 8 SERVINGS

8 cups vegetable stock (see
  Reference Chapter)
½ cup barley
1 bunch carrots, sliced thin
½ cup celery, diced

1/3 cup onions, chopped
1 cup tomatoes, chopped
1 1/3 cups fresh peas, shelled
Salt
2/3 cup parsley, chopped (garnish)

Simmer the barley in vegetable stock for 1 hour.

Prepare the vegetables and add to the stock. Cook covered for 20 minutes over low heat or until all the vegetables are soft. Taste for seasoning.

Serve in a tureen sprinkled with chopped parsley, accompanied by whole wheat crackers or rye bread.

Bohemian Vegetable Soup

YIELD: 8 TO 10 SERVINGS

2 gallons water or beef stock
½ cup barley
1 bunch carrots, peeled and chopped
2 onions, peeled and chopped
4 potatoes, peeled and diced
2 stalks celery, sliced
1 cup diced turnip

1 bay leaf
4 basil leaves or ½ teaspoon dried basil
1 bunch of parsley
2-3 tablespoons tamari (soy sauce)
4 tablespoons margarine
½ cup whole wheat flour

Put the water or beef stock or water fortified with beef base into a large pan. Bring to a boil. Add the barley and simmer for 1 hour.

Prepare the vegetables and add them and the tamari to the soup. Cook until the vegetables are almost tender.

Heat the margarine in a small saucepan. Stir in the flour and cook for 1 minute. Add 2 cups of the stock and stir until well blended. Add the mixture to the soup. Simmer until the soup thickens. Taste for seasoning, adding more tamari if necessary.

Serve the soup in a large tureen and accompany with slabs of thick dark buttered bread.

Lima Bean Soup

YIELD: 6 TO 8 SERVINGS

1½ cups dry lima beans	4 tablespoons corn oil
2 quarts vegetable stock (see Reference Chapter) or water	1/3-½ cup millet
3 stalks celery with leaves	¾ teaspoon ground sage
1½ large onions	1½ teaspoons caraway seed
1 tablespoon chopped parsley	4 tablespoons brewer's yeast (optional)
1½ cups chopped greens (lettuce, spinach, sorrel)	½ teaspoon nutmeg
	2 teaspoons salt
2-3 tomatoes	½ teaspoon fresh ground pepper
	Grated Parmesan or Cheddar cheese

Soak the beans overnight in the stock or water.

Chop the celery, onion, parsley, greens and tomatoes rather coarsely. Place in a large kettle with the lima beans, adding enough water to cover.

Add the oil, millet, sage, caraway seed, yeast if desired and seasonings. Mix well.

Cover and simmer 2 to 2½ hours, adding water if necessary. The vegetables should always be well covered.

Taste for seasoning and serve in individual bowls with grated cheese.

Celery Soup

YIELD: 8 SERVINGS

1 bunch of celery	*1 tablespoon whole wheat flour*
4 cups boiling water	*1 quart milk, scalded*
1 bay leaf	*Salt to taste*
1 large potato	*1/8 teaspoon nutmeg*
2 tablespoons butter or margarine	*Croutons*

Use a whole bunch of green celery (not the hearts). Wash well and chop coarsely.

Bring the water to a boil. Add the bay leaf and the potato, cut in small dice or grated. Cook 5 minutes.

Add the celery and continue cooking until the celery is tender.

Heat the butter in a small saucepan. Add the flour and whisk until blended. Gradually add the scalded milk and whisk until blended.

Discard the bay leaf and combine the two mixtures.

Season to taste with salt and nutmeg.

Serve very hot, garnished with croutons.

Potato Soup

YIELD: 1 GALLON

9 large potatoes	*¼ teaspoon pepper*
½ gallon vegetable stock (see Reference Chapter) or water	*1 teaspoon garlic powder*
1½ bunches green onions (scallions), finely chopped	*1 quart milk or cashew milk (see page 190)*
1 tablespoon salt	*Parsley, chopped*
2 tablespoons butter	*Croutons*

Peel and slice potatoes. Cook them in the stock with the onions and salt until the potatoes are soft.

Mash the potatoes with a potato masher.

Add butter, pepper and garlic powder.

Add the milk last and heat through, but do not boil. Taste for seasoning.

Dice slightly stale whole wheat bread in ½-inch cubes until you have 2 cups. Heat 4 tablespoons of corn oil in a skillet and sauté the croutons, shaking the pan frequently so that they brown on all sides. Drain on paper toweling and sprinkle with seasoned salt or Vege-Sal (available at health stores).

Serve the soup in soup plates, sprinkled generously with chopped parsley and croutons.

Hershel's Bean and Barley Soup

YIELD: 4 TO 6 SERVINGS

2 cups lentils
1 cup split peas
1 cup navy beans
1 cup barley
1 cup brown rice
1 gallon vegetable stock, beef stock
  or water

1½ tablespoons salt
1 large clove garlic
1 large onion, sliced thin
1½ teaspoons black pepper
2 teaspoons chili powder
Tamari (optional)
1 lemon, sliced thin

Wash the lentils, peas, beans, barley and rice very carefully.

Place them in a large soup pot and add the vegetable stock, beef stock or water.

Add the salt, garlic and onion. Bring to a boil and cover. Reduce heat and simmer for 2 hours or until the beans are tender. If the beans absorb too much of the liquid, add water.

When the beans are tender, add the pepper, chili powder and tamari if desired. Cook 15 minutes longer.

Serve in a soup tureen garnished with lemon slices.

Mexican Carrot Soup

YIELD: 8 SERVINGS

14 medium-size carrots
4 medium-size onions
4 stalks celery
8 cups vegetable stock or water

3 cups cashew milk (see page 190)
   or regular milk
Salt and pepper
Guacamole (see page 181)

Scrub but do not peel the carrots. Slice thin.

Peel and slice the onions.

Wash and slice the celery.

Put the vegetables in a saucepan with 1 cup of stock. Cover and simmer for 20 minutes.

Prepare the cashew milk, if desired.

Heat the milk in a double boiler.

Spin the cooked vegetables in a blender or food processor, adding the remaining stock or water.

Combine the vegetable mixture with the milk and heat (without boiling) for 15 minutes. Season highly with salt and pepper.

Make the guacamole.

Serve the soup in individual bowls with a dollop of guacamole for each serving.

Split Pea Soup

YIELD: 8 LARGE SERVINGS

2 pounds split peas
1 gallon vegetable stock (see Reference
   Chapter) or water
1 bay leaf
¼ teaspoon marjoram
¼ cup tamari (soy sauce) or to taste

3 potatoes
Butter or margarine
2 carrots, diced
2 medium onions, chopped
2¼ teaspoons caraway seed

Wash the peas, discarding any imperfect ones.

Bring the vegetable stock or water to a boil. Add the peas, bay leaf, marjoram and half the tamari. Reduce the heat, cover and simmer 1½ to 2 hours or until the peas are mushy.

Peel and slice the potatoes. Sauté them in 2 tablespoons of butter or margarine for 2 to 3 minutes, shaking the pan frequently. Remove to a bowl using a slotted spoon.

Scrub and dice the carrots, and using the same skillet sauté the carrots for 2 to 3 minutes, adding more butter or margarine if necessary. Remove to the bowl.

Peel and chop the onions and sauté them in the same skillet just until soft.

Add the sautéed vegetables and the caraway seeds to the peas. Cook just until the carrots are tender but still firm. Add more liquid if necessary. Season to taste with tamari.

Remove the bay leaf and serve the soup in a large tureen.

Cucumber Yogurt Soup

YIELD: 8 SERVINGS

1 medium to large cucumber
1 green onion (scallion)
1 tablespoon minced onion
2 tablespoons chopped green pepper
½ teaspoon minced garlic
1 teaspoon each: celery seed, chopped dill weed, fresh marjoram or oregano, fresh thyme, fresh minced basil, fresh chopped parsley, fresh chopped chives

1½ tablespoons tamari (soy sauce)
1 tablespoon lemon juice
1 quart tomato juice
2 cups vegetable broth (see Reference Chapter)
2 cups yogurt
Fresh ground pepper
4 tablespoons chopped fresh parsley

Wash and halve the cucumber and remove the seeds with a spoon. Do not remove the skin unless it is thick. Slice as thin as possible into a large bowl.

Prepare the onions, pepper and garlic and combine with the cucumber.

Measure out the herbs. If fresh herbs are not available use half the amount of the dried variety. Mix with the vegetables.

Add the tamari and lemon juice and mix well.

Finally add the tomato juice, vegetable broth and yogurt. Chill in the refrigerator until just before serving.

Serve in individual bowls, garnished with parsley. Accompany with strips of toasted whole wheat bread, buttered and sprinkled with toasted sesame seeds.

Tamari Noodle Soup

YIELD: 8 SERVINGS

2 cups sliced onions
4 cups shredded cabbage
2 cups sliced carrots
Corn oil

3 quarts water
1 tablespoon salt
½-1 cup tamari (soy sauce)
1 pound whole wheat noodles

Prepare the vegetables.

Heat 2 tablespoons of the oil in a deep kettle.

Sauté the onions until tender and remove them from the pan with a slotted spoon to a bowl.

In the same pan, sauté the cabbage until it is wilted. Stir frequently. Remove from the pan with a slotted spoon to the same bowl.

Repeat the process with the carrots, adding more oil if necessary.

Meanwhile bring the water to a boil. Add the salt and the sautéed vegetables. Cover and simmer 1 hour.

Add the tamari, according to taste, and the noodles. Add more water if necessary. Cook 10 minutes. Taste for seasoning.

ENTRANCING ENTREES

Luncheon and Dinner Dishes

O Blessed health!...

Thou art above all gold and treasure....

He that has thee, has little more to wish for.

—*Laurence Sterne* (Tristram Shandy)

The entree is traditionally the main event of the meal, the showpiece on which the cook lavishes her time and talent. It is also the theme-setter; salad and vegetable, soup and wine are chosen to complement it.

Nutritionally, too, the entree is central to the meal. It is the chief source of the protein needed for growth and for the repair and replacement of all the body's cells, and for the formation of hormones that control bodily functions.

The proteins in meat, fish, eggs and dairy products are "complete" proteins, so-called because they contain all the amino acids the human body needs. The proteins in fruits, vegetables and grains are "incomplete" since they contain some but not all of these essential amino acids. To provide complete proteins without serving meat it is necessary to combine vegetables and grains so that one provides what another lacks. This takes special knowledge and careful planning.

Unfortunately, while meat, eggs and dairy products are valuable sources of protein, they are also foods high in saturated fats and cholesterol.

We offer, then, a collection of recipes for both meat and meatless dishes chosen for moderation and balance, along with a few helpful hints:

The "complete protein" foods lowest in saturated fats are chicken (particularly the white meat), fish, shellfish, cheeses made from skimmed milk, and uncreamed cottage cheese. Serve these foods more often; serve red meats and bright yellow cheese less often.

Remove the skin from chicken before preparing it; most of the fat is stored just under the skin and will be discarded with it.

Serve casserole dishes that combine high-fiber vegetables and grains with small quantities of meat or cheese.

Use only as much salt as is absolutely necessary to make a dish palatable.

90

Fish Divan

YIELD: 6 SERVINGS

6 fish fillets (sole, turbot or flounder)
8 cups water
½ bay leaf
1/8 teaspoon thyme
4 sprigs parsley
2 tablespoons minced celery
1 tablespoon minced onion
½ cup cider vinegar
8 peppercorns

1½ teaspoons salt
2 packages frozen broccoli or
   2 pounds fresh broccoli
4 tablespoons butter or margarine
1 cup sliced mushrooms
4 tablespoons whole wheat flour
2 cups milk
Salt and pepper
6 slices Cheddar or Colby cheese

Order six fish fillets, each weighing approximately 6 ounces.

In a deep skillet combine the water with the bay leaf, thyme, parsley, celery, onion, vinegar, peppercorns and salt. If your fish dealer will give you bones and trimmings, add them too. Bring to a boil and boil uncovered for 20 minutes. Strain through a very fine sieve and cool.

Pour the cooled broth into the skillet. Place the fish in the pan carefully and bring to a simmer. Cook gently just until the fish flakes when pierced with a fork. Using a wide spatula, remove the fish to paper toweling to drain.

Cook the broccoli in lightly salted water so that it is tender but not overcooked. Drain well.

Heat the butter in a skillet and sauté the mushrooms until tender.

Add the flour gradually, stirring constantly until well blended and bubbling.

Add the milk gradually, stirring constantly, and stir until the mixture comes to a boil and thickens. Season to taste with salt and pepper.

Preheat the oven to 350 degrees F.

Place the broccoli in the bottom of a shallow oven-serving dish.

Arrange the fish fillets in a single layer over the broccoli.

Top with the cheese slices. Cover with the sauce and bake 25 to 30 minutes.

Arroz con Pollo (Chicken with Rice)

YIELD: 6 SERVINGS

2½ pounds choice chicken pieces

2½ tablespoons butter or margarine,
  softened

2 small cloves garlic, minced

2 teaspoons salt

1/8 teaspoon pepper

1/8 teaspoon paprika

3 slices bacon, diced

¼ cup chopped onion

¼ cup chopped green pepper

1 cup uncooked white or brown rice*

2 cups boiling chicken broth

½ cup chopped and drained tomatoes

Pinch of saffron (optional)

½ cup cooked green peas

Remove the skin from the pieces of chicken, wipe them with moistened paper toweling and arrange in a baking dish.

In a small bowl, combine the butter or margarine, 1 clove garlic, 1 teaspoon salt and the pepper and paprika.

Brush the seasoned butter on the chicken and bake at 350 degrees F. for 45 to 50 minutes, or until tender and nicely browned.

In a heatproof skillet, sauté the bacon until lightly browned.

Add the onion and green pepper and cook, stirring frequently, until the vegetables are tender but not brown.

Add the rice and cook, stirring frequently, for 2 minutes.

Add the hot chicken broth, the tomatoes, the saffron if desired, and the remaining 1 teaspoon of salt. Stir to blend seasonings.

Cover the skillet, using aluminum foil if it hasn't a snug-fitting lid, and bake at 350 degrees F. for 45 minutes, or until the rice is tender and all the liquid is absorbed.

To serve: Add the cooked green peas to the rice and fluff lightly with a fork. Transfer to a serving dish and arrange the chicken pieces on top.

*If you use brown rice you will need to increase the liquid by ½ cup (add more chicken broth or ½ cup water) and you will also need to increase the baking time by about 30 minutes (to 1 hour 15 minutes). When white rice is used, the two pans containing the chicken and the rice can go into the oven together; when brown rice is used, the rice mixture should go into the oven 30 minutes before the chicken.

Roast Stuffed Shoulder of Lamb

YIELD: 6 TO 8 SERVINGS

3-4 pound boned shoulder of lamb
Savory Mint Stuffing (see
   Reference Chapter)
Butter or margarine, softened

Rosemary
Salt and pepper
Mint leaves for garnish (optional)

Lay the meat out on a working surface and shape it as nearly as possible into a rectangle. Sprinkle the meat with salt and pepper.

Prepare the stuffing and spread it on the meat, leaving a 1-inch margin on all sides.

Roll the meat up like a jelly roll and tie it firmly with kitchen twine at 2-inch intervals.

Spread the outside of the meat roll with butter or margarine and sprinkle with rosemary.

Place the meat on a rack in an open roasting pan. Pour 1 cup of water into the pan.

Roast 60 to 75 minutes, according to the weight of the lamb, basting every 15 minutes. Sprinkle with salt and pepper before the last 15 minutes of cooking.

Transfer the meat to a heated platter. Pour any meat juices over the top. Garnish with fresh mint leaves and serve with mint jelly.

Baked Bran Swordfish Steaks

YIELD: 4 SERVINGS

4 swordfish steaks (4-6 ounces each)
2 cups wheat bran cereal
¾ cup milk
1 tablespoon salt
4 tablespoons butter or margarine,
   melted

4 lemon slices
2 tablespoons chopped green onions
   (scallions)
Salt and pepper

Preheat the oven to 400 degrees F.

Pulverize the bran in a blender and spread it on a plate.

Combine the milk and salt in a soup plate.

Melt the butter or margarine.

Butter a wire rack or trivet and place it in an open roasting pan. Preheat in the oven.

Wipe each steak with paper toweling, especially if you are using thawed frozen fish.

Dip each steak in the salted milk for 1 minute and then coat it evenly with the bran.

When all the steaks are prepared, place them on the hot buttered rack and dribble each one with a teaspoon of melted butter or margarine. Bake 18 to 20 minutes.

Meanwhile, simmer the green onions in the remaining butter or margarine.

To serve: Using a wide spatula, turn the steaks upside down on a serving platter to show the grill lines. Sprinkle with salt and pepper. Garnish with a slice of lemon and pour the onion butter over the fish. Serve immediately.

Baked Stuffed Haddock

YIELD: 4 TO 6 SERVINGS

*This fish needs no extra sauce, but the addition of Hollandaise
makes it a dinner party dish.*

4-5 pound whole fish (whitefish,
　scrod, haddock, etc.)

3 tablespoons butter or margarine

3 tablespoons chopped onion

4 tablespoons chopped celery

2 tablespoons chopped parsley

1 cup thinly sliced cucumber

1½ cups whole wheat bread crumbs

½ cup wheat bran cereal

1 teaspoon poultry seasoning

1 teaspoon salt

¼ teaspoon white pepper

¼ pound salt pork cut in long
　thin slices

Buy a whole fish, cleaned and scaled. Wash it inside and out and dry well with paper toweling.

Heat the butter in a skillet. Sauté the onion and celery until the onion is soft. Add the parsley and cucumber and stir gently for 1 minute.

Add the bread crumbs, cereal, poultry seasoning, salt and pepper; and stir over heat just until thoroughly blended.

Stuff the fish two-thirds full and close the opening with small skewers and kitchen twine.

Place the fish on a foil-lined baking sheet. Cut a few diagonal slits in the skin and cover with the salt pork strips.

Bake 30 to 40 minutes at 400 degrees F., depending on the size of the fish. It should flake easily but still be moist. Serve with the Broccoli-Cashew Casserole, if desired.

Hungarian Goulash with Buckwheat Dumplings

YIELD: 8 SERVINGS

Goulash tastes even better made a day ahead.
It can be reheated before adding the dumplings.

3 pounds chuck beef cut in
  2-inch cubes

4 cups sliced onion

4 tablespoons vegetable oil

3 tablespoons sweet paprika

2 teaspoons tomato paste

2 tablespoons red wine vinegar

1 quart water

1 teaspoon basic beef stock
  or 2 beef bouillon cubes

Salt and pepper

¼ pound salt pork

DUMPLINGS:

2 cups buckwheat flour

1½ teaspoons salt

4 teaspoons baking powder

1 egg

3 tablespoons melted butter
  or margarine

7/8 cup milk

2 tablespoons minced parsley

Prepare the beef and the onions.

Heat the oil in a Dutch oven or in a heavy electric skillet. Sauté the onions until golden, stirring frequently.

Add the paprika combined with the vinegar, ¼ cup of water and the beef. Cook 3 minutes, stirring continuously.

Add the tomato paste and the water, fortified with the basic beef powder or 2 bouillon cubes.

Wash the salt pork free of excess salt under running water. Place it on the goulash.

Cover the pan tightly and simmer gently for 2 hours.

Five minutes before the end of the 2 hours, prepare the dumplings: Sift buckwheat, salt and baking powder into a bowl. Beat the egg slightly and combine it with the melted butter, milk and parsley. Combine the liquid and dry ingredients, stirring just until the dry ingredients are moistened.

Remove the cover from the pan. Take out the salt pork and drop the dumpling batter by spoonfuls—12 of them—into the goulash. Cover and steam 10 to 12 minutes. Season the goulash to taste with salt and freshly ground black pepper.

To serve: Transfer the goulash to a well-heated serving dish. Sprinkle generously with freshly chopped parsley.

Stuffed Flank Steak

YIELD: 4 TO 6 SERVINGS

1½-2 pounds flank steak

MARINADE:
1 cup red wine
½ cup chopped onion
1/3 cup soy sauce
¼ cup oil
¼ teaspoon salt
¼ teaspoon pepper

STUFFING:
½ cup chopped onion
¼ pound sliced mushrooms
¼ cup chopped celery
1 tablespoon butter
½ cup beef broth or water
2 tablespoons oyster sauce
1 teaspoon crushed thyme
½ teaspoon pepper
3 cups whole wheat bread cubes

Begin preparation of this dish the day before or early on the day it is to be served. Cut a pocket in the flank steak and score the surface, or ask your butcher to do this.

Prepare the marinade: Combine the wine, onion, soy sauce, oil, salt and pepper in a shallow glass or enamel pan large enough to hold the steak. Let the steak stand in the marinade, in the refrigerator, overnight or for at least 3 hours.

Prepare the stuffing: Sauté the onion, mushrooms and celery in the butter until tender. Stir in the broth or water, the oyster sauce, thyme and pepper and bring to a boil. Stir in the bread crumbs.

Remove the steak from the marinade. Spoon the stuffing into the pocket and pin the open sides together with a metal skewer.

Broil in the oven or on charcoal, outdoors, 5 to 7 minutes on each side.

To serve: Transfer to a serving platter and garnish with sprigs of fresh parsley. The meat should be cut diagonally in thin slices.

Roast Duck Quarters with Corn Bread Stuffing

YIELD: 4 SERVINGS

For the host or hostess who dreads carving a duck at the table, here is the perfect solution.

1 4-5 pound duck

Salt, pepper and savory

Corn Bread Stuffing (see
    Reference Chapter)

2 cups chicken or vegetable stock

Parsley

Preheat the oven to 325 degrees F.

Wash the duck inside and out and dry thoroughly.

Sprinkle the inside cavity with salt, white pepper and savory. Bind the wings and legs to the duck with kitchen twine.

Place the duck on a rack in an open roasting pan and roast the bird, allowing 20 minutes per pound.

Heat 1 cup of chicken or vegetable stock with 2 tablespoons butter or margarine and baste the duck every 15 minutes with the mixture.

Prepare the stuffing, using 3 cups of corn bread crumbs.

Remove the duck and the rack and let the duck cool.

Add 1 cup of chicken or vegetable stock to the juices in the pan and bring to a boil over direct heat, scraping the juices from the bottom of the pan. Boil down to half its original quantity and pour the gravy into a bowl. Cool and chill until the fat rises to the top. Skim off and discard the fat.

Using kitchen shears, cut the duck into quarters and remove the backbone.

Forty-five minutes before serving, spread the stuffing in the bottom of an oven-serving dish. Cover with the duck pieces and bake 30 minutes at 300 degrees F. Serve with the gravy, warmed.

Layered Casserole with Wheat Germ

YIELD: 4 TO 6 SERVINGS

¾ pound zucchini (3 medium)
1 cup grated sharp Cheddar cheese
¾ cup wheat germ
1 egg
1 teaspoon salt
2 tablespoons whole wheat flour

½ pound lean ground beef
½ cup finely chopped celery
1 small onion, finely chopped
1 medium clove garlic, minced
¼ teaspoon pepper
1 8-ounce can tomato sauce

Shred or chop the zucchini and drain it in a sieve, pressing with the back of a spoon to remove as much moisture as possible.

Mix the drained zucchini with ½ cup of the cheese, ¼ cup of the wheat germ, the egg and ½ teaspoon salt. Press the mixture into the bottom of a 1½-quart baking dish. Sprinkle with the flour.

Crumble the ground beef into a skillet. Add the celery, onion, garlic, pepper and the remaining ½ teaspoon salt. Cook until the beef is browned. Pour off and discard any excess fat.

Preheat the oven to 400 degrees F.

Stir the remaining ½ cup of wheat germ and half of the tomato sauce into the meat mixture. Spoon it into the baking dish, over the zucchini layer.

Pour the remaining tomato sauce over the top and sprinkle with the remaining ½ cup of cheese. Bake 30 minutes or until well heated through.

Stuffed Artichokes

YIELD: 4 SERVINGS

4 artichokes
2 quarts water
1 teaspoon cider vinegar
1 teaspoon salt
½ cup whole wheat bread crumbs

½ cup wheat bran cereal,
   pulverized
1 clove garlic, minced
½ cup chopped parsley
1 small can anchovy fillets
Olive oil

Choose nice fat artichokes. Tear off the outer layer of leaves and cut off the top quarter. Snip off the spiny tops of the remaining leaves. Trim the bottom evenly so that the artichoke will sit gracefully on a plate. Peel the stems and set aside.

Bring the water, vinegar and salt to a full rolling boil. Add the artichokes and the peeled stems. Boil 25 minutes. Drain and cool.

Meanwhile, combine the bread crumbs, the bran which has been pulverized in a blender or food processor, the minced garlic, chopped parsley and the anchovy fillet, chopped very fine. Add enough of the anchovy oil to bind everything together. Mix until thoroughly blended.

Spread the leaves of the artichokes and stuff the mixture between the leaves using a teaspoon. Reform the artichokes and place them in an oiled casserole large enough so that they won't be squeezed but small enough so that the artichokes will be mutually self-supporting. Spoon a teaspoon of oil over each one.

Bake covered for 15 minutes at 350 degrees F. Serve with plenty of paper napkins, because fingers are the only possible tools for coping with all but the artichoke bottoms.

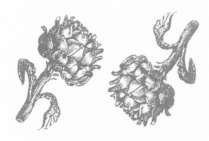

Dinner Frittata

YIELD: 3 TO 4 SERVINGS

*This is a dish with many variations. It is quick to prepare
and provides a hearty meal.*

1 teaspoon cooking oil
1 small white onion, diced
½ cup thinly sliced zucchini
½ cup thinly sliced fresh mushrooms
4 eggs
¼ cup milk
½ cup wheat bran cereal

¼ cup sliced black olives
½ cup diced cooked turkey or chicken
¼ cup diced mozzarella or
  Muenster cheese
¼ cup Parmesan cheese, grated
½ teaspoon garlic salt
Butter or margarine

Heat the vegetable oil in a skillet and sauté the onion, zucchini and mushrooms until the onion is translucent but not brown.

In a large mixing bowl beat the eggs until foamy. Stir in the milk and bran.

Add the sautéed vegetables, the olives, turkey or chicken, cheeses and garlic salt. Stir well.

Melt 1 to 2 tablespoons butter or margarine in a large, smooth skillet or omelet pan. Pour in the egg mixture and cook over medium heat until the eggs are set but not browned on the bottom.

Cautiously turn the omelet and cook the second side. (An easy way to turn the omelet: Slide it out of the skillet onto a large plate; then tip the plate so that it goes back into the skillet with the uncooked side down. Another way to cook the second side of the omelet: Place the omelet in the skillet under the broiler and cook until the top is set and looks dry.)

Turn out of the pan onto a serving dish and cut into 6 or 8 wedges.

Variations: Substitute diced ham or cooked shrimp or tuna for the turkey or chicken. Substitute artichoke hearts, thinly sliced green beans, chopped broccoli, chopped raw spinach or well-drained chopped tomatoes for the zucchini and mushrooms.

Spaghetti and Bran Meatballs

YIELD: 6 TO 8 SERVINGS

SPAGHETTI SAUCE:

1 large onion, chopped

1-2 cloves garlic, minced

1/3 cup vegetable oil

1 cup fresh sliced mushrooms

2 6-ounce cans tomato paste

*2 1-pound cans Italian plum
    tomatoes*

1 cup water

1 cup red wine

1 bay leaf

¼ teaspoon thyme

¼ teaspoon oregano

1 teaspoon sugar

MEATBALLS:

2 pounds ground beef

2 eggs, slightly beaten

1 medium-size onion, chopped

1 teaspoon salt

¼ teaspoon black pepper

2 slices whole wheat bread, crumbled

¾ cup wheat bran cereal

½ cup milk

Vegetable oil

*1½-2 pounds whole wheat or
    other spaghetti*

Parmesan cheese

Prepare the spaghetti sauce: Sauté the onion and garlic in the vegetable oil just until tender. Add the mushrooms and cook 2 minutes over low heat.

Add the tomato paste, tomatoes, water, wine and seasonings. Turn up the heat and bring the mixture to a boil. Reduce the heat, cover and simmer 30 minutes or longer. Remove the bay leaf.

While the sauce cooks, prepare the meatballs. Mix the ground beef with the eggs, chopped onion and seasonings.

Combine the bread crumbs and bran with milk enough to moisten them. Add to the meat and stir until all ingredients are blended.

Form the meat mixture into balls about 1½ inches in diameter, using your hands.

Heat a small amount of vegetable oil in a heavy skillet and brown the meatballs, a few at a time, shaking the pan so they will brown evenly. As the meatballs are browned, use a slotted spoon to transfer them to the cooking sauce. Let them simmer in the sauce, uncovered, 20 to 30 minutes.

While the meatballs simmer, cook the spaghetti. Bring to a boil a large kettle of salted water. Add a spoonful of vegetable oil. Add the spaghetti gradually so that the water doesn't stop boiling. Boil whole wheat spaghetti 8 to 10 minutes, or until just tender. Drain.

Serve the meatballs and sauce over the spaghetti, topping each serving with a small amount of grated Parmesan cheese.

French Spring Lamb with Fresh Shelled Beans

YIELD: 8 SERVINGS

Leg of spring lamb (7 pounds)	*Rosemary leaves*
6 pounds fresh shell (horticultural)	*Salt and pepper*
beans	*Butter or margarine*
2 cloves garlic	*2 tablespoons fresh chopped parsley*

Trim all fat possible from the lamb and pierce the surface in several places with the point of a sharp knife. Cut 1½ cloves of garlic in thin slivers and insert them.

Rub the surface with butter or margarine, rosemary leaves and freshly ground black pepper. (Do not sprinkle with salt until 15 minutes before the end of roasting time.) Let the roast stand at room temperature while shelling the beans.

Shell the beans and place them in a pan of cold water. Add a teaspoon of salt and the remaining half clove of garlic. Cover and bring to a boil. Cook gently for 20 to 25 minutes or until the beans are tender. Remove from the heat and let stand.

Roast the lamb at the appropriate time prior to serving, allowing 15 minutes per pound at 350 degrees F. for rare meat *à la française* or 20 to 25 minutes per pound for those who prefer lamb well done. Ten minutes before serving, transfer the lamb to a heated serving platter.

Put the beans with their cooking liquid into the roasting pan and stir gently to blend with the pan drippings over low direct heat until very hot. Add 2 tablespoons of butter and season with salt and pepper. Serve the beans around the roast and garnish with fresh chopped parsley.

Oriental Meat Balls with Rice

YIELD: 6 SERVINGS

2 slices whole wheat bread	1 tablespoon vegetable oil
1 pound lean ground beef	½ cup sugar
1 egg	½ cup vinegar
½ teaspoon powdered mustard	½ cup soy sauce
½ teaspoon powdered ginger	½ cup sherry or pineapple juice
1 teaspoon garlic salt	3 cups hot cooked rice
3 tablespoons cornstarch	(see Reference Chapter)

Moisten the bread with water and squeeze it dry. Combine the bread with the ground beef, egg, mustard, ginger and garlic salt and mix well. Shape into 1-inch balls.

Heat the vegetable oil in a skillet. When the oil is hot, roll the meatballs in cornstarch and cook them, turning frequently to brown all sides. Drain off any excess fat.

Combine the sugar, vinegar, soy sauce and sherry with the rest of the cornstarch. Pour this mixture over the meatballs.

Simmer, basting occasionally, for about 15 minutes or until the sauce thickens and the meatballs are glazed.

Serve the meatballs and sauce over the hot cooked rice.

Roast Chicken with Corn Bread Stuffing

YIELD: 4 TO 6 SERVINGS

1 4-5 pound chicken
Corn Bread Stuffing (see
   Reference Chapter)
Butter or margarine

GRAVY:
4 tablespoons pan fat or drippings
4 tablespoons unbleached white
   or whole wheat flour
2 cups chicken stock or broth

Wipe the inside of the chicken with a clean damp towel and sprinkle the inside with salt and a little white pepper.

Make the stuffing, using 3 cups of corn bread crumbs, and fill the body and neck cavity. Sew up the cavities with a kitchen needle and string or close the openings with small skewers. Truss the chicken and place it on a rack in an open roasting pan. Spread with a little butter or margarine.

Roast the chicken at 350 degrees F., allowing 25 minutes per pound. Baste occasionally with the juices in the pan.

Remove the chicken to a heated platter and keep warm.

There should be approximately 4 tablespoons of fat in the pan. If extra fat is needed, add more butter or margarine. Stir in the flour and cook over direct heat, scraping the juices from the bottom of the pan. Gradually add the chicken stock and whisk until the mixture is smooth and thick. Strain into a gravy boat.

Decorate the chicken with fresh watercress and serve with brown rice.

Shrimp Gumbo

YIELD: 6 1-CUP SERVINGS

¼ cup butter or margarine

2 cups chopped okra*

½ cup chopped onion

1/3 cup chopped celery

1/3 cup chopped green pepper

4 cups hot water

2 large tomatoes, peeled and chopped

1 clove garlic, minced

1 bay leaf

1 teaspoon salt

¼ teaspoon pepper

1/8 teaspoon thyme

1 pound fresh shrimp, shelled and
   deveined

Cooked brown or white rice
   (see Reference Chapter)

Melt the butter or margarine in a large heavy skillet or Dutch oven, over moderate heat.

Add the okra, onion, celery and green pepper. Sauté about 10 minutes, or until the vegetables are lightly browned and almost tender.

Add the water, tomatoes, garlic, bay leaf, salt, pepper and thyme. Bring to a boil, then cover and reduce heat. Simmer for about 50 minutes.

Add the shrimp and simmer just 10 minutes longer. Remove the bay leaf.

Serve over hot cooked rice, in bowls or soup plates.

*If using canned or thawed frozen okra, add it with the tomatoes in Step 3, as it will be too moist to sauté well.

Bran Hamburgers

YIELD: 6 TO 8 SERVINGS

2 pounds ground beef

2 eggs

¾ cup wheat bran cereal

1 small onion, finely chopped

2 tablespoons Worcestershire sauce

Salt and pepper to taste

Vege-Sal or seasoned salt, if desired

Combine all ingredients in a large mixing bowl. Stir until blended.

Shape into 6 medium-size or 8 small patties. Broil to taste in the oven or outdoors, over charcoal.

Variations: For a different taste or texture, add up to ½ cup grated cooked potato or grated cheese to the meat mixture.

Savory Stuffed Green Peppers

YIELD: 4 SERVINGS

4 green peppers, medium-size
1 tablespoon vegetable oil
½ pound ground beef (chuck or round)
1/3 cup chopped onion
1/3 cup chopped celery
1½ cups cooked brown rice (see
  Reference Chapter)

1 8-ounce can tomato sauce
¼ cup water
¾ teaspoon salt
½ teaspoon chili powder
Dash of pepper

Cut the green peppers in half lengthwise. Remove all seeds and membrane and wash carefully. Cook in boiling water for about 4 minutes, to soften slightly. Drain and set aside.

Heat the vegetable oil in a heavy skillet and cook the ground beef, onion and celery until the beef is gray and crumbly and the onion is soft. Remove from the heat and stir in the rice, tomato sauce, water and seasonings.

Spoon equal amounts of the beef-rice mixture into the pepper shells and arrange them in a shallow baking dish.

Bake at 350 degrees F. 20 to 25 minutes, or until the rice mixture is well heated through and the pepper shells are tender.

Raisin Ham Loaf

YIELD: 6 TO 8 SERVINGS

1 pound cooked ground ham
1 pound lean ground beef
¼ cup nonfat dry milk powder
1/3 cup water
2 eggs
2 tablespoons chopped onion
½ cup wheat bran cereal
½ cup wheat germ

¼ teaspoon thyme
½ cup raisins

SAUCE:
½ cup brown sugar
¼ cup vinegar or tart fruit juice
2 teaspoons dry mustard

Preheat the oven to 350 degrees F.

In a large mixing bowl, combine and stir together all the ham loaf ingredients.

In a saucepan, combine the ingredients for the sauce. Bring to a boil and cook 1 minute, stirring frequently.

Shape the meat mixture into a rectangular loaf and place it in a baking-serving dish or pan, allowing a little space around the edge of the loaf for the sauce.

Pour the sauce over and around the meat. Bake 1 hour.

Variation: Shape the meat mixture into 6 or 8 individual loaves or 12 to 16 small meatballs and arrange them in a baking dish or pan, then pour over the sauce. Bake 30 to 40 minutes.

Chicken Vegetable Salad

YIELD: 6 SERVINGS

1½ cups diced cooked chicken
1½ cups cooked green peas
1½ cups cooked (white or brown) rice
  (see Reference Chapter)
1½ cups finely diced celery

3 tablespoons diced pimientos
  (optional)
1 cup mayonnaise
2 teaspoons lemon juice
Lettuce, parsley, tomato

Combine in a large mixing bowl the chicken, peas, rice, celery and pimientos. (All ingredients should be chilled.)

In a small bowl, blend the mayonnaise and lemon juice. Pour over the salad and toss lightly.

Serve in lettuce cups, garnished with parsley sprigs and tomato wedges if desired.

Variations: Replace all or part of the chicken with cold cooked beef or pork.

Sauerbraten Meatballs

YIELD: 6 SERVINGS

1½ pounds ground beef
1 cup wheat bran cereal
½ cup milk or half-and-half
1 small onion, grated
1½ teaspoons salt
¼ teaspoon pepper
Flour

¼ cup butter or margarine
1 can condensed beef broth
1/3 cup coarse gingersnap crumbs
½ cup (packed) brown sugar
3 tablespoons vinegar
Whole wheat or other noodles, cooked
*   and drained*

In a large mixing bowl combine the bran cereal, milk, onion, salt and pepper. Let stand about 2 minutes or until the cereal is softened. Add the ground beef and mix until combined. Shape mixture into about 40 small balls (use about 1 level tablespoon of meat mixture for each one).

Roll the meatballs in flour to coat well.

Heat the butter or margarine in a large heavy skillet. Add the meatballs and turn them so they brown on all sides.

In a saucepan, heat the broth with ½ cup of water, the gingersnap crumbs, brown sugar and vinegar. Bring to a boil, then pour over the meatballs.

Simmer uncovered for 20 minutes, turning the meatballs once during the cooking time.

To serve, spoon the meatballs and sauce over the cooked noodles.

Vegetables Mornay Almondine

YIELD: 4 TO 6 SERVINGS

1 head cauliflower

1 bunch broccoli

2 green peppers

HERBED RICE:

2 cups uncooked brown rice

3 tablespoons vegetable oil

1/8-¼ teaspoon of each of the following:
  marjoram, basil, garlic powder
  and chopped parsley

4 cups water

SAUCE MORNAY (CHEESE SAUCE):

¼ cup butter or margarine

¼ cup vegetable oil

½ cup whole wheat flour

1 quart warm milk

8 ounces Cheddar cheese, grated

1 tablespoon stone-ground German
  or prepared Dijon-type mustard

½ teaspoon paprika

¼ teaspoon cayenne pepper

1½ teaspoons salt

½ teaspoon white pepper

TAMARI ALMONDS:

1 cup sliced almonds

2 tablespoons tamari (soy sauce)

Wash and separate into florets the cauliflower and broccoli. Remove seeds and white membrane from the green peppers and slice. Steam the vegetables in a rack over boiling water until tender but still slightly crisp. Set aside.

Prepare herbed rice: Heat the vegetable oil in a large heavy pan and sauté the uncooked rice until it is golden. Add the seasonings and continue cooking 2 minutes longer. Add the water, bring to a boil, then cover and reduce the heat. Simmer 45 minutes or until the rice grains are separated and tender.

Prepare the sauce: Melt the butter and combine it with the vegetable oil in a heavy saucepan over medium heat. Add the flour, whipping with a wire whisk until the mixture is smooth. Slowly stir in the warm milk. Simmer over low heat until the sauce begins to thicken, beating with the whisk, especially around the sides of the saucepan, to keep lumps from forming. Add the cheese. When it is melted, stir in the seasonings.

Prepare the tamari almonds: Spread the sliced almonds on a baking sheet and sprinkle the tamari over them. Bake at 350 degrees F. 5 to 10 minutes.

To assemble: Spread the rice in the bottom of a baking-serving dish. Arrange the steamed vegetables on the rice. Pour the sauce over all, and scatter the almonds on top.

Spinach Lasagna

YIELD: 4 TO 6 SERVINGS

1 pound fresh spinach (tough stems removed)

2 tablespoons vegetable oil

1 medium onion, chopped

2 cloves garlic, minced

2 teaspoons oregano leaves

½ teaspoon basil

¾ teaspoon salt

3 1-pound cans tomatoes (crushed or pieces, drained)

½ pound whole wheat or other lasagna noodles

1¼ pounds mozzarella cheese, sliced thin

1 pound ricotta cheese

Parmesan cheese, grated

Rinse the spinach leaves individually and place them in a saucepan. Cover and cook over medium heat, with just the water clinging to the leaves, until the spinach is steaming and wilted (about 2 minutes).

In another saucepan, heat the vegetable oil and sauté the onion, garlic, oregano and basil until the onion is soft. Stir in the salt and the tomatoes. Cover and cook 20 to 30 minutes.

Cook the lasagna noodles for 10 minutes in a large kettle of boiling water to which 1 tablespoon salt and 1 tablespoon oil have been added.

To assemble: Oil a 9-inch by 13-inch baking pan and pour in enough of the tomato sauce to cover the bottom. Add layers in the following order: noodles, spinach, ricotta, mozzarella, Parmesan, tomato sauce. Repeat until all ingredients are incorporated.

Bake at 350 degrees F. 35 to 45 minutes, or until the cheeses are melted and the sauce bubbles. Remove from the oven and let stand 15 minutes before cutting in squares and serving.

Oat Burgers

YIELD: 5 SERVINGS (2 EACH)

1 medium onion, diced

2 tablespoons butter or margarine

1 teaspoon minced garlic

½ ounce oregano

1 ounce presoaked sunflower seeds

¼ cup soy sauce

1½ cups water

3 cups uncooked oatmeal (rolled oats)

Melt the butter in a heavy saucepan and sauté the onion until transparent but not browned.

Stir in the garlic, oregano, sunflower seeds, soy sauce and water and bring to a boil. Remove from the burner and stir in the oatmeal. Let stand ½ hour or until cooled.

Use a ½-cup measure or an ice cream scoop to dip portions of the mixture onto an oiled cookie sheet. Shape the portions into round patties and bake at 350 degrees F. 30 minutes or until firm. Or, refrigerate the patties until firm; then fry them 3 minutes on each side in a little hot vegetable oil.

Serve the patties hot on whole wheat buns with mayonnaise, grilled onion slices, alfalfa sprouts and tomato and cucumber slices, as desired.

Cuban Black Beans and Rice

YIELD: 6 TO 8 SERVINGS

2 cups black beans

2 cups uncooked brown rice

1/3 cup oil (preferably olive)

1 green pepper, chopped

2 medium onions, chopped

2 cloves garlic, minced

1 bay leaf

½-1 teaspoon thyme

Salt and pepper

1 cup chopped onion

1 cup chopped green olives

½ cup grated Cheddar or Colby cheese

Soak the black beans overnight in a large bowl of water. Discard any beans that float to the top. Drain and rinse the beans and place in a pan with 1 quart of salted water. Bring to a boil and cook until tender (30 to 40 minutes). Drain, rinse and drain again.

Cook the rice (see Reference Chapter).

Heat the oil in a heavy skillet and sauté the green pepper, onion and garlic with the bay leaf and thyme until the vegetables are soft. Season with salt and pepper.

Add the beans and stir until well blended and a sauce develops.

Spread the rice—about 1 inch thick—in the bottom of a baking-serving dish. Cover with the bean mixture and sprinkle with the chopped onion and olives. Cover with the grated cheese.

Bake 20 to 30 minutes at 350 degrees F.

Meatless Bran Patties

YIELD: 6 TO 8 PATTIES

1 cup cooked oatmeal

1 small onion, chopped

3 tablespoons brewer's yeast (optional)

1 cup cottage cheese (dry)

2 eggs

1 cup fresh or canned mushrooms,
    chopped

½ cup walnuts or pecans

1 tablespoon tamari (soy sauce)

¼ teaspoon cayenne pepper

2 tablespoons sesame seeds

½ cup wheat bran cereal

Vegetable oil

1 can condensed cream of mushroom
    soup

In a large mixing bowl, combine all the ingredients except the vegetable oil and the soup. Stir together; then shape the mixture into 6 medium-size or 8 small patties.

Heat a small amount of vegetable oil in a heavy skillet. Brown the patties on both sides.

Transfer the patties to a baking-serving dish and top with the mushroom soup.

Bake at 350 degrees F. for 35 minutes.

Vegetable Stroganoff

YIELD: 8 SERVINGS

2 cups sliced carrots

1 cup sliced green peppers

3 cups sliced zucchini

2 cups cauliflower florets

8 ounces spinach noodles or
   whole wheat noodles

½ pint sour cream

2 tablespoons butter or
   margarine, melted

Salt and white pepper

MUSHROOM SAUCE:

½ cup butter or margarine

3 tablespoons unbleached white flour

3 tablespoons whole wheat flour

2 cups milk

2 cups concentrated vegetable stock

4 tablespoons chopped onion

½ pound mushrooms, sliced

Nutmeg

Tamari (soy sauce) to taste

Prepare the vegetables. Wash them well. Slice the carrots and green peppers. Steam them for 10 minutes or just until tender. Slice the zucchini and divide the cauliflower into florets. Steam them for 5 minutes. Drain and reserve the stock.

Cook the noodles, 6 minutes for the spinach variety, 7 minutes if using the whole wheat variety. Drain the noodles thoroughly and toss with the sour cream, butter, salt and a little white pepper.

Prepare the Mushroom Sauce: Heat 4 tablespoons of the margarine. Stir in the flour and cook for 2 minutes over very low heat. Add the milk and vegetable stock and whisk until thickened and smooth.

Heat the remaining margarine in a skillet and sauté the chopped onions until tender. Add the mushrooms and stir. Continue cooking until the mushrooms are tender.

Combine the sautéed onion and mushrooms with the sauce and season with a dash of nutmeg and tamari to taste.

Spread the noodles in an oven-serving dish. Cover with the vegetables and then with the sauce. Bake 30 minutes at 350 degrees F. If the dish is prepared in advance and kept in the refrigerator, allow 50 minutes for baking.

Lentil-Cheese Supper

YIELD: 6 TO 8 SERVINGS

1 pound lentils

2 cups water

1 1-pound can tomatoes (undrained)

1 cup chopped onion

2 cloves garlic, minced

1 bay leaf

2 teaspoons salt

¼ teaspoon black pepper

1/8 teaspoon each: marjoram, sage,
  thyme

2 carrots, sliced

1 green pepper, chopped

1 stalk celery, sliced

2 cups shredded sharp Cheddar cheese

2 tablespoons chopped parsley

Preheat the oven to 375 degrees F.

Rinse the lentils and pour them into a shallow 2-quart casserole or baking dish. Add the water, tomatoes and their liquid, the onion, garlic and bay leaf. Stir until well mixed together.

Blend together the salt, pepper and powdered herbs. Sprinkle them over the casserole and then stir.

Cover the casserole (use aluminum foil if there is no snug-fitting lid) and bake 30 minutes.

Remove the casserole from the oven and stir in the carrots, green pepper and celery. Return to the oven and bake 30 minutes longer.

Remove the casserole from the oven and sprinkle the shredded cheese over the top. Return to the oven just until the cheese melts. Sprinkle the chopped parsley over the top and serve at once.

Small Vegetarian Meat Loaf

YIELD: 2 TO 3 SERVINGS

½ cup walnuts
1½ cups cooked brown rice
   (see Reference Chapter)
1 cup tomato puree
2 teaspoons celery seed
¼ cup chopped onion
¼ cup chopped parsley

2 tablespoons soy flour or
   whole wheat flour
½ cup green pepper
3 eggs, slightly beaten
½ cup milk
8 ounces cubed sharp Cheddar cheese

Preheat the oven to 350 degrees F.

Combine all the ingredients except the cheese in a large mixing bowl. Stir until just blended.

Spoon half of the mixture into the bottom of an oiled small loaf pan. Scatter half of the cubed cheese over it. Add the rest of the mixture, to make another layer, and the remaining cheese.

Bake 45 minutes.

Chili con Queso

YIELD: 6 TO 8 SERVINGS

1 pound kidney beans
Vegetable oil
1 large onion, diced
3 carrots, sliced
1 small green pepper, chopped
1 can tomatoes
1 small can tomato paste
3 cups broth or water

1 clove garlic, minced
1 tablespoon chili powder
1 tablespoon salt
½ teaspoon pepper
½ teaspoon oregano
½ teaspoon cumin
1 cup grated Cheddar cheese

Soak the beans overnight. Cook them 1 hour in a pressure cooker, or follow the directions on the package.

Heat a little vegetable oil in a large heavy skillet or soup pot. Add the chopped onion and cook, stirring frequently, until the onion is transparent but not browned.

Add the carrots, green pepper, tomatoes, tomato paste, broth, the seasonings and the cooked beans. Bring to a boil, reduce heat and simmer 20 minutes or longer.

Serve in soup bowls, sprinkled with the grated cheese.

Leftovers: Store leftover Chili con Queso in the refrigerator. Use it to make the Southwestern Rice-Bean dish or reheat and spoon into tortillas with grated cheese and chopped lettuce to make tacos.

Oriental Vegetable Pancakes

YIELD: 6 SERVINGS

3 cups shredded cabbage
½ cup finely chopped onion
1 teaspoon celery seed
2 cups cooked brown rice
  (see Reference Chapter)
2 teaspoons salt
¼ teaspoon pepper
2 tablespoons soy sauce

8 eggs, beaten
Vegetable oil for frying

CHINESE SAUCE:
1½ cups chicken broth
1 tablespoon cornstarch
1 tablespoon soy sauce

Stir together the cabbage, onions, celery seed and rice.

In a large mixing bowl, beat the eggs and then beat in the salt, pepper and soy sauce. Fold in the cabbage-rice mixture.

Prepare the Chinese Sauce: In a saucepan, combine the chicken broth, cornstarch and soy sauce. Whisk over medium heat until thickened. Keep warm.

To make the pancakes, pour 1/3-cup portions of the cabbage-rice-egg mixture onto a hot, lightly oiled griddle. Brown on both sides and serve hot, with a little of the Chinese Sauce spooned over each pancake.

Deep Dish Vegetable Pizza

YIELD: 6 TO 8 SERVINGS

CRUST:

1 package active dry yeast

1 cup lukewarm water

1 tablespoon honey

1 tablespoon vegetable oil

1 teaspoon salt

2½ cups whole wheat pastry flour
    (not bread flour)

PIZZA SAUCE:

Vegetable oil

3 onions, diced

4 cloves garlic, minced

2 1-pound cans tomato pieces

1 6-ounce can tomato paste

1 tablespoon oregano

1 tablespoon chopped fresh basil

FILLING:

Any or all of the following: mushrooms,
    eggplant, yellow squash, zucchini,
    carrots, onions, green peppers, celery

3 tablespoons vegetable oil

Mozzarella or Colby cheese

Black olives, sliced

Prepare the crust: Dissolve the yeast in the lukewarm water. Stir in the honey, vegetable oil and salt. Combine in a large mixing bowl with 2 cups of the whole wheat pastry flour and stir until blended. Add the remaining ½ cup flour or as much as is needed to make a stiff dough. Knead until smooth. Roll on a floured surface to a rectangle that will line a 9-inch by 14-inch baking pan with sides (not a flat pizza pan). Refrigerate or freeze any leftover dough for later use.

Prepare the pizza sauce: Heat a little vegetable oil in a large, heavy pan and sauté the onions and garlic until the onion is translucent but not browned. Add the canned tomatoes and their liquid, about half of the can of tomato paste, the oregano and basil. Bring to a boil, then reduce the heat and simmer 10 minutes or until thickened. (If the sauce does not thicken sufficiently, add more of the tomato paste and cook a little longer.) Both crust and sauce may be prepared ahead of time and stored in the refrigerator until time to assemble the pizza.

Preheat the oven to 350 degrees F. Bake the crust 10 minutes.

Wash and peel, where necessary, the vegetables that are to go into the pizza. Heat the oil in a heavy skillet and cook the vegetables, stirring frequently, for 5 minutes. Cover the skillet, reduce the heat and cook the vegetables 7 minutes longer or until just tender. Drain well. Slice or grate the cheese.

Arrange the vegetables, the olives and the cheese in the partially baked crust.

Spread the pizza sauce over the filling.

Bake 15 minutes.

Variations: Replace ½ cup of the whole wheat flour in the crust with ½ cup yellow cornmeal or ½ cup bran.

California Party Quiche

YIELD: 10 SERVINGS

2 pounds zucchini	*1¼ pounds mild Cheddar or*
1 pound spinach	*Colby cheese, cubed*
2 large onions	*1 tablespoon oregano*
2 green peppers	*1 tablespoon chopped fresh basil*
15 eggs	*½ teaspoon salt*
	¼ teaspoon black pepper

Slice the zucchini. Wash the spinach, remove the large stems and chop coarsely. Peel and chop the onions. Slice the green peppers and discard the seeds and white membrane.

Cook the vegetables in a steamer rack over boiling water, just until tender. (Do not oversteam.) Mash the vegetables slightly with a fork or a potato masher.

Preheat the oven to 350 degrees F.

Beat the eggs in a blender or electric mixing bowl.

Stir together all the ingredients and pour into a greased 13-inch by 9-inch baking dish.

Bake 60 to 70 minutes, or until a wooden pick inserted near the center comes out clean.

Tamale Pie

YIELD: 6 TO 8 SERVINGS

1 cup cornmeal

4 tablespoons vegetable oil

¾ cup boiling water

1 can (14-ounce) garbanzo beans

½ cup chopped onion

2 cloves garlic, minced

1 cup sweet corn kernels
(preferably fresh)

1¾ cups diced tomatoes
(preferably fresh)

1 teaspoon kelp (optional)

¼ teaspoon oregano

½ teaspoon powdered basil

1 cup sliced ripe olives

¼ cup chopped green pepper

1 cup grated Cheddar or Colby cheese

Stir the cornmeal and 2 tablespoons of the oil into the boiling water.

Add ½ cup of the drained liquid from the garbanzo beans and the beans to the cornmeal mixture. Stir well.

Saute the onion and garlic in the remaining oil just until tender. Remove from the heat and stir in the corn, tomatoes, kelp if desired, oregano and basil.

Combine the mixtures and pour into a lightly oiled baking-serving dish.

Sprinkle the top with the sliced olives and chopped pepper. Cover with the grated cheese.

Bake at 375 degrees F., allowing 25 minutes if covered, 20 minutes if not.

Nut Burgers

YIELD: 6 SERVINGS

1 cup uncooked brown rice

½ pound cashews, ground in blender

½ pound walnuts, ground in blender

1 cup Colby cheese, grated

1 egg, slightly beaten

½ onion, chopped

Chili powder, hot sauce or other
seasonings (optional)

Whole wheat flour

Vegetable oil for frying

Cook the rice (see Reference Chapter).

Combine the ground nuts, rice, cheese, egg, onion and desired seasonings in a mixing bowl. Stir until well mixed.

Rinse the hands in cold water to prevent sticking; then shape the mixture into patties. Coat with the flour.

Heat 2 tablespoons of vegetable oil in a heavy skillet and fry the patties, a few at a time, adding more oil as needed, until browned on both sides. (Watch closely, to prevent burning.)

Serve the patties on whole wheat buns or in Whole Wheat Pita Pouches.

Stuffed Manicotti Noodles

YIELD: 4 TO 6 SERVINGS

SAUCE:

2 cups tomato sauce (see Reference
   Chapter)

1 can (6 ounces) tomato paste

2 tablespoons butter or margarine

1 cup sauterne wine

4 vegetable bouillon cubes

2 teaspoons basil

FILLING:

1 tablespoon butter or margarine

1 tablespoon vegetable oil

1 large onion, chopped

2 stalks celery, chopped

3 cloves garlic, minced or grated

1 tablespoon chopped parsley

1 teaspoon salt

¼ teaspoon pepper

¼ teaspoon nutmeg

2 10-ounce packages of frozen chopped
   spinach, thawed

1 8-ounce package of Swiss cheese,
   grated

Manicotti noodles

Parmesan cheese

Prepare the tomato sauce. Combine it with the remaining ingredients in a large saucepan and simmer gently for 20 minutes.

Prepare the filling: Heat the butter and vegetable oil in a heavy skillet. Add the onion, celery, garlic and parsley and cook, stirring frequently, until the onion is soft and limp. Add the seasonings and mix well. Drain the spinach very thoroughly pressing out the excess moisture with the back of a spoon. Add to the sautéed vegetables and stir in the grated cheese.

Bring 6 quarts of water to a full rolling boil. Add 1 tablespoon of salt. Put in the manicotti gradually so that the water never ceases to boil. Stir gently once and boil 6 minutes or until the manicotti are just tender. Pour off the hot water and fill the kettle with cold water.

When the manicotti are cool enough to handle, withdraw them from the water and place on toweling to drain.

Using a large tipped pastry bag or a teaspoon, fill the manicotti with the spinach mixture and lay them in a single layer in a lightly oiled baking-serving dish, allowing a little space between for expansion.

Pour the sauce over all and sprinkle with Parmesan cheese.

Cover with aluminum foil and bake for 45 minutes at 350 degrees F.

THE GARDEN OF EARTHLY DELIGHTS

Vegetables and Grains

There comes the morning with
the golden basket in her right hand
bearing the wreath of beauty,
silently to crown the earth.

—*Rabindranath Tagore*

You don't have to hate meat to love vegetables, but a great many people do, regarding the choice as moral (the sacredness of living things), hygienic (why eat dead animals?) or nutritive (which is the way *we* like to think of vegetables). They're good for you, so why not eat 'em?

Some of the high-powered emotion so amusingly engendered by the vegetable cult has had fallouts in very high places. Bernard Shaw, with his usual and probably deliberately infuriating way of heaping praise upon himself, said: "It seems to me, looking at myself, that I am a remarkably superior person, when you compare me with other writers, journalists and dramatists; and I am perfectly content to put this down to my abstinence from meat." Other vegetarians of transcendental stature were Albert Einstein, Jean-Jacques Rousseau, Richard Wagner, Leo Tolstoy, Mahatma Gandhi, Leonardo da Vinci, Percy Bysshe Shelley, Albert Schweitzer and that renowned humanitarian, Adolf Hitler. It has been rumored, but incorrectly, that Count Tolstoy was so enamored of vegetables that the first version of his immortal novel was entitled *War and Peas.* This is probably historically inaccurate although it is factually true that while he was loudly proclaiming his vegetarian principles every day, during the night hours he was frequently caught making forays to the kitchen refrigerator for a snack of some succulent meat tidbit. In much the same way, some years ago in Battle Creek, Michigan, where Doctor Kellogg ran his world-famous sanatorium on a vegetarian diet, it was a recognized fact that some backsliding patients were known to slip out at night and frequent meat-easies where they would gorge on steak before returning to the good doctor's abstemious regime.

The romance of vegetables is well established. Corn was known to the Aztec, Mayan and Incan cultures in the New World an estimated 6,000 years before

124

Columbus landed near their shores and brought its bounty to the world. The ancient Egyptians worshipped the onion as the symbol of the universe—one rounded layer within the other, a veritable firmament of inner and outer skins, not awfully out of the way in its concept of constellations within galaxies. An inscription on the pyramids built nearly 5,000 years ago indicates that the workmen erecting these gigantic monuments ate not only onions but garlic, proof that the hero sandwich is not a recent invention.

Green beans, navy beans, red kidney beans and spotted pinto beans came from this hemisphere, and the potato as well, although the dear old spud came to North America from South America by way of Europe, where the Spanish explorers introduced it first to Iberia, thence to England and Ireland. That encouraged the founding of the first vegetarian society in Britain in 1847, and we got around to it in the United States with our own American Vegetarian Convention in 1850, where the wearing of the green was *de rigueur*. Said Mr. Horace Greeley, founder of the *New York Herald Tribune* (and erroneously blamed for proclaiming "Go West, Young Man"), "Other things being equal, I judge that a strict vegetarian will live ten years longer than a habitual flesh eater, while suffering on the average about half as much from sickness as the carnivorous must."

Too often vegetables are the forgotten heroes of the American diet, possibly because we haven't given them the full chance they deserve. We do here! We have sought out all kinds of combinations, and you'd be surprised how new flavors come from such explorations.

A few stoveside hints:

Undercook rather than overcook, to preserve both fiber and flavor.

In preparing vegetables, don't ever let them stand around. When you are ready to cook is when you start to shred and slice.

If you are boiling vegetables, use as little water as possible.

If you can steam them, do so. This best preserves everything that is good in vegetables.

If vegetables are to be sautéed, cooked together, a good general rule is to start with the heavier ones since they take longer to cook. You can judge pretty well by weight and density. Cabbage takes longer than onions, which take longer than mushrooms. Add the short-order vegetables as you go and you'll come out pretty well in *le finis*.

Stuffed Eggplant

YIELD: 8 SERVINGS

4 medium eggplants

Boiling water

2 onions, chopped

4 tablespoons (½ stick) butter or
  margarine

½ cup cooked brown or white rice

2-3 large tomatoes

1 cup grated Cheddar cheese

Salt

Cayenne pepper

Cut the eggplants in half lengthwise and lower them into a large kettle of boiling water. Cook 5 minutes only, lift out and drain.

Scoop some of the pulp out of the center of each eggplant and chop it coarsely.

Sauté the chopped onions in the butter or margarine until soft but not brown. Combine with the rice, tomatoes, cheese and the chopped eggplant pulp. Season with salt and a little cayenne pepper.

Arrange the eggplant shells in an oiled baking pan and spoon the stuffing mixture into them. Cover with foil and bake at 350 degrees F. for 30 to 40 minutes.

Provencale Vegetable Casserole

YIELD: 4 SERVINGS

2 large onions, coarsely chopped

2 cloves garlic, minced

Vegetable oil

2 green peppers, chopped

2-3 small zucchini, sliced

2 medium eggplants, peeled and diced

2 large potatoes, peeled and diced

½ pound mushrooms, sliced

1 pound (2-3) ripe tomatoes, peeled and
  chopped

1 6-ounce can tomato paste

2 bay leaves

1¼ tablespoons chopped parsley

½ teaspoon oregano

½ teaspoon thyme

Wheat germ (optional)

2 tablespoons margarine

Sauté the chopped onions and minced garlic in a little vegetable oil, in a large heavy skillet.

Add the green peppers, zucchini, eggplants, potatoes and mushrooms and cook over medium heat, stirring frequently, 3 to 5 minutes.

Bring the tomatoes, tomato paste and herbs to a boil, stirring until blended.

Transfer the vegetables to a large casserole or deep baking-serving dish. Spread the tomato mixture over the top and sprinkle with the herbs.

Top with a layer of wheat germ, if desired, and dot with the margarine.

Bake at 350 degrees F. for 1 hour and 15 minutes.

French Peas

YIELD: 6 SERVINGS

3 cups shelled fresh peas	*2 teaspoons sugar*
6 tablespoons butter or margarine	*½ teaspoon salt*
¼ head garden lettuce	*2 tablespoons butter or margarine*
6 sprigs parsley, tied together	*1 egg yolk*
12 tiny onions	

Combine in a saucepan all of the ingredients except the 2 tablespoons butter or margarine and the egg yolk. Cover with a pie pan holding ¼ inch of water (this will cook the peas evenly) and cook over low heat 35 minutes, or until the peas are just tender.

Remove the peas from the heat. Discard the parsley. Pour ½ cup of the cooking liquid into a small bowl. Add the 2 tablespoons of butter or margarine and the egg yolk and stir until blended. Pour this mixture back into the peas and cook, stirring constantly, just until the sauce thickens slightly. Serve immediately.

Rainbow Vegetable Banquet

YIELD: 8 SERVINGS

1 cup whole hulled millet

1 quart water

1 teaspoon salt

1 cup chopped zucchini

1 cup chopped green beans

1 cup chopped cauliflower

1 cup fresh corn or peas

1 cup chopped rutabaga

1 cup diced carrots

1 cup diced onion

1 bay leaf

1 teaspoon tarragon

1 cup chopped mushrooms

4 cloves garlic, minced

Vegetable oil

Vegetable stock

Tamari (soy sauce)

1 cup grated cheese (Cheddar, Gruyère or Parmesan)

Chopped cooked beets for garnish

Combine the millet, water and salt in a saucepan. Bring to a rapid boil, stirring often. Cover, reduce the heat and simmer for approximately 45 minutes or until tender.

Meanwhile prepare all the vegetables.

Parboil the zucchini, green string beans, cauliflower for 3 minutes and the peas or corn for 5 minutes. Drain, reserving the liquid.

Using the same vegetable stock, adding whatever water is necessary to cover the vegetables, cook the rutabaga, carrots and onion with the bay leaf and tarragon for 10 minutes. Drain but still reserve the vegetable stock. Remove the bay leaf.

Meanwhile sauté the mushrooms and garlic in 2 tablespoons of oil just until tender. Do not brown. Set aside.

Spread the cooked millet in the bottom of a casserole or an oven-serving dish. Sprinkle with the mushrooms, garlic and the oil they were sautéed in and a tablespoon or two of tamari. Cover with the vegetables and sprinkle with a cupful of the vegetable stock. Top with the grated cheese and the chopped cooked beets.

Cover and bake 30 to 40 minutes at 325 degrees F. If the dish gets too dry add a little more vegetable stock and tamari.

Cheese Zucchini Casserole

YIELD: 2 TO 3 SERVINGS

1 pound (2-3 small) zucchini, cut up   *1 tablespoon butter or margarine*
1-2 ounces cream cheese, cut in bits   *Salt and pepper to taste*
1 egg, beaten slightly   *1 cup Cheddar cheese, grated*

Simmer the cut up zucchini in very little water until soft.

To the drained cooked zucchini add the cream cheese, egg, butter and salt and pepper to taste. Stir until blended.

Pour the mixture into an oiled baking-serving dish and sprinkle the grated Cheddar cheese over the top.

Bake, uncovered, at 350 degrees F. just until the cheese melts and the mixture begins to bubble.

Zucchini Rice Casserole

YIELD: 6 SERVINGS

6 zucchini, sliced ½ inch thick   *1 onion, finely chopped*
1 cup boiling water   *Salt*
4 eggs, beaten   *1 teaspoon marjoram*
1 pound cottage cheese   *1 tablespoon chopped chives*
2 cups cooked white or brown rice   *1 cup Parmesan cheese*

Boil the zucchini in water for 5 minutes and reserve the liquid for stock.

Combine the eggs, cottage cheese, cooked rice, onion, salt to taste and marjoram in a mixing bowl.

Spoon half the drained zucchini in a baking dish. Top with half the rice mixture and repeat the 2 layers. Sprinkle the chives and the Parmesan cheese over the top.

Bake at 350 degrees F. for 45 minutes.

Zucchini Onion Mélange

YIELD: 6 TO 8 SERVINGS

2 pounds zucchini, sliced

1 large onion, sliced

2 tablespoons olive oil

1 can stewed tomatoes

½ can tomato sauce

1 teaspoon garlic salt

½ teaspoon oregano

1 teaspoon lemon juice

2 tablespoons chopped parsley

Heat the oil in a large skillet or heavy saucepan and sauté the zucchini and onion for several minutes, stirring frequently.

Stir in the tomatoes and tomato sauce, garlic salt, oregano and lemon juice.

Cover and simmer over reduced heat until the zucchini and the onion are cooked through, about 15 minutes.

Serve in a heated vegetable dish sprinkled with the chopped parsley.

Frijoles (Refried Beans)

YIELD: 4 TO 6 SERVINGS

2 tablespoons cooking oil

1-2 onions, chopped

½ green pepper, chopped

2-3 cups cooked pinto beans, mashed or
   sieved

¼-½ cup grated Colby cheese

Dash of Tabasco or hot sauce

½-1 teaspoon tamari (soy sauce)

Chili pepper or cayenne pepper to taste

Garlic powder to taste

Heat the oil in a heavy skillet and sauté the onion and green pepper until tender.

Add enough beans to cover the bottom of the skillet, then the cheese and seasonings.

Cook, stirring frequently, just until the beans are heated through and the seasonings blended. Serve immediately, as is or in tacos.

Mixed Vegetable Casserole with Cheese

YIELD: 8 SERVINGS

*1 head cauliflower or 2 10-ounce
  packages frozen cauliflower*
*1 pound fresh peas, shelled, or 1
  10-ounce package frozen peas*
4 carrots, diced
½ pound small pearl onions
4 tablespoons butter

4 tablespoons whole wheat flour
2 cups milk
1 teaspoon salt
1 teaspoon brewer's yeast (optional)
2/3 cup grated sharp Cheddar cheese
Paprika

Prepare the vegetables. If using all fresh vegetables, which is preferable, wash the cauliflower carefully and cut it into florets, discarding all but the tender stems. Steam the vegetables separately until half cooked. Put them into a lightly buttered casserole or oven-serving dish.

Melt the butter and stir in the flour. Cook 2 minutes over low heat and add the milk. Whisk vigorously until the mixture is thick and smooth. Add the cheese and continue to whisk until the cheese melts. Add the salt and taste for seasoning. Remember the vegetables have not been salted.

Pour the sauce over the vegetables and sprinkle with paprika. Bake uncovered at 350 degrees F. for 20 to 25 minutes. The vegetables should be tender but not mushy.

Broccoli Cashew Casserole

YIELD: 6 TO 8 SERVINGS

1 large bunch broccoli or 2 packages
   frozen broccoli
1 pound whole wheat or spinach noodles
2 tablespoons butter or margarine
8 ounces Swiss cheese, cubed
1/3 cup whole wheat flour

2 cups milk
¾ cup Parmesan cheese
¼ cup poppy seeds
2 egg yolks
2 cups cashews
Salt and pepper

If using fresh broccoli, wash carefully and cut off the thick stems. Quarter the florets and cut the tender stems in bite-size pieces. Boil in salted water for 3 minutes and drain thoroughly. Or thaw the frozen variety and drain well.

Cook the noodles in a large kettle of boiling salted water for 6 to 7 minutes or just until tender. Do not overcook. Drain and rinse very briefly in cold water. Drain again and toss with the butter or margarine. Set aside.

In a saucepan toss the cheese cubes with the flour and stir in the milk. Place over moderately high heat and stir until thick and smooth. Add ½ cup of the Parmesan cheese and the poppy seeds and continue to cook until thoroughly blended. Remove from the heat.

Beat the egg yolks well, and add a little of the hot sauce gradually. When those ingredients are blended, add the mixture slowly to the rest of the sauce, stirring vigorously. Season to taste with salt and pepper.

Spread a little of the cheese sauce in the bottom of a lightly oiled baking-serving dish. Cover with a layer of noodles and then with a layer of broccoli. Sprinkle with ¾ cup of cashews and pour over half the remaining sauce. Repeat the layering process. Garnish the top with the rest of the Parmesan cheese and the remaining ½ cup of cashews.

Bake 20 to 30 minutes at 325 degrees F. If this is prepared in advance and kept in the refrigerator, allow 40 minutes for baking.

Spinach Stuffed Artichoke Bottoms

YIELD: 4 TO 8 SERVINGS

8 large fresh artichokes or
  1 can (16 ounces) artichoke bottoms
1 package chopped frozen spinach
  (thawed)

1 cup cheese sauce (see
  Reference Chapter)
Salt and pepper
¼ teaspoon nutmeg
½ cup finely chopped cashews

If large fresh artichokes are available, wash them and cook in boiling salted water for 30 to 35 minutes. Remove from the water and turn upside down in a colander. When they are cool enough to handle, remove all the leaves and the chokes, leaving just the bases. Place the artichoke bottoms in a lightly oiled or buttered oven-serving dish.

If using the canned variety, drain them well on paper toweling before placing them in the baking dish.

Drain the spinach, pressing out the moisture with the back of a spoon.

Make the sauce and flavor it well with salt, pepper and nutmeg.

Combine the spinach and sauce and divide the mixture among the artichoke bottoms.

Bake 20 minutes at 350 degrees F. Five minutes before the end of the cooking time, sprinkle each artichoke with chopped cashews.

Serve two per serving as a vegetable or as an entree. This also makes a delicious garnish for roast lamb in which case one per person is sufficient.

Eggplant and Cheese Casserole

YIELD: 6 SERVINGS

4 medium eggplants   *Milk*
Boiling water   *6 eggs, well beaten*
6 slices whole wheat bread   *3 cups grated Cheddar cheese*

Peel the eggplants, cut them into cubes and cook in boiling water just until tender. Drain and mash, using a fork or a wire potato masher.

Pour over the bread enough milk to cover and let stand 5 minutes. Squeeze the excess milk from the bread, pull the bread apart and add the soaked crumbs to the eggplant. Mix well.

Fold the beaten eggs and the grated cheese into the mixture and turn it into an oiled baking-serving dish. Bake at 350 degrees F. 1 hour, or until set and nicely browned on top.

Down Home Corn Casserole with Cheese

YIELD: 6 TO 8 SERVINGS

2 green peppers, chopped   *1¼ cups fine bread crumbs*
1 onion, sliced thinly   *1 teaspoon salt*
2 cloves garlic, minced   *¾ teaspoon paprika*
2 tablespoons vegetable oil   *1 tablespoon honey*
1½ cups raw corn kernels   *¾ teaspoon basil*
1 cup fresh tomatoes, peeled and   *½ teaspoon cayenne*
  chopped   *Grated Cheddar or Colby cheese*
¾ cup celery, chopped

Sauté the green peppers, onion and garlic in vegetable oil, over moderate heat, until the onions are golden.

In a large mixing bowl combine the sautéed vegetables with all the other ingredients except the cheese. Stir until well mixed. Pour into an oiled casserole and top with the cheese.

Cover the pan and bake at 350 degrees F. for 30 minutes; then remove the cover and increase the oven temperature to 400 degrees F. Bake 10 minutes longer, to brown the top.

Stir-Fried Winter Vegetables

YIELD: 4 TO 6 SERVINGS

3-4 tablespoons vegetable oil	1 cup mung bean sprouts (see Reference
1 small onion, chopped	Chapter)
1 clove garlic, minced	1 cup alfalfa sprouts (see Reference
4 medium carrots, shredded	Chapter)
½ head cabbage, grated	Cayenne pepper (optional)

Heat the vegetable oil in a large skillet or heavy saucepan. Over medium heat sauté the onion and garlic until the onion is transparent.

Increase the heat and add the carrots and cabbage. Cook, stirring frequently or continually, for about 5 minutes.

Lower the heat. Add the sprouts and just a little water, not more than ¼ cup. Cover and simmer just until the sprouts are wilted down. The vegetables should still be slightly crisp. Season with cayenne if desired.

Serve with tamari (soy sauce) on cooked rice if desired.

Variations: Other combinations of vegetables good for stir-frying are (1) yellow summer squash, zucchini, onions and tender young green beans; (2) onions, cauliflower, broccoli and coarsely chopped spinach; (3) onion, celery, mushrooms, snow peas and mung bean sprouts; and (4) onions, garlic, zucchini, yellow squash and tomato, served with grated Parmesan cheese rather than soy sauce.

Crunchy Sweet Potato Casserole

YIELD: 6 TO 8 SERVINGS

*This dish is delicious with roast turkey, roast goose,
roast duck or ham in any form.*

2 pounds (6-8) sweet potatoes

1/3 cup butter or margarine

½ cup honey or molasses (unsulfured)

2 eggs, beaten

½ cup milk

1/3 cup chopped pecans

1/3 cup shredded coconut

2 tablespoons unbleached flour

2 tablespoons melted butter

Peel, halve and boil the potatoes in lightly salted water until soft. Drain well and mash with a potato masher or with an electric beater. There should be 4 cups.

Beat in the butter, 2 tablespoons of honey or molasses, beaten eggs and milk. When they are well blended, spread the mixture into a lightly buttered 1½- to 2-quart casserole.

Stir together the pecans, coconut and flour. Add the rest of the honey or molasses and the melted butter. When they are well blended, spread the mixture over the sweet potatoes.

Bake 1 hour at 325 degrees F.

Banana-Sweet Potato Casserole

YIELD: 4 SERVINGS

*2 cups cooked and mashed sweet
 potatoes*

1 cup mashed ripe bananas (3 medium)

¾ teaspoon curry powder

1/3 cup sour cream

½ teaspoon salt

1 egg

Thomas Hart Benton
CRADLING WHEAT

Combine all the ingredients in a large mixing bowl and beat until fluffy. Turn the mixture into an oiled 1-quart casserole dish.

Bake, uncovered, at 350 degrees F. for 20 minutes, or until puffed and lightly browned.

Oven-Baked Vegetables

YIELD: 8 TO 10 SERVINGS

2 cups peeled yams, cut into large chunks

2 cups peeled potatoes, cut into large chunks

1 cup zucchini, sliced

½ cup tomatoes, cut into strips

½ green pepper, cut into strips

1 cup sliced onion

2 cloves garlic, minced

¾ cup vegetable oil

½ cup soy sauce

¼ cup honey

½ cup lemon juice

½ teaspoon sweet basil, marjoram, pepper or coriander

Salt and pepper

Cook the yams and potatoes in boiling water 15 minutes.

Prepare the remaining vegetables.

In a large mixing bowl, combine the yams, potatoes, zucchini and tomatoes.

Heat ½ cup of vegetable oil in a skillet and sauté the green pepper, onion and garlic until the onion is transparent. Add to the other vegetables in the mixing bowl and mix gently.

In another bowl, mix together the remaining ½ cup oil, the soy sauce, honey and lemon juice. Add salt and pepper to taste and herbs as desired. Pour over the vegetables and mix gently.

Transfer the mixture to an oiled casserole. Cover and bake at 375 degrees F. 45 minutes.

Homemade Sauerkraut

*Raw cabbage contains up to 50 milligrams of vitamin C
per 100-gram serving. About half of the vitamin C is lost
during the fermentation that turns raw cabbage into sauerkraut,
but sauerkraut is still a remarkably nutritious food that is
also inexpensive and low in calories.
Making sauerkraut can be an interesting project for the
whole family. Trudy Dendurent of Pella, Iowa, wrote to
give us the method used in the old days on the family farm:*

"Take nice solid cabbage (white) and remove any loose leaves. To shred it, an old-fashioned cabbage cutter mounted on a board is best. Have ready a big stone jar or a five- or ten-gallon glass jar, depending on how much kraut you want to make. Put in it a clean white sack—like a pillowcase—and turn the top of the sack down around the top of the jar. Put the cut cabbage in it, a layer of cabbage and then a couple of tablespoons of salt* sprinkled on the cabbage. Then take a potato masher and pound it down. Keep alternating cabbage and a little salt and pounding until the juice comes on it, until you have as much as you want. Then take the part of the sack at the top and twist it down and put a plate with a weight on top. Set it in a cool place for a week or so. When a scum comes on the plate take it up and wash the plate and put it back on. When the cabbage has softened and soured it is kraut, and you can put it up in jars if you wish."

The method recommended today is basically the same but suggests a few precautionary measures to avoid contaminating the sauerkraut with dirt or bacteria:

1. Ahead of time, wash well all equipment that is to be used and scald it with boiling water.

2. Use a square of clean white cloth (muslin or cheesecloth) to cover the top of the cabbage rather than lining the container with a bag—then, when scum appears (indicating bacterial action), you can discard the cloth and replace with a new or freshly washed one. Skim off any scum visible on the surface of the cabbage before recovering it with the cloth, the washed and scalded plate and the weight. A round piece of wood that fits neatly inside the jar can be used instead of a plate. A jar of

water makes a good weight to hold it down snugly, so that juice drawn from the cabbage will rise above it.

3. During the fermentation process the jar should stand where the temperature is 68 to 72 degrees F. At a cooler temperature the cabbage may not ferment, and at a higher temperature it is likely to spoil before fermentation is complete. The process will usually take 5 to 6 weeks. During this time inspect the jar daily. Gas bubbles indicate that fermentation is proceeding normally, but scum indicates the presence of harmful bacteria, so it should be removed promptly. When gas bubbles cease to appear and when the cabbage has a pleasantly sour taste fermentation is complete.

4. For long-term storage, can the sauerkraut by the hot water bath method, processing pint jars 15 minutes in boiling water and quart jars 20 minutes.

Note: Use canning salt, rather than table salt which may contain additives. The proper proportion is about 3 tablespoons of salt to 5 pounds of finely shredded cabbage.

Mushroom Barley Skillet

YIELD: 6 TO 8 SERVINGS

This is good as a meatless main dish or as an accompaniment to a baked ham slice.

2 cups cooked whole barley	*1 teaspoon salt*
4 tablespoons butter	*½ teaspoon pepper*
1 large onion, minced	*½ teaspoon garlic powder*
2 cups (1 pound) sliced mushrooms	*½ cup chopped parsley*

Cook the barley (see Reference Chapter).

Heat the butter in a large skillet. Add the onions and sauté until tender.

Add the sliced mushrooms and cook 3 to 5 minutes, stirring frequently. The mushrooms must be just tender.

Stir in the barley and seasonings and cook, stirring frequently, until the barley is well heated. Serve immediately with the chopped parsley sprinkled on top.

Italian Green Beans with Filberts

YIELD: 8 SERVINGS

Filberts (hazelnuts) are very high in both fiber and flavor. This nut sauce is good with many vegetables.

2 pounds Italian green beans or 3
   10-ounce packages frozen Italian
   beans
¼ pound butter or margarine

½ cup chopped filberts
½ teaspoon lemon juice
Salt and pepper

Prepare the fresh green beans by snipping off the ends with scissors.

Cut the beans or leave them whole according to size and preference. Cook in a small amount of boiling salted water for 10 to 12 minutes or just until tender. Do not overcook. If using the frozen variety, subtract 2 minutes from the directed cooking time.

Heat the butter in a small skillet and sauté the nuts, stirring frequently. Do not let them burn, which they are prone to do if not carefully supervised. Remove from the heat. Add the lemon juice and pour over the drained beans. Season with salt and pepper and serve hot.

Cauliflower au Gratin

YIELD: 4 SERVINGS

1 medium head cauliflower, broken
   into florets
2 cups milk
4 tablespoons whole wheat flour
2 cups mild Cheddar or Colby cheese,
   cubed

½ teaspoon dry mustard
Salt to taste
½-1 cup wheat germ
Paprika

Break the cauliflower into florets and steam it on a rack over boiling water, until it is about half cooked.

Heat the milk (do not boil).

Toss together the flour and cheese cubes. Add to the milk and stir until the cheese melts. Stir in the salt and mustard.

Pour into an oiled baking-serving dish enough of the cheese sauce to cover the bottom. Distribute the cauliflower evenly in the dish. Pour on the remaining cheese sauce and sprinkle the wheat germ and paprika over the top.

Bake at 350 degrees F. for 20 minutes.

Mushroom Stuffed Summer Squash

YIELD: 6 TO 8 SERVINGS

6-8 small summer squash
4 tablespoons butter or margarine
4 tablespoons unbleached white or
   whole wheat flour
1½ cups milk

1 teaspoon onion flakes
½ cup grated sharp cheese
1 8-ounce can mushroom pieces
Salt and pepper

Wash the squash and boil it, whole, for 10 minutes. Drain.

In a saucepan heat the butter until melted and blend in the flour. Add the milk and stir until smooth. Add the onion flakes, cheese and mushroom pieces. Cook over very low heat, or with an asbestos pad under the saucepan, for 15 minutes. Watch closely, as the sauce will burn readily. Taste and add salt and pepper as needed.

Halve the squash and scoop out the seeds. Place the squash, skin side down, in an oiled baking-serving dish. Fill the centers with the sauce.

Cover the dish and bake at 350 degrees F. 20 minutes. Uncover and bake 10 minutes longer.

Garlic Rice

YIELD: 6 SERVINGS

*This is delicious with lamb cooked rare in
the French manner.*

2 cloves garlic

3-4 teaspoons vegetable oil

1½ cups brown rice

2 potatoes, cubed

6 cups water or chicken broth

1 teaspoon salt

Heat the vegetable oil in a large skillet or heavy saucepan. Crush the garlic cloves in a garlic press or mince very fine and sauté them for 2 or 3 minutes.

Add the uncooked rice and cook, stirring frequently, until the rice is golden.

Add the potatoes, water or broth and salt. Bring to a boil; then reduce heat, cover and simmer 30 to 40 minutes or until the rice is fluffy and tender.

Fruited Rice

YIELD: 6 SERVINGS

3 cups cooked brown rice (cook in
  chicken broth for extra flavor)

1 cup sliced carrots

3 tablespoons vegetable oil

1 cup sliced green onions (scallions)

2 cups sliced, cored, unpeeled apples

1 teaspoon salt

½ cup seedless raisins

1 tablespoon sesame seeds

Cook the rice (see Reference Chapter).

Sauté the carrots in the oil over moderate heat for about 10 minutes, stirring frequently.

Add the onions and apples and cook 10 minutes longer. (The vegetables should be crisp-tender but not browned.)

Add the rice, salt and raisins. Continue cooking over low or moderate heat, stirring constantly, until the rice is heated through.

Sprinkle with the sesame seeds and toss lightly.

Spinach Rice Provençale

YIELD: 8 SERVINGS

4 cups cooked brown rice	*2 eggs, beaten*
2 pounds fresh spinach	*1 cup grated Parmesan cheese*
1 large onion, chopped	*Salt*
1 clove garlic, minced	*Butter or margarine*
Olive or vegetable oil	

Cook the rice (see Reference Chapter) and set aside.

Wash the spinach leaves carefully and remove the coarse stems.

Heat the oil in a large heavy saucepan. Add the onion and garlic and sauté 3 minutes or until the onion is transparent but not browned.

Add the spinach and cover tightly. Cook 3 minutes over moderate heat. Uncover and stir, then cook a few minutes longer. Remove from the heat.

When the spinach has cooled slightly, stir into it the beaten eggs, ½ cup of the Parmesan cheese, and salt as needed.

Spread the rice in the bottom of a large baking dish. Cover it with the spinach mixture. Sprinkle the remaining ½ cup of Parmesan cheese over the top and dot with butter or margarine. Bake at 375 degrees F. 20 minutes.

Variation: Add a layer of sliced fresh tomatoes or chopped, drained canned tomatoes before topping with the cheese and dotting with the butter.

Vegetarian Rice

YIELD: 6 TO 8 SERVINGS

1 cup uncooked brown rice
1 tablespoon vegetable oil
½ cup chopped onion
½ cup chopped green pepper
2 cups sliced zucchini

3 small tomatoes, cut in wedges
2¾ cups chicken broth
1 teaspoon salt
1 clove garlic, pressed

Heat the vegetable oil in a heavy skillet and sauté the uncooked rice over moderate heat 2 or 3 minutes.

Oil a shallow 2½-quart casserole and spread the sautéed rice evenly over the bottom of it.

Add the onion, green pepper, zucchini and tomatoes, layering them over the rice.

Bring the chicken broth to a boil and add the salt and garlic to it. Pour the broth gently over the rice and vegetables.

Cover the casserole tightly (use foil if the dish has no snug-fitting lid) and bake at 350 degrees F. for 1 hour and 15 minutes, or until the rice is tender and the liquid absorbed.

Rice Fritters

YIELD: 12 FRITTERS

A great way to use leftover rice.

¼ cup sesame seeds
2 eggs, separated
¼ cup milk
2/3 cup brown rice, cooked (see
  Reference Chapter)

2 tablespoons whole wheat flour
1/8 teaspoon pepper
Vegetable oil

Place the sesame seeds in a moderately hot skillet and cook them, stirring constantly to prevent burning, until they are toasted and golden. Set aside.

In a mixing bowl, beat the egg yolks and blend in the milk, cooked rice, flour and the toasted sesame seeds.

In another bowl, beat the egg whites until stiff.

Fold the egg whites into the rice mixture. Fry by spoonfuls on a hot, lightly oiled griddle, turning once to brown both sides. Serve as a side dish or, with honey, as a dessert.

Wild Rice with Mushrooms

YIELD: 6 TO 8 SERVINGS

2 cups uncooked wild rice
½ cup (1 stick) butter or margarine
½ pound mushrooms, sliced
3 tablespoons whole wheat flour

¼ teaspoon nutmeg
2 cups chicken broth
Salt and pepper

Wash the rice in several waters or rinse thoroughly under cold running water, in a large wire strainer. Cover the rice with clean water and allow to stand 2 or 3 hours. Drain and cover with boiling water. Stir in 1 teaspoon salt and allow to stand 30 minutes.

Melt half the butter (4 tablespoons) and sauté the mushrooms until almost dry.

Add the remaining butter and allow it to melt, then add the flour and stir until it is well blended with the melted butter. Season with the nutmeg, salt and pepper.

Add the chicken broth and cook, stirring, until the sauce begins to thicken.

Drain the rice and spread it in an oiled casserole or baking dish. Pour the mushrooms and sauce over the rice. Cover with a snug-fitting lid and bake at 350 degrees F. for 45 minutes.

Rice with Spinach and Water Chestnuts

YIELD: 4 SERVINGS

½ cup uncooked brown rice
¼ cup chopped onion
3 tablespoons butter
¼ cup liquid from rice or water
½ cup sliced water chestnuts

¼ teaspoon salt
1 package (10 ounces) frozen chopped
  spinach, cooked and drained
2 tablespoons grated or shredded
  Parmesan cheese

Cook the rice (see Reference Chapter).

In a large heavy saucepan melt the butter and sauté the onion over moderate heat.

Add the rice, cooking liquid or water, sliced water chestnuts, salt and the drained spinach.

Continue cooking over low or moderate heat, stirring constantly, until the rice is heated through.

Transfer to a serving dish and sprinkle the Parmesan cheese over the top.

Mushroom Rice

YIELD: 6 SERVINGS

3 cups cooked brown rice (in beef broth)
3 tablespoons vegetable oil
1 cup sliced onions
½ pound fresh mushrooms, sliced
3 tablespoons chopped fresh parsley

3 tablespoons brewer's yeast (optional)
¼ cup wheat germ
¼ teaspoon basil
½ teaspoon cumin seeds

Cook the rice (see Reference Chapter).

Heat the oil in a large skillet or heavy saucepan and sauté the onions, mushrooms and parsley until the onions are tender.

Add the cooked rice. (For extra flavor, cook the rice in beef broth rather than water.)

Add the yeast if desired, the wheat germ, basil and cumin seeds. Continue cooking over moderate heat, stirring constantly, until the rice is heated through. Taste and correct the seasoning as needed.

Brown Rice Patties

YIELD: 12 PATTIES

3 cups cooked brown rice	*1 teaspoon salt*
¼ cup chopped fresh parsley	*¼ teaspoon pepper*
1 cup grated carrots	*2 eggs, beaten*
½ cup finely chopped onions	*½ cup whole wheat flour*
1 clove garlic, minced	*¼ cup vegetable oil*

Cook the rice (see Reference Chapter).

Combine all the ingredients except the vegetable oil in a large mixing bowl. Stir until well mixed.

Using your hands, divide the mixture and shape it into 12 patties of equal size.

Heat the vegetable oil in a heavy skillet and fry the patties until nicely browned on both sides, adding more oil if necessary.

Green Rice Bake

YIELD: 6 SERVINGS

¾ cup uncooked white or brown rice

1 package (10 ounces) frozen broccoli, chopped

½ cup onions, chopped

1 tablespoon butter or margarine

1 can condensed cream of mushroom soup

½ cup grated Cheddar cheese

Cook the rice (see Reference Chapter).

Cook the broccoli in a small amount of water just until tender. Drain and set aside.

In a large skillet or heavy saucepan, melt the butter or margarine and sauté the onion until tender and golden but not browned. Add the rice, soup and broccoli and stir until mixed together well.

Oil a shallow 1½-quart baking-serving dish or casserole and pour the broccoli-rice mixture into it. Top with the cheese.

Bake at 350 degrees F. for 30 minutes.

Brown Rice O'Brien

YIELD: 6 SERVINGS

3 cups cooked brown rice (in beef broth)

2 tablespoons vegetable oil

1 cup chopped green onions with tops

½ cup chopped green pepper

3 tablespoons chopped pimientos

Salt and pepper

Cook the rice (see Reference Chapter).

Heat the vegetable oil in a heavy saucepan and sauté the onions and green peppers until tender.

Add the rice, pimientos, salt and pepper, and toss lightly to mix. Taste and adjust seasoning as necessary.

Southwestern Rice Bean Dish

YIELD: 6 TO 8 SERVINGS

1 pound dry kidney beans

2 cups uncooked brown rice

Water

Vegetable oil

1 green pepper, chopped

2 onions, chopped

2 cloves garlic, minced

1 16-ounce can tomatoes

2 teaspoons tamari (soy sauce)

1 teaspoon chili powder

1/8 teaspoon cayenne (optional)

Salt and pepper

1 cup grated Monterey Jack or
    Cheddar cheese

2 tablespoons chopped parsley

Ripe olives, sliced, for garnish

Soak the beans for several hours or overnight. Discard any imperfect beans, drain, and place in a heavy kettle. Add water to cover. Bring to a boil, then cover and reduce heat. Simmer for 30 minutes.

Drain the liquid from the canned tomatoes and combine it with enough water to make 4½ cups. Bring to a boil. Add the rice slowly, so the water continues to boil. Stir in 1 teaspoon salt. Cover, reduce heat and simmer 40 to 50 minutes or until the rice is dry.

Heat a little vegetable oil in a skillet and sauté the green pepper, onion and garlic until the onion is golden.

Stir together the drained beans, rice, sautéed vegetables and drained tomatoes. Add the seasonings and salt and pepper to taste and pour the mixture into a large casserole or heatproof serving dish.

Bake at 350 degrees F. 1 hour.

Remove the casserole from the oven and sprinkle the chopped parsley and grated cheese over the top. Garnish with a few ripe olives, sliced. Return the casserole to the oven and bake 5 minutes longer or until the cheese melts.

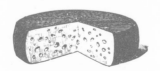

Bulgur Pilaf

YIELD: 4 SERVINGS

2 tablespoons butter or margarine

2 tablespoons chopped onion

2 tablespoons chopped green pepper

2 tablespoons chopped celery

1 cup uncooked bulgur or cracked
   wheat

2 cups chicken or beef broth, or
   1 chicken bouillon cube dissolved
   in 2 cups boiling water

½ teaspoon salt or to taste

Melt the butter in a heavy saucepan. Sauté the onion, green pepper and celery over moderate heat until the onion is soft and golden.

Add the dry bulgur or cracked wheat and cook, stirring frequently, for 5 minutes.

Add the broth and salt. Bring to a boil, then cover and reduce heat. Cook until all the moisture is absorbed and the grain is light and fluffy, about 20 minutes for bulgur or up to 40 minutes for cracked wheat.

Taste and correct seasoning as needed. Serve as a side dish with meat, poultry or vegetables.

Variation: Before serving stir in 1 small can sliced mushrooms or 1 cup sliced fresh mushrooms sautéed in 2 tablespoons of butter or margarine.

Wild Rice-Stuffed Peppers

YIELD: 4 SERVINGS

½ cup uncooked wild rice

2¾ cups boiling water

½ teaspoon salt

4 medium green peppers

1 cup diced cooked chicken

¾ cup leftover chicken gravy or
   thickened chicken broth

½ cup chopped water chestnuts

1 tablespoon butter

4 tablespoons fine bread crumbs

Salt and pepper

Wash the rice in several waters or rinse it under cold running water, in a wire strainer, until the water runs clear.

Stir the rice into the boiling water and add the salt. Cover, reduce heat and simmer 45 minutes or until the rice is tender and all the water is absorbed.

While the rice is cooking, wash the green peppers. Cut off the stem end and remove all seeds and membranes. Blanch (partially cook) the hollow pepper cases by simmering them 3 to 5 minutes in boiling water. Remove and drain. Arrange the pepper cases, upright, in a baking dish.

Heat the butter in a small skillet. Stir in the crumbs and cook until lightly browned.

Stir together the rice, chicken, gravy or broth and chopped water chestnuts. Taste and correct seasoning, as needed. Stuff the rice mixture in the peppers and cover tops with the buttered crumbs. Bake at 350 degrees F. for 30 minutes.

Herbed Spaghetti

YIELD: 3 OR 4 SMALL SERVINGS

*8 ounces whole wheat or other
  spaghetti
Water
Salt
3 tablespoons butter or margarine*

*2 tablespoons mixed chopped fresh
  herbs (2 teaspoons parsley, 2
  teaspoons chives, 1 teaspoon basil,
  1 teaspoon tarragon)*

Cook the spaghetti in a large kettle of boiling, salted water until just tender (8 to 10 minutes for whole wheat spaghetti).

Drain the spaghetti, then return it to the saucepan with the butter or margarine and the suggested herbs or those of your own choosing. Mix well and serve at once.

Summertime Spaghetti

YIELD: 6 TO 8 SERVINGS

1½ pounds whole wheat or other spaghetti
Boiling water
Vegetable oil
2 teaspoons salt
Butter or margarine
2 green peppers, chopped
2 medium onions, chopped

1 pound fresh mushrooms, sliced
2 cups tomatoes, chopped and drained
1-2 cloves garlic, minced
Salt
½ teaspoon oregano
1 cup Parmesan cheese
3 ounces mozzarella cheese

Stir the spaghetti into a large kettle of boiling water to which 2 teaspoons of salt and a little vegetable oil have been added. Cook 5 to 7 minutes, or just until tender. Rinse under cold water and drain.

Melt a small amount of butter or margarine in each of 2 skillets. Sauté the green peppers and onions in one, the mushrooms in the other.

Oil a large shallow casserole or baking-serving dish. Spread half of the cooked spaghetti in the bottom. Over it layer half of the pepper and onion mixture, half of the tomatoes and half of the mushrooms. Sprinkle with half of the garlic, salt, oregano and Parmesan cheese. Repeat the layers, using the remaining spaghetti, pepper and onion, tomatoes, mushrooms, garlic and a little more salt, oregano and Parmesan cheese. Top with thin slices of mozzarella cheese.

Bake covered at 350 degrees F. for 20 minutes. (Cover the casserole or pan with aluminum foil if there is no close-fitting lid.) Uncover and bake 10 to 15 minutes longer.

TAKING YOUR LEAVES

Salads and Salad Dressings

Salad gets its name from the Latin word *sal* for "salt" and hence you run across the English *sallet*, meaning any number of uncooked tender leaves of herbs and plants. Chaucer himself mentions a fourteenth-century gourmet who favored, and flavored, a sallet of "garlic, onions and lettuce."

"Lettuce" could be any one of hundreds of varieties available today, derived from plants growing wild across Asia and Europe over the centuries. Thomas Jefferson, that great experimenter in both diet and democracy, grew about twenty varieties of lettuce in the humble garden behind royal Monticello. Mr. Jack Bibb, soldier in the War of 1812, one-time legislator and citizen of Frankfort, Kentucky, grew such bouffant and tasty heads behind *his* house that now his name is tossed in fame and he is immortalized in the leafy heavens of the sallet.

Oh, but the unknowns who also blazed a green trail in the garden variety, taking the thyme to seize the salad days! Your grandmother and her mother knew sweet basil, borage, chervil, chicory, chives, dill, fennel, mustard, parsley, pennyroyal, peppergrass, purslane, winter savory, sorrel and watercress, as well as spinach, beet greens and the humble dandelion. With these, the doughty ladies fought off family visits of jaundice, hysterics, coughs, sore throat, colic, consumption, toothache, corns and the pip.

They knew! The *Domestic Oracle* of 1826 declared that salads are "proper for all seasons, but particularly from the beginning of February to July, in which period they are in greatest perfection, and consequently act most effectually in cleaning and attenuating the blood. . . . So again from the middle of September to the end of January, fresh salading of every kind is grateful to the stomach, and will have the

154

effect of removing obstructions, relieving shortness of breath and correcting the humours generated by gross food."

A charming "Summer Salad" was made of lettuce, mustard, cresses, sorrel and young onions, "garnished with nasturtium flowers."

Our own variations may not have as much diversity as some of those antiquarian goodies, but perhaps we have done even better in capturing for you the freshness and health-giving-est of garden greens.

A word about fiber: It's found in all plant foods, as it makes up the walls that surround all cells in the stems, leaves and fruit of plants—but there isn't much of it in the tender, succulent vegetables that taste good in salads. You'd have to eat salad all day long to get fiber equal to that in one bowl of bran cereal! To increase the fiber content of salads, add wheat bran cereal as you would croutons, and serve the salads with whole wheat, pumpernickel or rye bread.

A few rules of green thumb:

The best place to eat a salad really is in the garden. Once the greens and vegetables are picked, the action of enzymes sets in to spoil the green freshness and steal away precious vitamins.

Refrigeration slows the process of spoilage but does not stop it, so pick or purchase only the salad ingredients you can use up in a hurry.

Water washes away nutrients, so do not soak or wash greens until you are ready to prepare your salad.

Light and oxygen are spoilers, too—so wrap your salad ingredients snugly or store them in covered containers.

Obviously heat will wilt your salad, so keep everything in the refrigerator until the very last minute.

Use lots of spinach, parsley, watercress, romaine and endive—the dark green greens contain the most of what's good for you.

Keep your greens away from copper as it, and other metals to a lesser degree, can destroy vitamin C and other nutrients.

Make a still life, an arrangement, of your salad—it tastes better that way. And don't forget that lettuce leaves are not there just to hold the other salad ingredients—they're not *plates*, they're there to be eaten.

So, *salud salad!*

Tossed Salad

YIELD: 8 GENEROUS SERVINGS

2-3 large handfuls fresh spinach
2-3 heads romaine lettuce
1 small head cauliflower
2-3 carrots
1 medium onion
1 green pepper
½-1 cup soaked sunflower seeds
½-1 cup rye, alfalfa, lentil or bean
*   sprouts (see Reference Chapter)*

Dash of kelp (optional)
Salt and pepper to taste
2-3 tablespoons apple cider vinegar
6-8 tablespoons safflower or vegetable
*   oil*
2-3 tomatoes
2-3 hard-cooked eggs, chopped fine
½ cup croutons or bran cereal
½-1 cup grated Colby or Cheddar cheese

Wash the vegetables and drain them on paper toweling.

Tear the spinach and lettuce into bite-size pieces, discarding coarse stems.

Grate the carrots. Chop the cauliflower quite fine.

Chop the onion and green pepper.

Combine the vegetables in a large salad bowl and toss.

Add the seeds and sprouts and toss again.

Add the seasonings, cider and oil and toss again.

Arrange on top the tomatoes, cut into wedges, the eggs, croutons or bran and the cheese. Serve immediately.

Green and White Choux Salad

YIELD: 6 TO 8 SERVINGS

1 large head cauliflower
1 bunch broccoli
1 cup mayonnaise
1 teaspoon chopped tarragon

1 tablespoon chopped parsley
2 teaspoons chopped chives
1 clove garlic, minced (optional)
Lettuce leaves

Trim the cauliflower and cook it, stem side down, in boiling salted water for 15 minutes. Transfer to a colander to drain and cool.

In the same water, cook the broccoli for 5 minutes. Drain and cool the broccoli.

In a small bowl stir together the mayonnaise, tarragon, parsley, chives and the garlic, if desired, to make the salad dressing.

Place the cauliflower, right side up, in a shallow serving bowl. Cut the broccoli florets apart, leaving only about 1½ inches of stem. Insert the broccoli florets into the cauliflower head. Cover with plastic wrap and chill in the refrigerator until serving time.

To serve, surround the cauliflower with lettuce leaves and spoon a little of the dressing over all. Serve the rest of the dressing in a side dish.

Potato Salad

YIELD: 8 TO 10 SERVINGS

1/3 cup vinaigrette dressing

1/3 cup mayonnaise

1 teaspoon prepared mustard

4 cups diced cooked potatoes

2 hard-cooked eggs, chopped

1½ cups chopped celery

1 cup cottage cheese, drained

½ cup wheat germ

½ cup chopped pimiento

1/3 cup chopped green pepper or
  pickles

3 tablespoons minced onion

3 tablespoons chopped parsley

1-2 teaspoons salt

¼ teaspoon black pepper

Garnish: salad greens, radishes and
  ripe olives

In a large bowl combine the salad dressing, mayonnaise and mustard. Mix well.

Add the potatoes and eggs. Stir and let stand 20 minutes or longer.

Add all the other ingredients except those for garnish. Mix well, taste for seasoning and refrigerate 2 hours or longer.

Serve bordered with salad greens, with radishes and olives dotted over the top.

Wheat Germ-Corn Salad

YIELD: 4 SERVINGS

1/3 cup wheat germ

1 small can (7-ounce) whole kernel corn
 or 1 cup cooked fresh corn kernels

1/3 cup finely sliced green onion
 (scallions)

1/3 cup minced parsley

1/3 cup chopped carrot

1/3 cup chopped celery

3 tablespoons vegetable oil

2 tablespoons lemon juice

½ teaspoon basil, crumbled

¼ teaspoon oregano, crumbled

¼ teaspoon salt

Salad greens

Sliced cucumber

Combine the wheat germ with the canned or fresh corn, which has been thoroughly drained.

Prepare the green onions, parsley, carrot and celery. Toss with the corn mixture.

Combine the oil, lemon juice, herbs and salt and mix with the vegetables.

Line a salad bowl with crisp salad greens and fill the center with the salad mixture.

Wash a medium-size fresh cucumber and slice it very thin. Do not remove the skin unless it has been waxed to preserve it. Place the slices decoratively over the corn salad.

Wheat Germ Stuffed Tomatoes

YIELD: 4 SERVINGS

4 large tomatoes (3-inch diameter)

1 avocado

½ cup wheat germ

½ cup chopped celery

2 tablespoons finely chopped onion

2 tablespoons minced parsley

2 tablespoons lemon juice

½ teaspoon salt

1/8 teaspoon pepper

Wash the tomatoes and cut off the top ¾ inch from each tomato. Scoop out the seeds and pulp with a spoon, leaving a ¾-inch shell. Turn upside down on a rack to drain.

Peel the avocado. Halve the avocado and remove the seed. Dice the flesh quite fine.

Mix the wheat germ, celery, onion, parsley, lemon juice, salt, pepper, avocado and tomato pulp.

Spoon the mixture into the tomato shells. If desired sprinkle with additional wheat germ and garnish with parsley.

Yogurt-Three Bean Salad

YIELD: 8 SERVINGS

½ cup dry garbanzo beans	*1 tablespoon honey*
½ cup dry kidney beans	*¾ teaspoon garlic salt*
½ cup dry black turtle beans	*¼ teaspoon curry powder*
1 cup yogurt	*½ teaspoon basil*
4 teaspoons lemon juice	*3 tablespoons fresh chives, chopped*
½ cup nonfat dry milk powder	*3 tablespoons fresh parsley, chopped*

Soak the beans separately overnight. Cook them separately until tender. Drain thoroughly. The canned varieties of these beans may be substituted. They should be well drained. Combine the cooked beans in a nonmetal bowl.

Whisk the yogurt in a small bowl.

Blend the lemon juice with the dry milk to make a thin paste and combine with the yogurt.

Mix the honey, garlic salt, curry powder, basil, chives and parsley and add to yogurt.

Pour the dressing over the beans. Cover and refrigerate overnight.

Variation: Cooked or canned green beans can be added to make a 4-bean salad. (Be sure they are well drained.)

Vegetable Rice Vinaigrette

YIELD: 8 SERVINGS

2 cups uncooked white or brown rice

1 bay leaf

1 clove garlic

1 tablespoon lemon juice

1 teaspoon salt

10-ounce package frozen peas

1 pound raw mushrooms

1 small onion

1 carrot

¾ cup vinaigrette dressing

2 heads Boston or Bibb lettuce

½ cup chopped walnuts or sunflower
   seeds

Bring 6 cups of water and 1 teaspoon of salt to a full rolling boil. Add the rice and stir until the mixture boils. Add the bay leaf, garlic clove, lemon juice and salt. Cover and cook over reduced heat until all the liquid is absorbed. The brown rice will take 35 to 40 minutes, the white rice less time. Discard the bay leaf and garlic. Fluff the rice with a fork and cool.

Meanwhile, cook the peas just until tender. Do not overcook. Drain and cool.

Wash and dry the mushrooms. Cut them lengthwise, using both cap and stem.

Chop the onion very fine and sliver the carrot.

Toss the rice and vegetables with the dressing and chill in the refrigerator.

Toast the walnuts or sunflower seeds.

Serve the rice mixture on salad leaves and sprinkle with the toasted nuts or seeds.

Tomato Rice Salad

YIELD: 4 TO 6 SERVINGS

1 cup uncooked brown rice

3 large ripe tomatoes

2 green peppers, cut into strips

½ teaspoon salt

¼ teaspoon pepper

2 tablespoons vegetable oil

1 tablespoon vinegar or lemon juice

1 teaspoon prepared mustard

Bring 3 cups of water and 1 teaspoon of salt to a full rolling boil. Gradually add 1 cup of brown rice. Bring to a boil. Reduce the heat to low, cover the pan and cook 35 to 40 minutes or until the liquid is completely absorbed. Put the rice in a wooden bowl and fluff it with a fork. Cool completely.

Slice the tomatoes and cut the green peppers into strips. Add to the rice.

Mix the salt, pepper, oil, vinegar or lemon juice and mustard well. Add to the contents of the bowl and toss lightly.

Superb Rice Salad

YIELD: 6 TO 8 SERVINGS

1 cup uncooked brown rice
½ cup minced onions
1 cup chopped celery
1 cup drained, cooked green peas

6 hard-cooked eggs, diced
2 tablespoons diced pimiento
½ cup mayonnaise

Cook the rice as in the preceding recipe.

Prepare the remaining ingredients. Combine with the rice in a bowl and toss lightly.

Turn the mixture into a lightly oiled 9-inch ring mold or other mold holding 6 cups. Press down with the back of a spoon. Chill.

At serving time, invert the mold onto a serving plate bordered with lettuce leaves and garnish as desired. If a ring mold is used, the center may be filled with a small bowl of pickled beets.

Turnip Salad

YIELD: 4 SERVINGS

2 cups turnip strips   *1 tablespoon Dijon-type mustard*
1 cup mayonnaise   *2 tablespoons chopped parsley*
1 teaspoon caraway seeds (optional)   *Boston or Bibb lettuce leaves*

Peel medium-size white turnips and cut them into matchstick-sized strips.

Bring a pan of salted water to a full boil. Throw in the strips. As soon as the water boils, drain the strips and place in a bowl of ice water. Refrigerate for at least 2 hours. Drain and dry thoroughly.

Combine the turnip strips with the mayonnaise, caraway seeds if desired, mustard and chopped parsley. Keep very cold.

Serve on lettuce leaves, as a salad course with French Bread, or Whole Wheat Pita Pouches (see page 34).

Tabbouleh Salad

YIELD: 6 TO 8 SERVINGS

2 cups bulgur

4 cups boiling water

2¼ cups fresh chopped parsley

1½ bunches green onions

1½ cups chopped fresh mint (optional)

1 tablespoon salt

2 teaspoons black pepper, ground

½ cup olive oil

½ cup lemon juice

4 large tomatoes

1-2 heads garden lettuce

Combine the bulgur and the boiling water. Let stand ½ hour or until the water is absorbed.

Mix in the parsley, onion, fresh mint if desired, salt and pepper.

Add the oil and lemon juice.

Wash the tomatoes. Chop them coarsely and toss with the rest of the ingredients. Chill the mixture in the refrigerator.

Serve the salad on individual plates lined with well-washed and dried lettuce leaves.

Mushroom and Bean Salad

YIELD: 3 OR 4 SERVINGS

2 cups small fresh mushrooms

3-4 scallions or green onions

1½ cups cooled cooked lima or
* navy beans*

1/3 to ½ cup mayonnaise or yogurt

Chopped parsley

Slice the mushrooms and scallions or green onions. Combine with the beans and enough mayonnaise or yogurt to make the mixture hold together. Top with the chopped parsley.

Cauliflower Salad

YIELD: 4 TO 6 SERVINGS

1 small head cauliflower

1/3 to ½ cup mayonnaise
   mixed with 2 tablespoons of yogurt

1-2 carrots, grated

1-2 tablespoons chopped black olives

Watercress

Pimiento strips or paprika

Chopped parsley

Wash the cauliflower well and divide into florets.

Combine the mayonnaise and yogurt with the grated carrots and chopped olives.

Arrange the cauliflower on a bed of watercress and top with the mayonnaise mixture. Garnish with narrow strips of pimiento or a sprinkling of paprika and chopped parsley.

Gourmet Sprout Salad

YIELD: 4 SERVINGS

2 heads Bibb lettuce

4 green onions (scallions)

1 cup sprouted mung beans (see
   Reference Chapter)

1 cup sprouted wheat seeds or alfalfa
   seeds (see Reference Chapter)

4 large radishes

2 stalks celery, sliced thin

½ cup sunflower seeds

¼ cup wheat germ

1/3 cup Italian dressing

1 avocado

Wash the Bibb lettuce or other fresh garden lettuce. Dry well and tear into pieces into a wooden bowl.

Cut the onions, celery and radishes in thin slices. Add them to the salad bowl along with the sprouts, seeds and wheat germ.

Toss lightly with the Italian dressing.

Peel, halve and seed the avocado. Cut lengthwise into thin strips and spread decoratively over the top. Serve immediately.

Celery and Leek Salad

YIELD: 4 TO 6 SERVINGS

1 small head celery
2-3 small leeks

1 orange
1 tablespoon chopped parsley

Wash the celery and leeks well. Save some of the celery leaves for garnishing the salad; the rest of the leaves and the tough outer stalks can be used to make vegetable stock for soup. Make celery curls from several of the choice celery stalks by cutting thin strips and chilling them in ice water for one hour. Chop the remaining celery into a salad bowl.

Cut the leeks into very thin slices. (Use only small leeks, which have a delicate flavor, in a salad.) Add to the chopped celery.

Grate a little rind from the orange, then squeeze it. Stir together the orange juice, grated rind and parsley and pour over the salad. Stir and chill.

Just before serving, garnish with the reserved celery leaves and celery curls.

Sunshine Salad

YIELD: 6 TO 8 SERVINGS

4 cups cooled cooked bulgur (see
    Reference Chapter)
1 cup each alfalfa and mung bean
    sprouts (see Reference Chapter)

½ cup toasted sunflower seeds
1/3 cup vinaigrette or Italian salad
    dressing

Combine the bulgur, sprouts and sunflower seeds in a large salad or mixing bowl. Toss lightly.

Sprinkle the salad dressing over the ingredients and toss again.

Cover the bowl and refrigerate 1 hour or longer before serving.

Lentils Vinaigrette

YIELD: 6 TO 8 SERVINGS

1 pound dry lentils
3 small onions sliced thin

Vinaigrette or Italian salad dressing
2 tablespoons chopped parsley

Soak the lentils overnight. Pick out any shells that float to the top and drain the lentils. Place them in a saucepan, cover with cold water and add the onions. Cook just until tender, 20 to 45 minutes depending on the kind of lentils you have (some are processed so as to cook quickly).

Drain thoroughly and cool the lentils.

Before serving, combine the cooled lentils with 2/3 to 1 cup of a French or Italian salad dressing made with garlic. Do not add too much, as the salad should not be soupy. Taste and add salt if needed.

Pile the salad on a serving dish and sprinkle with chopped parsley.

Bulgur Vegetable Salad

YIELD: 6 SERVINGS

1½ cups cooked bulgur
1/3 cup cider or wine vinegar
1½ tablespoons sugar
½ teaspoon salt
1/3 cup finely chopped onion

1½ cups cooked green beans, drained
3 tomatoes, chopped and drained
½ cup diced celery
2 hard-cooked eggs (optional)

Combine the cooled, cooked bulgur with the vinegar, sugar, salt and the chopped onion. Blend well and chill, covered, in the refrigerator for 2 hours or longer.

Shortly before serving time fold in the beans, tomatoes and celery. Serve on lettuce leaves, garnished with sliced hard-cooked eggs if desired.

Citrus Crunch Salad

YIELD: 6 TO 8 SERVINGS

2 cups grapefruit and orange segments, drained

3 heads Bibb lettuce, washed and chopped

¾ cup diced celery

½ cup wheat germ

½ cup sprouted mung beans (see Reference Chapter)

½ cup sprouted wheat berries or alfalfa (see Reference Chapter)

½ cup sunflower seeds

1 cup seedless white grapes, whole

¼ cup vinaigrette dressing

¼ cup mayonnaise

Use fresh fruit or well-drained canned fruit.

Wash the lettuce and dry it carefully. Tear it into small pieces. Any fresh garden lettuce can substitute for Bibb lettuce.

Assemble the remaining ingredients but do not mix until just before serving.

Apple Slaw

YIELD: 4 TO 6 SERVINGS

1 small head green cabbage, finely shredded

1 carrot, grated

4 scallions or green onions, sliced

2 tablespoons chopped celery

1 tablespoon chopped green pepper

1 large apple, cored and finely chopped

1-2 tablespoons honey

½ teaspoon salt

1 tablespoon wine vinegar

1 tablespoon mayonnaise

Dash cayenne pepper

In a large salad bowl, combine the prepared cabbage, carrot, scallions, celery, green pepper and apple.

In a small bowl, beat together the honey, salt, wine vinegar, mayonnaise and cayenne pepper.

Pour the dressing over the salad mixture and toss lightly. Chill at least 20 minutes before serving.

Variations: For Mock Waldorf Salad, stir in ½ cup chopped walnuts and ½ cup wheat germ or ½ cup bran.

Cheese Waldorf Salad

YIELD: 4 SERVINGS

1 large or 2 small apples
¾ cup chopped celery
½ cup chopped walnuts
2/3 cup yogurt

Lettuce
Chopped basil and/or chervil (optional)
Cottage cheese

Core and chop, but do not peel, the apples. Combine the apples with the celery, nuts and yogurt.

Prepare a bed of lettuce leaves. Heap the apple mixture in the center and spoon cottage cheese around it. Top with a sprinkling of chopped herbs, if desired.

Parsley Dressing

YIELD: 2 CUPS

1 bunch parsley
2 cloves garlic, minced
¾ cup olive oil

¾ cup peanut, corn, safflower or
   olive oil
½ cup lemon juice
1 teaspoon salt

Paul Gauguin
STILL LIFE WITH APPLES

Put everything in a blender. Blend until smooth; then store in a covered jar, in the refrigerator. Olive oil combined half and half with one of the other oils is recommended.

Zippy Tomato Dressing

YIELD: 2 CUPS

1 16-ounce can V-8 juice

2 teaspoons prepared mustard

Juice of 1 lemon

¼ cup cider vinegar

2 garlic cloves, minced

2-3 scallions, chopped

1 tablespoon chopped parsley

Blend together. Store in a covered jar, in the refrigerator.

Creamy Caraway Dressing

YIELD: 2 CUPS

2 cups sour cream

2 tablespoons lemon juice

1 teaspoon caraway seeds

¾ teaspoon sesame seeds

¾ teaspoon salt

Dash of pepper

2 tablespoons water

Combine the ingredients and blend until smooth. Refrigeration improves the flavors, so chill before serving.

French Cream Cheese Dressing

YIELD: 2/3 CUP

3 ounces cream cheese

1 tablespoon minced onion

½ teaspoon dry mustard

1 teaspoon salt

2 tablespoons chopped parsley

¼ cup safflower, corn or peanut oil

2 tablespoons lemon juice

Dash of black pepper, to taste

Beat the cream cheese until smooth.

Blend in the remaining ingredients.

The dressing can be thinned with a small amount of milk if desired.

Mayonnaise

YIELD: 1½ CUPS

1 egg

½ teaspoon dry mustard

1 teaspoon salt

1 teaspoon honey (optional)

3 tablespoons cider vinegar

1 tablespoon lemon juice

Dash of Tabasco

1-1¼ cups vegetable oil (half olive oil and half safflower oil recommended)

Place all the ingredients except the oil in a blender and spin on medium speed until well blended.

Set the blender speed on low and gradually add the oil, pouring it in a thin steady stream. The mixture may become thick at first, but it will smooth out as the last of the oil is added. (Some cooks recommend adding 1 tablespoon of hot water after the oil, to stabilize the mixture.)

Vinaigrette Dressing

YIELD: ¾ CUP

4 tablespoons tarragon vinegar

10 tablespoons corn or peanut oil

¾ teaspoon salt

Freshly ground pepper to taste

¼ teaspoon dry mustard

Place all the ingredients in a sealed container and shake until well blended. Store in the refrigerator.

Herbed Salad Dressing

YIELD: 1½ CUPS

¼ cup tamari (soy sauce)

1 cup vegetable oil

1 tablespoon oregano

1 tablespoon sweet basil

Juice from freshly squeezed lemon

Blend the ingredients and store in a covered jar in the refrigerator.

Yogurt-Thousand Island Dressing

YIELD: 1 CUP

1 hard-cooked egg, chopped

1½ tablespoons finely chopped black
  olives

1 teaspoon minced onion

½ cup minced celery

2/3 cup low-fat yogurt

2 tablespoons ketchup

Combine all ingredients in a glass jar with a tight-fitting lid. Shake to blend well, then store, covered, in the refrigerator.

Italian Dressing

YIELD: 1 CUP

4 tablespoons red wine or cider
  vinegar
1-2 cloves garlic, minced
½ teaspoon crumbled leaf oregano
1 teaspoon salt

1/8 teaspoon freshly ground black
  pepper
6 tablespoons olive oil
6 tablespoons corn oil

In a glass jar, mix together the vinegar, garlic, oregano, salt and pepper. Let stand 1 hour or longer. Just before serving, add the oils, cover the jar and shake to mix well.

LUCKY BREAKS

Snacks, Sandwiches and Beverages

To lengthen thy life, lessen thy meals.
Eat sparingly and defy the physician.
Light supper makes long life.
That you may sleep soundly, eat lightly.

—*Old Proverbs*

These are the foods Americans eat with their fingers, on the run, between meals, or late at night. The pastry an office worker has at his coffee break. The "nibblings" served with cocktails. Children's after-school snacks and the refreshments served at their parties. Sandwiches packed in lunchboxes and picnic baskets. The bedtime drink.

There is nothing nutritionally wrong with eating small meals at odd hours but there is something very wrong with many of the foods consumed at such times.

One reason Americans buy so many soft drinks (221 16-ounce cans for every man, woman and child in one recent year) may be that it's much easier to buy a soft drink than to buy an apple or a banana!

Here, then, is a plea for the wholesome and healthful snack: fresh fruit, raisins, carrot or celery sticks, skimmed milk with whole-grain bread or crackers. The recipes that follow suggest ways to add variety to the menu that eschews "junk food" in favor of good nutrition.

Goodies which are good for you fortunately have a lot of eye appeal, so snackify them around the house and you'll find they disappear quickly enough and start sweet tooths well on their way to becoming wisdom tooths. Stash pecans ordered fresh from Georgia where they'll be picked up for a pick-me-up. Sink toothpicks into fresh California dates and set up an oasis in every room. Mixtures of seeds and nuts are chewy choose-ables for other snack bowls. Treat yourself to one of the magic apple cutters which eliminate the core and provide eight eatable segment-chunks simply for the trouble of making a pressing decision. Incidentally, the chunks will be fresh-appearing for hours after cutting, and more tasty apple-with-lemon-wise, if you sprinkle them with a dash of ascorbic acid (vitamin C)—which is also a boon to any scurvy knaves who may wander into your ménage.

174

Granola

YIELD: ABOUT 12 CUPS

*Granola recipes need not be followed exactly. The ingredients
and proportions can vary according to taste and availability. Serve
granola as a breakfast cereal with milk or as a between-meal
snack, dry. For a quick lunch, stir it into yogurt.*

1 cup sorghum molasses	*8 cups uncooked oatmeal (rolled oats)*
½ cup vegetable oil	*2 cups flaked rye*
1 teaspoon vanilla extract	*½ cup sesame seeds*
2 teaspoons salt	*1 1/3 cups unsweetened flaked coconut*

Preheat the oven to 275 degrees F.

Combine the molasses, vegetable oil, vanilla and salt. Stir until blended. Set aside.

Combine the oatmeal, flaked rye, sesame seeds and coconut in a very large mixing bowl. Stir until mixed.

Pour the molasses-oil mixture over the dry ingredients and stir until blended.

Spread the mixture on cookie sheets and bake 40 to 45 minutes or until golden brown, stirring every 5 minutes during baking time. Or, cook small quantities in a skillet over medium or low heat until golden brown.

Allow the mixture to cool, then store in glass jars with tight-fitting lids.

Variations: (1) Substitute flaked wheat or buckwheat groats for the rye flakes. (2) Add ½ cup chopped pecans, ½ cup chopped walnuts and ½ cup cashew pieces. (3) Add 1 cup roasted peanuts.

Jan's Super Granola

YIELD: ABOUT 10 CUPS

1 cup honey

1 cup vegetable oil (cold-pressed oil
   recommended)

4 cups uncooked oatmeal (rolled oats)

2 cups flaked rye

1 cup poppy seeds

1 cup pumpkin seeds

1 cup sunflower seeds

2 cups sesame seeds

1 cup unsweetened flaked coconut

1 cup powdered whey or nonfat dry
   milk powder

1 cup wheat germ

1 cup chopped almonds (optional)

Preheat the oven to 275 degrees F.

In a small bowl combine the honey and oil. Stir until blended.

In a very large bowl combine the oatmeal, flaked rye, poppy seeds, pumpkin seeds, sunflower seeds, sesame seeds, coconut and powdered whey or milk. Stir until mixed evenly.

Pour the honey-oil mixture over the dry ingredients and stir until blended. If the mixture is too dry, add a little more oil and honey.

Spread the mixture on cookie tins and bake 40 to 45 minutes, or until an even golden-brown color, stirring once every 5 minutes of the baking time. Cool and store in covered glass jars, in the refrigerator.

Branola

YIELD: ABOUT 11 CUPS

½ cup vegetable oil

¾ cup honey

3 cups wheat bran cereal

3 cups uncooked oatmeal (rolled oats)

1 cup sesame seeds

1½ cups wheat germ

1½ cups unsweetened flaked coconut

1 cup chopped mixed nuts

¾ cup brown sugar

Preheat the oven to 275 degrees F.

Combine the vegetable oil and honey and stir until blended. Set aside.

Combine the dry ingredients in a large bowl and stir.

Add the oil-honey mixture to the dry ingredients and stir until blended.

Spread the mixture on 1 very large or 2 regular-size cookie sheets. Bake about 45 minutes, stirring every 5 minutes during baking time.

Allow the mixture to cool, then store in a container with a tight-fitting lid.

Hiker's "Gorp"

YIELD: ABOUT 11 CUPS

This high-energy mixture was originated by a nutrition class at Antioch College as an easy-to-carry food for backpackers and mountaineers. Supplemented with cheese and vitamin C, it should provide all the elements of a complete diet. It can also serve, at home, as a breakfast food or a nutritious snack.

3 cups uncooked oatmeal (rolled oats)
½ cup vegetable oil
2 cups roasted peanuts
1 cup sunflower seeds
1 cup yellow cornmeal

1 cup nonfat dry milk powder
1½ cups raisins
1 cup chopped dates
1 cup chopped dried apricots

Stir together the oatmeal and vegetable oil.

Toast the mixture on cookie sheets in a 275-degree oven or in a skillet over medium low heat, stirring frequently during baking or cooking time, until golden brown. Allow to cool.

In a large mixing bowl combine the toasted oatmeal with all the other ingredients. Stir until well blended. Store in glass jars with tight-fitting lids, for home use, or package small quantities in sturdy plastic bags for the hiker.

Peach Nut Chews

YIELD: 2 TO 3 DOZEN

2 cups dried peaches
2 cups dates
2 cups raisins
½ cup honey

1 cup chopped walnuts
1 teaspoon salt
Flaked coconut, sesame seeds or finely
chopped sunflower seeds, for coating

Put the dried peaches and dates through a food chopper.

In the top of a double boiler combine the dried peaches, dates, raisins and honey. Cook over boiling water until the fruit is softened.

Remove from the heat and stir in the walnuts and salt. Allow the mixture to cool partially.

Spread the coconut, sesame seeds or chopped sunflower seeds on waxed paper.

Use your hands to form the fruit mixture into small balls and roll them in the coating. (Rinse your hands frequently in cold water to keep them from getting sticky.) Store the Peach Nut Chews between layers of waxed paper, in the refrigerator.

Super Seed Mixture

YIELD: 1 QUART

Serve this seed mixture by the spoonful, as a between-meal
snack that is satisfying and nutritious.

½ cup sesame seeds
1 cup sunflower seeds
¼ cup (or more) pumpkin seeds
½ cup flax seeds
¼ cup chia seeds
1 teaspoon celery seeds

¼ teaspoon caraway seeds
1 tablespoon (or more) poppy seeds
1 tablespoon unhulled buckwheat
1 tablespoon wild rice or brown rice
1½ cups pineapple juice

Combine in a mixing bowl all the seeds and grains suggested, or as many as are readily available. Stir until mixed.

Pour the pineapple juice over the seeds. Stir until all are moistened.

Transfer the seed mixture to a wide-mouth quart jar and store in the refrigerator. Within 24 hours the seeds should swell enough to fill the jar to the top.

Brazil Nut Chips

YIELD: 2 CUPS

Brazil nuts are not only delicious but are very high in fiber content. They make a wonderful snack any time of day. Served warm they are especially good. At receptions they can be served in a heatproof dish and kept warm over a candle or other low heating device.

1 pound Brazil nuts   *Salt, Vege-Sal or seasoned salt*
1 tablespoon butter or margarine,
melted

Shell the nuts by cracking them with a hammer on a wooden board.

Place the shelled nuts in a pan of cold water and bring them slowly to a boil. Simmer 3 minutes. Drain, and while the nuts are warm, slice them with a very sharp knife as thin as possible.

Spread the nuts out on a baking sheet and sprinkle with the melted shortening.

Bake the nuts at 375 degrees F. for 5 minutes or until lightly browned. Sprinkle with the preferred salt.

Breaded Carrots

YIELD: ABOUT 24 PIECES

2 eggs
2/3 cup milk
6 drops Tabasco liquid pepper sauce
½ cup wheat bran cereal
*2 tablespoons melted shortening or
    vegetable oil*

1 cup unbleached white flour
1 teaspoon baking powder
½ teaspoon salt
*1 pound uncooked carrot chunks,
    ½-inch pieces*

In a small mixing bowl, beat the eggs for 1 minute. Add the milk, liquid pepper sauce and cereal. Let stand about 2 minutes or until the cereal is soft. Stir in the shortening or oil.

Stir together the flour, baking powder and salt. Add to the cereal mixture, mixing until well blended.

Preheat oil in a deep fryer to 375 degrees F. Lower the basket into the hot oil before adding carrots. Dip carrots in the batter. Carefully lower them into the hot fat using tongs. Fry until golden brown. Drain on absorbent paper. Serve warm.

Ann's Broiled Mushrooms and Cheese

YIELD: 16 TO 24 PIECES

1 pound mushrooms
½ pound Muenster cheese

*Spike, Vege-Sal (available in health
    stores) or garlic salt*

Buy medium-size mushrooms of uniform size. Remove the stems and wash them gently. Dry on a paper towel. Place them on a lightly buttered baking sheet.

Break the cheese in small pieces and fill each mushroom cap.

Sprinkle with spike, Vege-Sal or garlic salt.

Bake at 400 degrees F. until the cheese is melted. Serve immediately.

Guacamole

YIELD: 16 TO 24 SERVINGS, AS A DIP

2 avocados, mashed

1 ripe tomato

¼ cup green onions, minced

½ teaspoon salt

1 teaspoon chili powder

2 cloves garlic, minced

Dash of cayenne pepper

2-3 tablespoons lemon juice, or to taste

Peel and halve the avocados. Remove the seed and place in a small wooden bowl.

Dip the tomato in boiling water just long enough to loosen the skin. Peel and halve the tomato. Squeeze out the seeds; cut the tomato in pieces into the bowl.

Add the remaining ingredients and mash with a silver fork. Add the lemon juice to taste.

Serve as a dip with corn chips.

Variations: For the first course of a dinner party or for a lunch or brunch dish, spread guacamole on slices of buttered whole wheat toast.

Soybean Dip

YIELD: ABOUT 2 CUPS

1 15-ounce can soybeans or 2 cups
cooked soybeans, drained

3 cloves garlic, minced

2 teaspoons salt

½ teaspoon Tabasco or other liquid
pepper sauce

¼ cup lemon juice

Place the soybeans in a blender and spin until smooth.

Add the remaining ingredients and blend well. Transfer to a covered bowl and store in the refrigerator until serving time. Serve as a dip with raw vegetables (cauliflower florets, carrot and celery sticks) or corn chips.

Carrot Yogurt Squares

YIELD: 16 SQUARES

An ideal finger food for brown baggers, sportsmen and spectators, too.

2 cups whole wheat flour
½ cup unbleached white flour
2 teaspoons baking soda
1 teaspoon baking powder
1 teaspoon salt
1 teaspoon grated lemon peel

8 ounces plain or mandarin orange
  yogurt
1 cup finely grated carrots
½ cup molasses
1 egg, beaten
½ cup chopped nuts

Preheat the oven to 350 degrees F. Oil a 9-inch square baking pan and dust it with flour.

Stir together the flours, baking soda, baking powder and salt. Set aside.

In a large mixing bowl combine the grated lemon peel, yogurt, grated carrots, molasses and beaten egg. Stir until blended.

Stir in the chopped nuts.

Add the dry ingredients all at once and stir just until combined.

Spread the batter in the prepared pan and bake 25 to 30 minutes or until the edges pull away from the sides of the pan. Cool and cut into squares.

Cheese Wafers

YIELD: ABOUT 5½ DOZEN WAFERS

¾ cup unbleached white flour
½ teaspoon salt
Dash of cayenne pepper
½ cup margarine or butter, softened

½ pound (2 cups) shredded Cheddar
 cheese
1½ cups wheat bran cereal

Preheat the oven to 350 degrees F.

Stir together the flour, salt and cayenne pepper. Set aside.

In a large mixing bowl, beat the margarine or butter and the cheese together until they are light and fluffy.

Add the bran cereal. Stir until blended.

Add the dry ingredients and stir just until all are moistened.

Drop the batter by teaspoonfuls onto ungreased cookie sheets. Flatten each mound of batter by pressing with a fork dipped in flour.

Bake 12 minutes or until lightly browned around the edges. (Do not overbake.) Remove at once from the cookie sheets and cool on wire racks or paper toweling.

Stuffed Celery Sticks

YIELD: 8 TO 12 SERVINGS

1 2½-ounce can smoked oysters
1 cup cottage cheese
2 tablespoons cream

1 teaspoon tamari (soy sauce)
Celery
Paprika

Chop the oysters. Combine them with the cottage cheese, cream and tamari. Stir until blended.

Fill the cavities in crisp celery sticks with the cheese mixture and sprinkle with a little paprika. Store in the refrigerator until serving time.

Madge's Hummous

YIELD: ABOUT 2 CUPS

*A staple food of the Mediterranean countries, hummous makes a nutritious
and satisfying snack food. Serve it as a dip or spread, with
crackers or pita bread, or top ½ cup of hummous with a serving of
green salad for a luncheon dish.*

*2 cups cooked garbanzos (chickpeas)
   or 1 15-ounce can of garbanzos
½ cup of the cooking liquid or liquid
   drained from the canned garbanzos
½ cup tahini (mashed sesame seeds)*

*3 cloves garlic, minced
1 tablespoon olive oil
2 teaspoons salt
¼ cup fresh lemon juice*

Start preparing the hummous at least 24 hours before it is to be served. Soak the
garbanzos overnight, then simmer 2 hours or longer, until very tender.

Combine the cooked garbanzos, cooking liquid and tahini in the blender and spin
until smooth. Add the other ingredients and spin until blended. Add more liquid if
needed to bring the consistency to that of mashed potatoes.

Transfer to a covered bowl and refrigerate 8 hours or longer before serving.

Cheese Ball

YIELD: 16 TO 24 SERVINGS

*2 8-ounce packages cream cheese,
   softened
½ pound Cheddar cheese, shredded
2 tablespoons chopped onion
1 tablespoon chopped green olives
2 teaspoons Worcestershire sauce*

*1 teaspoon lemon juice
1 teaspoon salt
Dash of cayenne pepper
Chopped pecans
Stuffed olives (garnish)*

Combine the 2 cheeses in a mixing bowl and stir until blended.

Sprinkle the chopped onion, chopped olives and the seasonings over the cheese. Stir until combined, then use your hands to shape the mixture into a round ball.

Spread the chopped pecans on waxed paper and roll the cheese ball over them until entirely coated. Wrap the cheese ball in waxed paper or plastic wrap and chill in the refrigerator 2 hours or longer.

Serve the cheese ball as an appetizer or party snack, garnished with a few stuffed olives cut into 4 petals, if desired. Provide whole wheat crackers, small slices of party rye bread and knives for slicing and spreading the cheese.

Sesame Seed Crackers

YIELD: 2 TO 3 DOZEN

1 cup whole wheat flour	1 teaspoon salt
½ cup unbleached white flour	¼ cup vegetable oil
¼ cup soy flour	1/3 cup (or more) cold water
¼ cup sesame seeds	

Preheat the oven to 350 degrees F.

Combine the flours, sesame seeds and salt in a mixing bowl. Stir until well mixed.

Form a well in the center of the dry ingredients and pour in the oil. Stir to blend, then add cold water as needed to make dough that holds together in a ball, as when making pie pastry.

Place the dough on an oiled baking sheet and roll it to 1/8-inch thickness. Use a knife to mark the dough into squares without cutting through. Bake 20 minutes or until crisp and golden.

Eggplant Openface Sandwich

YIELD: 4 SERVINGS

4 slices eggplant
1 egg, beaten
¼ cup milk
½ cup whole wheat flour
¼ teaspoon salt
1/8 teaspoon oregano
4 slices whole wheat or rye bread

4 tablespoons Tomato Sauce (see
*   Reference Chapter)*
4 tomato slices
4 slices mild Cheddar or mozzarella
*   cheese*
Additional oregano

Slice the eggplant in ½-inch rounds. Soak the slices in salted water for 30 minutes or sprinkle with salt and let stand at room temperature.

Drain the eggplant slices and pat dry with paper toweling. Dip each in a mixture of beaten egg and milk, then dredge in whole wheat flour that has been seasoned with the salt and oregano.

Place the eggplant slices on an oiled baking sheet and bake at 400 degrees F. until the top side of each is browned. Turn slices, adding a little more oil to the baking sheet, and bake until the other side is browned.

Toast the bread.

On each slice of bread spread 1 spoonful of tomato sauce. Add 1 eggplant slice and 1 tomato slice; top with the cheese. Sprinkle a little oregano over the top and place under the broiler until the cheese melts.

Eight Sandwiches for Peanut Butter Enthusiasts

1. Combine peanut butter and banana slices between slices of whole wheat bread.

2. Combine peanut butter and crisp cooked bacon between slices of whole wheat or rye bread.

3. Place a thin slice of ham on whole wheat bread. Spread peanut butter over the ham and arrange banana slices on the peanut butter. Top with a second slice of

bread. Spread the outsides of the sandwich with softened butter or margarine and grill in a skillet over low heat, turning once to brown both sides.

4. Spread peanut butter on one slice of whole wheat bread. Spread mayonnaise on another. Combine with crisp bean sprouts or lettuce leaves between the two slices.

5. Spread peanut butter on whole wheat bread. Top with banana slices and crisp bean sprouts and a second slice of bread.

6. Combine peanut butter, sunflower seeds and lettuce between slices of whole wheat bread.

7. Spread peanut butter on one slice of whole wheat bread and mayonnaise on another. Combine with banana slices and a dribbling of honey between the two slices.

8. Spread one slice of whole wheat bread with peanut butter. Sprinkle wheat germ generously over the peanut butter and top with a second slice of bread.

Spinach Openface Sandwich

FOR EACH SERVING:
Fresh spinach
Salt

1 slice whole wheat or rye bread
1 slice mild Cheddar or mozzarella
   cheese
Dash of oregano

Remove any tough stems from the spinach, wash the leaves well and place them directly in a saucepan. The water that clings to the leaves will be enough liquid for cooking them. Steam the leaves about 5 minutes, until wilted down and just tender.

Drain off any liquid left in the pan and save it for vegetable stock. Chop the spinach and season it with a little salt.

Toast the bread.

Spoon the chopped spinach onto the toasted bread. Top with the slice of cheese and sprinkle a little oregano over it.

Place in a preheated oven or under the broiler until the cheese melts.

Meatless Reuben Sandwich

FOR EACH SERVING: *Onion*

1 slice rye bread   *Green pepper*

Zucchini   *1 slice mild Cheddar or Swiss cheese*

2-3 tablespoons sauerkraut

Drain the sauerkraut well, placing it in a wire strainer and then pressing with the back of a spoon to force the liquid out.

Cut the zucchini into thin slices. Cut thin rings from the onion and green pepper. Toast the bread.

Spoon the drained sauerkraut onto the toasted bread. Arrange 4 or 5 zucchini slices on top, then add a few onion and green pepper rings. Top with the cheese slice.

Place in a preheated oven or under the broiler until the cheese melts.

Yogi Tea

YIELD: 4 SERVINGS

4 whole cardamom seeds   *Boiling water*

3 whole cloves   *Black or jasmine tea*

4 whole peppercorns   *Milk*

½ stick cinnamon   *Honey*

1 slice ginger root (optional)

Tie the spices in a cheesecloth bag.

Bring 1 cup of water to a boil and add the spice bag. Reduce the heat and simmer for 20 minutes.

Add 1 teaspoon of loose tea or 1 teabag and simmer 3 minutes longer.

Warm a teapot by rinsing it with very hot water. Strain the tea into it.

Add 1 cup of milk and boiling water as needed (about 2 cups) to make 4 servings. Sweeten with honey as desired, in the teapot or in individual cups.

Fruit Milk Shake

YIELD: 1 SERVING

1 cup cold milk
½ teaspoon vanilla extract
1 cup fruit: bananas, strawberries,
*   blueberries, apricots, peaches, etc.*

1 tablespoon honey
1 tablespoon wheat germ (optional)

Thawed frozen fruit (unsweetened) may be used in this recipe. Combine all ingredients in the blender and spin until smooth.

Clem's Fruit Slush

YIELD: 18-24 SERVINGS

Julie Moore of Kirksville, Missouri, contributes this recipe for
a summertime refresher both children and adults will enjoy.
Offer it to guests as a substitute for soft drinks
and junk foods.

½ cup sugar
½ cup honey
2 cups hot water
1½ quarts orange juice (or 2 small
*   cans of frozen orange juice*
*   concentrate plus 6 cans of water)*

6 ripe bananas, sliced
3½ cups crushed pineapple
2 cups sliced strawberries (or 16
*   ounces of frozen strawberries)*

In a large bowl combine the sugar and honey with the hot water and stir until they dissolve. Allow to cool; then add all the other ingredients and place in your freezer. Remove and stir well after 4 hours, then return to the freezer. Stir every few hours thereafter for 24 hours, or until all the "slush" has been eaten.

Banana Carob Shake

YIELD: 1 SERVING

1 cup milk
1 banana, ripe
1 teaspoon carob powder

1 teaspoon honey
1 drop vanilla extract
¼-½ teaspoon cinnamon

Combine all the ingredients in the blender and spin 1 minute or until blended and smooth.

Cashew Milk

YIELD: 4 SERVINGS

A beverage with interesting flavor; it is nutritious and it can be used in recipes instead of milk.

1 cup cashew pieces
1 quart water
1 tablespoon vegetable oil

2 tablespoons honey
1 teaspoon salt

Combine all the ingredients in the blender and spin 3 minutes or until well blended and smooth.

THE SATISFYING CONCLUSION

Desserts and Candies

Excessively corpulent and excessively lean persons
are alike condemnable. A body which is neither
too stout nor too lean, but strikes the mean as
regards plumpness, is the best. A lean frame
should have the preference to a stout one.

—*Sushruta (5th Century BC)*

As a youngster was heard to remark: "Dessert is what you have to eat the rest of the stuff to get to." Or, as put more diplomatically by a noted chef: "Dessert is the happy memory a dinner guest takes with him when he leaves the table." These tempting creations that round out a meal are as delicious as they are important, and have been elevated to the point of ritual—the blowing out of candles on a birthday cake, young marrieds cutting their cake with a flower-decked knife. In fact, fine desserts are "as American as apple pie."

Our aim has been to offer desserts that are significant in their nutritional content, a not so difficult task when you consider that many of the ingredients that give flavor are excellent sources of essential nutrients and fiber. A good cook will know the value of made-from-scratch pastries and puddings where all that tickles the taste buds is so plainly healthful.

Fruit is a natural for desserts: raisins, dates, nuts, seeds and coconut, all are filled with nature's sweetness, vitamins and minerals. Combine these good sources of fiber with bran cereal, rolled oats or wheat germ and your desserts will pack nutritional punch. But let it be noted, desserts are to gloriously round out a meal and not to ingloriously round out a figure, so eat sparingly. Never be ashamed to present your guests with a hearty apple, cored and sliced into bite-size morsels, as an after-dinner treat. You would need to devour three pounds of apples to equal the calorie content of a candy bar. Tempt your family with fresh strawberries, raspberries, blackberries for dessert, and pineapple which is a bright decoration as it ripens in the kitchen. These fruits are not luxuries, but rather investments in good health.

Sour Cream Poppyseed Cake

YIELD: 8 TO 10 SERVINGS

½ cup butter or margarine

½ cup poppy seeds

1 cup honey

4 egg yolks

1 teaspoon vanilla extract

2 cups whole wheat pastry flour

1 teaspoon baking soda

¼ teaspoon salt

8 ounces sour cream or yogurt

4 egg whites

FROSTING:

8 ounces cream cheese

2 tablespoons milk

2 tablespoons maple syrup

Preheat the oven to 350 degrees F. Grease a 10-inch tube pan (angel food cake pan) and dust it with flour.

In a large mixing bowl cream the butter or margarine with the poppy seeds.

Beat in the honey, egg yolks and vanilla extract.

In another bowl stir together the flour, baking soda and salt.

Add the dry ingredients to the mixing bowl, half at a time, beating well after each addition.

Stir in the sour cream or yogurt.

Beat the egg whites until they stand in peaks; then fold them gently into the batter.

Pour the batter into the prepared pan and bake 1 hour.

Invert the pan on a rack and let stand 5 minutes. Run a spatula around the edge to loosen and remove the cake from the pan. Cool thoroughly.

Make the frosting: Soften the cream cheese. Whip it until fluffy, then add the milk and maple syrup and beat until smooth.

Raspberry Hazelnut Torte

YIELD: 8 SERVINGS

6 eggs (room temperature)

1/8 teaspoon salt

6 tablespoons brown sugar

6 tablespoons ground hazelnuts*

3 tablespoons pulverized wheat
   bran cereal

½ pint cream, whipped*

¼ cup confectioners' sugar
   (optional)

1 quart raspberries

Preheat the oven to 325 degrees F.

Butter two 9-inch cake pans and dust them with flour.

Separate the eggs between two mixing bowls.

Beat the egg whites with the salt until stiff but not dry.

Using the same beater, beat the egg yolks until lemon colored. Still beating, gradually add the sugar, hazelnuts and cereal. Stir in a quarter of the egg whites very thoroughly and then fold in the rest very gently.

Divide the batter between the two cake pans and bake on a middle rack for 15 minutes.

Remove from the oven and let stand 5 minutes before turning out on a wire rack. Cool completely.

Just before serving, spread the layers with the whipped cream or topping. Place one layer on a dessert platter. Cover with raspberries and top with the second layer. Spread with the rest of the raspberries.

*Walnuts may be substituted for the hazelnuts and the less caloric whipped topping for the whipped cream.

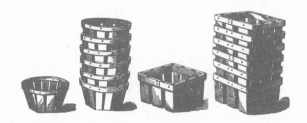

Fresh Apple Cake with Fluffy Frosting

YIELD: 9 TO 12 SERVINGS

1½ cups unbleached white flour

2 teaspoons baking soda

½ teaspoon salt

1 teaspoon cinnamon

1 teaspoon nutmeg

½ cup butter or margarine, softened

1 cup sugar

2 eggs

4 cups pared finely chopped apples

1 cup wheat bran cereal

FLUFFY FROSTING:

1 tablespoon unbleached white flour

¼ cup milk

¼ cup butter or margarine, softened

¼ cup sugar

½ cup chopped nuts (optional)

Preheat the oven to 350 degrees F. Oil generously a 9-inch square baking pan.

Stir together the flour, soda, salt, cinnamon and nutmeg. Set aside.

Cream together the butter or margarine and the sugar. Add the eggs and beat until fluffy.

Stir in the apples, the bran cereal and the dry ingredients.

Spread the batter in the prepared pan; bake 1 hour or until the cake begins to pull away from the sides of the pan. Allow the cake to cool.

Make the frosting: Measure the flour into a small saucepan. Add the milk gradually, stirring until smooth. Cook over low heat, stirring constantly, until the mixture thickens. Cool. Combine the soft butter or margarine and the sugar in a mixing bowl and beat until light and fluffy. Add the cooled flour mixture and beat until the mixture is of spreading consistency. Spread on the cake and top with chopped nuts, if desired.

Yogurt Carrot Cake

YIELD: 9 TO 12 SERVINGS

4 large eggs
1 cup vegetable oil
2 cups honey
1 cup yogurt
4 cups whole wheat pastry flour

2 teaspoons soda or baking powder
½ teaspoon salt
1 tablespoon cinnamon
2 cups carrots, grated

Preheat the oven to 350 degrees F. Oil a 9-inch by 13-inch baking pan and dust it with flour.

Break the eggs into a large mixing bowl and beat until frothy.

Add the vegetable oil, honey and yogurt. Beat until smoothly blended.

In another bowl stir together the flour, baking soda or baking powder, salt and cinnamon.

Add the dry ingredients, half at a time, to the liquids, mixing well after each addition.

Fold in the grated carrots.

Pour the batter into the prepared pan and bake 45 minutes or until a wooden pick or cake tester inserted near the center comes out dry.

Pie Pastry

*Pastry made with part white flour is lighter and more delicate than
that made with all whole wheat pastry flour. If you prefer to use all whole
wheat flour, sift it twice. Save the particles of bran left in the sifter and
add to flour that is to be used for making bread.*

*1 cup whole wheat pastry flour plus
    1 cup unbleached white flour or 2
    cups whole wheat pastry flour,
    sifted twice*

1 teaspoon salt
2/3 cup margarine (cold)
*3 tablespoons (approximate) ice
    water*

Combine the flours and salt in a mixing bowl and stir until blended. Add the margarine and cut in, using a pastry blender or 2 knives, until there are no lumps larger than small peas.

Add just enough ice water to make the mixture hold together in a ball.

Roll half at a time into a circle large enough to line or cover a 9-inch pie pan. Use white flour on the pastry board and roller, or roll between sheets of waxed paper.

To bake an unfilled pie shell, preheat the oven to 425 degrees F. With the tines of a fork, prick the bottom and sides of the crust in numerous places. Bake 12 to 14 minutes or just until lightly browned.

Bran Cereal Pie Crust

YIELD: 1 9-INCH PIE CRUST

¾ cup wheat bran cereal
1 cup unbleached white flour

½ cup butter or margarine
2 tablespoons milk

Preheat the oven to 400 degrees F.

Combine the cereal and flour in a small mixing bowl.

Add the butter or margarine and cut in, using a pastry blender or 2 knives, until the mixture resembles coarse meal.

Add the milk and stir until all ingredients are moistened.

Press the crumbly mixture evenly around the sides and in the bottom of a 9-inch pie pan. Prick the bottom and sides with a fork.

Bake 12 minutes or until lightly browned. Cool crust before filling.

Pecan Pie

YIELD: 1 9-INCH PIE

*Dates add natural sweetness and extra fiber to this pie, an
all-time favorite but a dessert not recommended for dieters.*

3 eggs

¾ cup date sugar or ½ cup finely
   chopped dates (optional)

2 tablespoons whole wheat pastry
   flour

½ teaspoon salt

1 cup sorghum molasses

2 tablespoons butter or margarine,
   melted

1 teaspoon vanilla extract

1½ cups pecan pieces

1 9-inch unbaked pie shell

Preheat the oven to 350 degrees F.

In a mixing bowl, beat the eggs until foamy.

Add the date sugar or chopped dates, the flour and salt.

Stir in the molasses, melted butter or margarine and the vanilla extract.

Stir in the pecans.

Pour into the pie shell and bake for 45 minutes. Cool the pie before cutting and serving it.

Fluffy Apricot Cheese Pie

YIELD: 1 9-INCH PIE

1 cup chopped dried apricots

2 eggs, separated

1 teaspoon lemon juice

½ teaspoon grated lemon peel

½ cup date sugar or brown sugar

1 tablespoon whole wheat flour

½ teaspoon salt

2 cups ricotta cheese

1 9-inch unbaked pie shell

Rinse the apricots and place them in a saucepan with just enough water to cover them. Bring to a boil; then reduce heat and simmer for 5 minutes.

Preheat the oven to 350 degrees F.

In a mixing bowl, stir together the egg yolks, lemon juice and grated lemon peel.

Combine the date sugar or brown sugar, flour and salt. Add gradually to the egg mixture, beating continuously.

Stir in the ricotta cheese.

Beat the egg whites until they stand in stiff peaks, then gently fold them into the cheese mixture.

Arrange the cooked apricots in the bottom of the unbaked pie shell. Pour the cheese-egg mixture over them and bake for 40 minutes.

Blueberry Crisp

YIELD: 6 SERVINGS

*4 cups fresh blueberries or 2
   15-ounce cans, drained
1/3 cup water or syrup from canned
   berries
2 teaspoons lemon juice*

*4 tablespoons butter or margarine
1/3 cup (packed) brown sugar
1/3 cup unbleached white flour
¾ cup uncooked oatmeal (rolled oats)*

Preheat the oven to 375 degrees.

Wash the fresh berries and pick over carefully, removing any stems or unripe berries. Place the berries in a baking dish 6 inches by 10 inches or 8 inches square.

Pour in the water or syrup and the lemon juice and stir to mix well.

In a mixing bowl, cream the butter or margarine and beat in the brown sugar.

Combine the flour and uncooked oatmeal and add together to the butter-sugar mixture. Mix until evenly colored and crumbly.

Sprinkle the oatmeal mixture over the blueberries and bake 40 minutes or until well browned.

Poached Stuffed Pears

YIELD: 2 TO 4 SERVINGS

2 Anjou pears   ½ cup boiling water
1 tablespoon honey   1 tablespoon sugar
2 tablespoons golden raisins   1 slice lemon
2 tablespoons chopped walnuts

Peel and halve the pears and scoop out the core with a spoon, leaving a cavity big enough for the stuffing.

Combine the honey, raisins and walnuts and mix well. Fill the cavities with the stuffing.

Place the pears in a buttered casserole. Add the water around the edge of the dish. Sprinkle the pears with the sugar and put the lemon slice on top.

Cover and bake 30 to 35 minutes or until the pears are just tender but not soft. Serve warm plain, with vanilla ice cream or with cottage cheese.

Strawberry Melon Bowl

YIELD: 10 TO 12 SERVINGS

½ watermelon   2 tablespoons orange liqueur or 1
1 honeydew melon   tablespoon undiluted orange juice
2 cantaloupes   concentrate
2 cups strawberries, stems removed   Mint sprigs for garnish
1 2/3 cups dry white wine

Halve the melons and scoop out balls, using a melon ball cutter. Place the balls in a large glass dessert bowl, one kind at a time to form layers.

Top with the strawberries.

Pour the wine and liqueur or orange concentrate over the fruit.

Cover the bowl and chill for 2 hours of longer. Serve very cold, garnished with the mint sprigs.

Louise Moillon

STILL LIFE WITH CHERRIES, STRAWBERRIES AND GOOSEBERRIES

Raspberry Strawberry Cheese

YIELD: 6 TO 8 SERVINGS

1½ pounds cottage or pot cheese
1 pint all-purpose cream
½ teaspoon salt
3-4 tablespoons honey

1 pint fresh raspberries
1 pint small fresh strawberries,
  preferably wild

Beat the cheese smooth in a blender or food processor. If the blender is small do a third at a time, adding the cream gradually. When the cheese and cream are smooth, add the salt and as much honey as your sweet tooth dictates. Blend well.

Place the mixture in a cheesecloth-lined colander or sieve. Hang the container over a bowl so that the cheese can drain overnight. Place in the refrigerator.

Puree the raspberries in a blender and strain to remove the seeds.

Wash and hull the strawberries. If using large cultivated berries, slice them, saving a few whole berries for garnish.

To serve, unmold the cheese onto a dessert platter. Remove the cheesecloth and spread with the raspberry puree. Cover with the fresh strawberries. If the berries are very tart sprinkle with a little sugar.

Lemon Lime Squares

YIELD: 16 SMALL SQUARES

½ cup butter or margarine, softened
½ cup (packed) brown sugar
1 cup unbleached white flour
¼ teaspoon salt
1 1/3 cups wheat bran cereal

1 14-ounce can sweetened condensed
  milk
1 teaspoon grated lemon peel
¼ cup lemon juice
¼ cup lime juice

Preheat the oven to 350 degrees F.

Cream together the butter or margarine and the brown sugar. Beat until fluffy.

Stir in the flour, salt and bran cereal. Mix until evenly blended.

Press half of the crumbly mixture into a 9-inch square pan and bake 10 minutes or until lightly browned. Set aside to cool.

Pour the condensed milk into a mixing bowl. Gradually add the lemon peel, lemon juice and lime juice, stirring continuously.

Pour over the baked crust and sprinkle the remaining crumbly mixture over the top.

Return to the oven and bake 30 minutes or until the filling is set and the topping lightly browned.

Cool completely; then cut into small squares.

Raspberry Cups

YIELD: 8 CUPS

1 recipe pie pastry
1 pint raspberries

1 jar (6 oz.) currant jelly

Make the pastry, using all or part whole wheat pastry flour as desired, and roll it out between sheets of wax paper to a thickness of 1/8 inch. Carefully remove the top sheet and cut the pastry into 8 2½-inch circles using a fluted cookie cutter. Cut right through the paper.

Oil lightly the backs of a set of small muffin tins. Drape the pastry circles on the backs of the muffin tins, removing the wax paper. Press the pastry close to the tins.

Bake 15 minutes at 400 degrees F. Cool.

Turn the pastry cups right side up on a dessert plate. Fill with the raspberries.

Heat the jelly, whisking just until it is smooth. Spoon the jelly over the raspberries. Serve plain, with whipped topping or with sour cream.

Raspberry Fig Compote

YIELD: 6 SERVINGS

1 pound dried figs
3 lemon slices
½ cup honey
1 pint raspberries

1½ teaspoons cornstarch
1 teaspoon lemon juice
½ cup shaved almonds

Place the figs in a saucepan with the lemon slices. Cover with cold water by 1 inch. Bring to a boil. Cover and simmer for 30 minutes or until the figs are tender.

Drain the juice from the figs into a small saucepan. Discard the lemon slices and reserve the figs. Boil the juice down to half its original quantity. Add 6 tablespoons of the honey. Stir until the mixture boils and set aside to cool. Pour over the figs.

Puree the raspberries in a blender and drain to remove the seeds.

Put the raspberry juice into a small saucepan and bring to a boil. Add the cornstarch dissolved in 1 tablespoon of water and stir until the mixture begins to thicken. Remove from the heat and add the lemon juice and the remaining honey (2 teaspoons of Cointreau may be substituted for the lemon juice, if preferred). Cool and chill.

To serve, put the figs and their sauce into a dessert bowl or into individual dessert glasses. Cover with the raspberry sauce and sprinkle with the almonds.

Orange Rice Valencia

YIELD: 8 TO 10 SERVINGS

1 cup uncooked white (or brown) rice
3½ cups milk
2 tablespoons butter or margarine
1 envelope unflavored gelatin
1 cup fresh orange juice
½ teaspoon salt
1/3 cup honey

1 tablespoon grated orange rind
1 cup heavy cream, whipped, or 1½
  cups whipped topping
4 large oranges, peeled and
  sectioned
1/3 cup Grand Marnier or Curaçao
  (optional)

Put the rice into a heavy saucepan with the milk and butter. Bring to a boil, then reduce heat and stir once with a fork. Cover and simmer 30 minutes, or until all the liquid is absorbed and the rice is tender. (If using brown rice, increase the milk to 4 cups and the cooking time to about 45 minutes.)

Sprinkle the gelatin over the orange juice and stir it into the hot rice. Add the salt, honey and the grated orange rind. Mix well; then place in the refrigerator until thoroughly cooled, about 1½ hours. Stir occasionally while cooling.

Fold the whipped cream or topping into the rice mixture. Turn into a serving dish or into an oiled 7-cup mold. Return to the refrigerator to chill 3 to 4 hours longer.

Shortly before serving time, place the orange sections in a bowl and pour the liqueur over them. Stir gently to mix. Unmold the rice onto a serving platter and arrange the orange slices on top.

Danish Raspberry Coupe

YIELD: 4 SERVINGS

1 10-ounce package frozen
  raspberries, thawed
2 tablespoons potato starch

¼ cup white wine (sweet or dry) or
  ¼ cup water
6 tablespoons heavy cream

Puree the raspberries in a blender.

Transfer the raspberries to a small saucepan and bring to a boil. Add the potato starch dissolved in either white wine or water. Stir constantly until the mixture begins to thicken.

Pour the mixture into 4 dessert glasses. Chill in the refrigerator.

Just before serving, gently pour 1½ tablespoons of cream over the surface of each dessert.

Note: If water is used in place of the white wine add 1 teaspoon of lemon juice. Potato starch is best for making this dessert but you can use cornstarch if potato starch isn't available.

Rhubarb and Strawberry Sauce

YIELD: 6 TO 8 SERVINGS

3 cups fresh rhubarb
1-1½ cups honey

¼ cup water
1 pint fresh strawberries

Cut the rhubarb into small pieces.

Place in a saucepan with the honey and water. Stir over moderately high heat until the mixture boils. Reduce the heat, cover and simmer for 10 minutes. Wash the strawberries briefly. Hull them and slice fairly thick.

Remove the rhubarb from the heat and stir in the strawberries. Chill before serving.

Macadamia Maple Parfait

YIELD: 8 SERVINGS

6 large eggs

1½ cups heated maple syrup

¼ teaspoon salt

¼ teaspoon almond extract

1 pint all-purpose cream

1 cup chopped macadamia nuts

Demerara (or granulated) sugar

Beat the eggs in the top of a double boiler until frothy.

Place the double boiler over simmering water and continue beating while adding the hot syrup in a steady stream. Add the salt and almond extract and continue beating until the mixture thickens. Remove from the heat and pour into a bowl to cool.

Whip 1½ cups of the cream until it stands in stiff peaks. Fold in the cooled maple mixture and half the chopped nuts. Pour into parfait glasses and place in the freezer. Freeze at least 2 hours.

To serve, whip the remaining cream until stiff. Place a little cream in each glass. Sprinkle with the Demerara sugar. Add a little more cream and top with the remaining chopped nuts.

Bran Walnut Surprise Bombe

YIELD: 6 TO 8 SERVINGS

1 pint raspberry sherbet or

   1 pint pistachio ice cream

1 pint whipping cream

½ cup wheat bran cereal

½ cup walnuts

2 cups mashed bananas

½ teaspoon almond extract

¼ cup confectioners' sugar

Let the frozen sherbet or ice cream stand at room temperature while preparing the rest of the recipe.

Whip the cream fairly stiff.

Chop the bran and walnuts very briefly in a blender or food processor.

Mash enough bananas to yield 2 cups.

Fold the bran, nuts, bananas, almond extract and sugar into the cream and stir until blended.

Line a 2-quart melon mold or other decorative mold with the cream mixture. Lacking a mold, use a bowl that can be put in the freezer. Leave a hole in the center of the cream.

Place the sherbet or ice cream in the hole and smooth the whipped cream over it. Cover with aluminum foil and if possible with a tight-fitting cover. Otherwise use a double sheet of aluminum foil, and tie it securely.

Freeze for a minimum of 3 hours before unmolding onto a dessert platter.

This will keep for weeks in the freezer.

Avocado Honey Ice

YIELD: 6 TO 8 SERVINGS

For an unusually nutritious and satisfying sweet, serve this frozen dessert topped with yogurt.

2 large lemons

2 ripe avocados

5 tablespoons honey

Yogurt (optional)

Squeeze the lemons and pour the juice into a bowl.

Halve the avocado and slice the pulp into the lemon juice, working quickly to avoid discoloration of the avocado pulp.

Mash the avocado and add the honey, stirring until the mixture is smooth. Spoon into a freezer tray and freeze until solid.

Carob Chip Cookies

YIELD: 14 DOZEN SMALL COOKIES

1 cup butter or margarine   *1 teaspoon baking powder*

1½ cups light brown sugar   *1 teaspoon salt*

2 eggs, lightly beaten   *1-2 teaspoons vanilla extract*

1 teaspoon water   *1 cup chopped nuts (pecans or walnuts)*

1 cup wheat bran cereal   *1 cup carob chips (or chocolate chips)*

2 cups whole wheat flour

Preheat the oven to 350 degrees F.

In a large mixing bowl, cream together the brown sugar and butter.

Add the eggs and water and blend well. Stir in the bran cereal. Let stand 2 minutes or until the cereal is softened.

Stir together the dry ingredients: the flour, baking powder and salt. Add to the sugar-egg-cereal mixture, half at a time, and stir until blended.

Stir in the vanilla extract, nuts and carob chips.

Drop by teaspoonfuls onto an oiled cookie sheet and bake 10 to 12 minutes.

Honey Butter Cookies

YIELD: 3 TO 4 DOZEN

½ cup butter or margarine, softened   *1 teaspoon baking soda*

½ cup chunky peanut butter   *½ teaspoon baking powder*

½ cup mashed banana   *½ teaspoon salt*

1 cup honey   *½ teaspoon cinnamon*

1½ cups whole wheat flour   *¼ teaspoon nutmeg*

Cream together the butter and peanut butter.

Stir together the mashed banana and honey; then add them to the butter mixture. Stir until blended.

In another bowl combine and blend the flour, baking soda, baking powder, salt, cinnamon and nutmeg.

Combine the dry and moist ingredients, stirring just until all the dry ingredients are moistened.

Chill the dough 1 hour or longer.

When ready to bake the cookies, preheat the oven to 350 degrees F. Drop the dough by spoonfuls on oiled cookie sheets and bake 10 to 15 minutes or until done in the centers and lightly browned.

Spicy Apple Oatmeal Cookies

YIELD: 4 DOZEN OR MORE

1 cup sorghum molasses
1 cup apple juice
2/3 cup vegetable oil
2½ cups whole wheat pastry flour
1½ teaspoons cinnamon
½ teaspoon ground nutmeg

¼ teaspoon ground cloves
½ teaspoon salt
1 cup sunflower seeds
2½ cups diced apples
3 cups uncooked oatmeal (rolled oats)

Preheat the oven to 350 degrees F.

In a large bowl combine the molasses, apple juice and vegetable oil. Stir until blended.

In another bowl mix together the flour, cinnamon, nutmeg, cloves and salt.

Add the dry ingredients to the liquids, a third at a time, blending well after each addition.

Fold in the sunflower seeds and diced apples.

Fold in the oatmeal.

Drop the batter by tablespoonfuls on oiled cookie sheets and bake 12 to 14 minutes or until done and lightly browned.

Wheat Germ-Peanut Bars

YIELD: 3 DOZEN SMALL BARS

½ cup butter or margarine, softened
½ cup (packed) brown sugar
1 egg
1 teaspoon vanilla extract

1 cup wheat germ
½ cup whole wheat flour
¼ teaspoon baking soda
¾ cup chopped salted peanuts

Preheat the oven to 325 degrees F. Oil a 13-inch by 9-inch baking pan.

Combine the butter and sugar and cream until light and fluffy.

Beat the egg vigorously with a fork or wire whisk. Add 2 tablespoons of the beaten egg and the vanilla to the butter-sugar mixture and beat well.

In another bowl stir together ¾ cup of the wheat germ, the flour and baking soda. Add with ½ cup of the peanuts to the other mixture and stir until blended.

Press the dough into the prepared pan. Brush the remaining egg over the top of the dough. Sprinkle with the remaining ¼ cup of wheat germ and ½ cup chopped peanuts.

Bake 15 to 20 minutes or until lightly browned. Cool in the pan; then break into irregular pieces or cut into small squares.

Apple Cheese Squares

YIELD: 18 SQUARES

CRUST:
¾ cup butter or margarine, softened
¼ cup brown sugar
2½ cups uncooked oatmeal (rolled oats)

FILLING:
1½ cups applesauce

1 teaspoon cinnamon
1/3 cup honey
1 cup grated Cheddar cheese

TOPPING:
¼ cup chopped walnuts
¼ cup grated Cheddar cheese

Preheat the oven to 350 degrees F. Oil a 9-inch by 13-inch baking pan.

Cream together the butter or margarine and the brown sugar. Add the oatmeal and stir until evenly mixed. Press half of this crust mixture into the prepared pan. Reserve the rest.

In a mixing bowl combine the applesauce, cinnamon and honey. Stir until blended. Fold in the 1 cup of grated cheese. Pour over the prepared crust.

Sprinkle the remaining crust mixture over the filling.

Top with the chopped walnuts and ¼ cup of grated cheese.

Bake 10 to 12 minutes, or until the filling is just set and the crust lightly browned. Cool partially, then cut into squares and remove from the pan.

Banana Sunflower Cookies

YIELD: 3 DOZEN

2 cups whole wheat pastry flour   *2/3 cup peanut butter*
1 teaspoon cinnamon   *2/3 cup sorghum molasses*
¾ teaspoon salt   *1 egg, beaten*
½ cup mashed banana   *1 cup chopped sunflower seeds*

Preheat the oven to 350 degrees F.

Stir together the flour, cinnamon and salt. Set aside.

In a large mixing bowl combine the mashed banana, peanut butter, molasses and egg. Stir until blended.

Add the dry ingredients and the sunflower seeds to the banana mixture and stir just until all the dry ingredients are moistened. Do not beat.

Drop the batter by spoonfuls, 2 inches apart, on oiled cookie sheets. Bake 10 minutes or until lightly browned.

Oatmeal Apple Pandowdy

YIELD: 8 TO 10 SERVINGS

4 cups cooking apples, thinly sliced

1 teaspoon salt

¼ teaspoon nutmeg

1 teaspoon cinnamon

1/3 cup molasses

6 tablespoons butter or margarine

1 cup unbleached white flour

½ cup uncooked oatmeal (rolled oats)

2 teaspoons baking powder

½ cup (packed) brown sugar

1 egg

2/3 cup milk

Preheat the oven to 350 degrees F. Oil a 9-inch square pan.

Spread the apple slices in an even layer in the pan. Sprinkle with ½ teaspoon of salt, the nutmeg and cinnamon. Drizzle the molasses over all and dot with 2 tablespoons butter. Bake for 10 minutes.

While the apples are in the oven prepare the cake topping. Stir together the flour, rolled oats and baking powder. In another bowl cream together the remaining 4 tablespoons butter or margarine and the brown sugar. Add the egg and beat until fluffy. Add the dry ingredients and the milk alternately, beating well after each addition.

Spread the batter over the hot apple slices and return to the oven. Bake for 30 minutes, or until the apples are tender and the cake lightly browned. Serve warm, with milk or whipped topping.

Whole Wheat Brown Betty

YIELD: 6 SERVINGS

1½ cups whole wheat bread crumbs

3 tablespoons vegetable oil

5 apples, cored and thinly sliced

1½ cups applesauce

¼ teaspoon cinnamon

¼ teaspoon nutmeg

1 teaspoon grated lemon rind

¼ teaspoon vanilla extract

1/8 teaspoon salt

½ cup raisins

Preheat the oven to 400 degrees. Oil a deep 2-quart baking-serving dish.

Sprinkle the 3 tablespoons vegetable oil over the bread crumbs and stir to mix well. Spread a third of the crumbs in the bottom of the prepared baking dish.

Spread half the apples over the crumbs.

Stir together the applesauce, cinnamon, nutmeg, lemon rind, vanilla extract and salt. Pour half of this mixture over the apples.

Spread another third of the crumbs over the apples. Sprinkle on half of the raisins. Spread on the remaining apples.

Pour on the remaining applesauce mixture. Sprinkle on the remaining raisins. Sprinkle the remaining crumbs over the top.

Cover (use foil if the baking dish has no lid) and bake 40 minutes.

Turn the oven up to 400 degrees F. Uncover the dish and bake 15 minutes longer or until nicely browned.

Serve warm, with hard sauce or whipped topping if desired.

Layered Custard Dessert

YIELD: 6 SERVINGS

3 eggs

2 cups milk

½ cup granulated sugar

1/8 teaspoon ground nutmeg

1/8 teaspoon salt

1 teaspoon vanilla extract

1 cup wheat bran cereal

1/3 cup raisins

½ cup finely chopped nuts

Preheat the oven to 375 degrees F. Butter 6 custard cups or one 1½-quart baking dish.

In a mixing bowl, beat the eggs until foamy.

Add the milk, sugar, nutmeg, salt and vanilla extract. Stir until blended.

Stir in the bran cereal, raisins and nuts.

Pour the custard mixture into the cups or baking dish. Set the cups or dish in a large baking pan and pour about 1 inch of hot water around them. Bake 45 minutes or until a knife inserted near the center of a custard comes out clean.

Apricot Bars

YIELD: 32 BARS

2/3 cup dried apricots	*¼ teaspoon salt*
½ cup butter or margarine, softened	*1 cup (packed) brown sugar*
¼ cup granulated sugar	*2 eggs*
1 cup unbleached white flour	*½ teaspoon vanilla extract*
½ cup wheat bran cereal	*½ cup chopped walnuts*
½ teaspoon baking powder	*¼ cup sifted confectioners' sugar*

Rinse the dried apricots and place them in a saucepan with water to cover. Bring to a boil and simmer 10 minutes. Drain, cool and chop.

Preheat the oven to 350 degrees F.

Combine the butter or margarine, granulated sugar and ½ cup of the flour. Beat until smooth. Stir in the wheat bran cereal and spread the mixture in the bottom of an unoiled 8-inch square pan. Bake 25 minutes or until lightly browned.

While the crust is baking, sift together the remaining flour, baking powder and salt. Set aside.

In a mixing bowl combine the brown sugar and the eggs. Beat until smooth.

Add the dry ingredients and stir until blended. Stir in the vanilla, walnuts and chopped apricots. Spread over the baked crust and return the pan to the oven. Bake 35 minutes or until lightly browned.

Allow to cool; then sprinkle confectioners' sugar over the top and cut into bars.

Carob Candy

YIELD: ABOUT ½ POUND

2 tablespoons honey	*¼ cup chopped pecans*
1 tablespoon water	*1 teaspoon vanilla*
1 cup sunflower meal or sesame meal	*¼ cup ground pecans*
2 tablespoons carob powder	

Combine the honey and water.

Beat in the sunflower or sesame meal, the carob powder, chopped pecans and vanilla.

Chill the mixture for 15 minutes.

Roll into small balls and coat with pecans that have been finely ground in a blender.

Store in the refrigerator between sheets of waxed paper.

Peanut Butter Sesame Eggs

YIELD: 2½ DOZEN

¼ cup sesame seeds or 1/8 cup sunflower seeds plus 1/8 cup chopped walnuts
¾ cup chunky or smooth peanut butter
½ cup honey
1 teaspoon vanilla extract

2 tablespoonfuls boiling water
¾ cup nonfat dry milk powder
1 cup uncooked oatmeal (rolled oats)
Additional toasted sesame seeds or chopped nuts for coating

If you are using sesame seeds, preheat the oven to 200 degrees F. Spread the sesame seeds in a shallow pan and toast them 20 minutes or until they are lightly browned.

In a mixing bowl combine the peanut butter, honey, vanilla extract and boiling water. Stir until blended.

In another bowl stir together the dry milk powder, the oatmeal and the toasted sesame seeds or sunflower seeds and nuts.

Gradually add the dry ingredients to the peanut butter mixture, stirring until blended. Use your hands if the dough becomes too stiff.

Shape the dough into 1-inch "eggs" and roll them in additional toasted sesame seeds or chopped nuts. Store in the refrigerator until serving time.

Date Delights

YIELD: ABOUT 3 DOZEN

½ cup butter or margarine
1/3 cup honey
2 cups chopped dates

2 cups granola
2 cups finely chopped nuts or grated
unsweetened coconut for coating

Melt the butter or margarine in a saucepan over low heat.

Add the honey and dates and cook, stirring constantly, until the dates are very soft.

Remove from the heat and stir in the granola.

Spread the chopped nuts or coconut on waxed paper.

When the mixture is cool enough to handle, shape it into small balls and roll them in the coating. Store in the refrigerator, between sheets of waxed paper.

Butter Crunch Logs

YIELD: 4 DOZEN SMALL COOKIES

1 cup butter or margarine
¼ cup honey
¼ cup barley malt or other sweetener
1 tablespoon vanilla extract

5 cups granola without raisins
Carob Frosting, if desired
(See Reference Chapter)

Combine the butter, honey, barley malt and vanilla in the blender and spin until smooth and creamy.

Transfer the butter-honey mixture to a large mixing bowl and stir in the granola, one cup at a time. When the ingredients are well blended, use your hands, wet, to shape the mixture into 4 logs. Chill in the refrigerator.

If frosting is to be used, spread it over the outsides of the logs and return them to the refrigerator.

To serve, slice the logs into thin circles.

WAVE A
MAGIC WAND

Microwave Cookery

Look to your health and if you have it praise God,
and value it next to a good conscience; for health is
the second blessing that we mortals are capable of;
a blessing that money cannot buy....

—Izaak Walton

Your microwave oven will usher you into the electronic age with time saving you will find absolutely astonishing—as your ancestor might if he jetted back east after traveling west by prairie schooner.

And just as that ancestor might have to substitute a new and simpler trick of fastening a seat belt for his old skills of harnessing and driving a team, you will have to make some adjustments in your ways of preparing food. All will be shortcuts, for saving time is what microwave cooking is all about.

The secret is in those little waves of electromagnetic energy produced inside the oven. We are all accustomed to cooking by external heat which is literally hot air. The heat gets at your food, cooks the outside first and then gradually makes its way in to the center. Microwaving is quite different. There's no heat except inside the food that is being cooked. The energy waves go right into the food and are absorbed by it. In somewhat Einsteinian fashion they reach the very molecules in the food, causing them to jostle each other until friction produces heat.

All parts of the food—inside and out—cook simultaneously. (You needn't over-cook the outside to get the inside tender.) Food cooks without drying out. Meanwhile the cook and the kitchen stay cool as cucumbers because there's no energy going to waste in the form of hot air.

An unexpected dividend of pleasure: no pans to scrub when dinner is over. You will be cooking in the same dishes you serve in, or in throwaway paper containers, or even on dinner plates.

You will find yourself doing a lot of things you didn't do before because they were too much bother and you didn't want to stay around the kitchen waiting for them. Things that are fun, but practical, too.

Like turning leftover bread into seasoned croutons.

Toasting nuts. Making popcorn. Drying home-grown herbs. Freshening and heating leftover rolls.

Warming sauces, toppings and syrups.

Producing quick meals on any schedule for the members of the family who must eat and run.

Cooking hot cereal for breakfast: Just combine in a large cereal bowl the proper amounts of cereal and water, like 1/3 cup old-fashioned rolled oats with 1 cup water. Stir once, cover and microwave 1 minute. Stir again and microwave 1 minute. Stir again and let stand 1 minute outside the oven. *Voilà!* The kind of smooth and creamy oatmeal grandmother simmered on the back of the stove for hours.

The quick, clean performance of the microwave oven appeals to busy cooks of both sexes, and the fact that it uses so little electricity makes it even more attractive in this energy-conscious age. But what is most important is *how* it cooks one of nature's most precious gifts to man—fresh vegetables.

In this nationwide swing back to natural foods, garden plots are to be found in almost every backyard, no matter how small, and apartment dwellers are growing fresh vegetables in window boxes and on balconies. Especially in the garden season, frozen and canned vegetables are taking a back seat and their country cousins are riding high.

To have both microwave ovens and fresh vegetables on center stage at the same time is a very happy happening, and we are at the start of a new culinary era.

Freshly picked vegetables from your own garden or from a nearby farm, quickly prepared in the microwave oven, provide an eating experience that cannot be surpassed, and even vegetables from the supermarket's produce counter which may be days or even weeks old are somehow remarkably restored to freshness by this method of cooking. Most vegetables are cooked with a minimal amount of water so that vitamins and minerals are retained along with garden-bright color.

For lucky owners of microwave ovens, we offer these recipes with a gourmet twist that you can produce in short order. Follow the directions that came with the oven as to the proper utensils to use (no metal in any form is a safe rule to follow).

When you have made these recipes, strike out on your own. Be creative. You will find that the drudgery has been taken out of cooking vegetables, and you will find them tasting better than ever.

Asparagus Polonaise

YIELD: 4 SERVINGS

1½ pounds fresh asparagus

2 tablespoons water

Salt and white pepper

2 hard-cooked eggs, finely chopped

2 tablespoons finely chopped parsley

4 tablespoons melted butter

3 tablespoons fine white bread crumbs

½ teaspoon salt

½ teaspoon paprika

Wash the asparagus and cut off the tough ends. Place the asparagus all heading in the same direction in a 1½-quart casserole. Add the water and cover.

Microwave 5 minutes. Rearrange the asparagus to insure equal cooking and cook 5 minutes longer. Remove from the oven. Sprinkle quickly with salt and pepper and cover again. Let the asparagus stand 5 minutes.

Mix together the hard-cooked egg and parsley.

Stir the melted butter into the bread crumbs.

Drain the asparagus thoroughly and place it on a glass or ovenproof serving dish. Sprinkle with the egg and parsley mixture. Spread with the bread crumb mixture and sprinkle it all with salt and paprika. Place in the microwave oven and cook 3 minutes.

Honeyed Beets

YIELD: 2 TO 4 SERVINGS

4 medium-size beets

4 tablespoons honey

2 tablespoons lemon juice

1 tablespoon butter or margarine

½ teaspoon cornstarch

2 tablespoons sherry

Salt and pepper

Cut off all but an inch of the beet stems. Wash clean without piercing the skin. Place the beets in a glass bowl and cover with water. Cover and microwave without turning for 15 to 20 minutes, according to the age and size of the beets. Let stand until cool. A fork inserted in the center will test for doneness.

Peel and slice the beets and place in a shallow ovenproof serving dish. In a saucepan combine the honey, lemon juice, butter and the cornstarch mixed with the sherry. Bring to a boil and cook 4 minutes, stirring frequently. Pour the mixture over the beets and microwave 1 minute. Give the dish a quarter turn and cook 1 minute longer. Season with salt and pepper before serving.

Bran Stuffed Mushrooms

YIELD: 3 OR 4 SERVINGS

8 medium to large mushrooms
2 tablespoons butter or margarine
2 slices bacon
2 tablespoons soft whole wheat bread crumbs

2 tablespoons pulverized wheat bran cereal
1/8 teaspoon thyme
¼ teaspoon salt
1/8 teaspoon freshly ground black pepper

Choose mushrooms of uniform size. Wash briefly and remove the stems. Dry the caps well.

Heat the butter for 40 seconds on an oven-serving plate. Place the mushrooms in a circle on the plate.

On another plate place the 2 strips of bacon and cover with a paper towel.

Microwave both for 2 minutes, turning the mushrooms once during the process.

Chop the mushroom stems by hand or in a food processor. Mix with the bread crumbs, wheat cereal, thyme, salt and pepper and 1 tablespoon of bacon fat.

Crumble the bacon into the mixture.

With a small piece of paper toweling pat dry the centers of the cooked mushrooms and fill with the stuffing.

Just before serving, microwave the mushrooms uncovered for 1 minute. Give the plate a quarter turn and cook 1 minute longer. Let stand 3 minutes before serving.

Broccoli Puree

YIELD: 4 SERVINGS

1 pound fresh broccoli   *1/8 teaspoon nutmeg*
1 cup milk   *Salt and pepper*
3 tablespoons butter or margarine   *1 tablespoon slivered almonds*
2 tablespoons flour

Remove the large leaves and tough ends from the broccoli stalks.

Wash the broccoli in cool water and slit each stem once or twice up to the flowerets.

Place the broccoli in a 1½-quart casserole with 4 tablespoons of water. Cover with wax paper and microwave 8 minutes, turning the dish 3 times during the process. Let stand 3 minutes.

Remove the broccoli with a slotted spoon to a blender or food processor. Measure the remaining liquid into a cup and fill the cup with milk. Add 2 tablespoons of the butter and the flour to the blender and spin the broccoli, adding the milk mixture gradually. Add the nutmeg. Mix until smooth. Season to taste with salt and pepper.

Meanwhile heat the remaining butter in a custard cup for 30 seconds in the microwave oven. Stir in the almonds and microwave 3 minutes, stirring once or twice.

Place the broccoli in a 1-quart serving casserole. Microwave 2 minutes. Stir well, smoothing the top, and cook 2 minutes longer. Sprinkle with the almonds and serve.

Glazed Turnips

YIELD: 4 SERVINGS

6 white turnips   *2 tablespoons honey*
6 tablespoons concentrated chicken *Salt and pepper*
  broth

Peel and slice the turnips quite thin. Lay them in an ovenproof pie plate. Add 4 tablespoons of the chicken broth.

Cover with wax paper and microwave for 8 minutes, turning the plate every 2 minutes.

Combine the honey with the rest of the broth. Pour over the turnips and microwave 4 minutes uncovered, turning the plate halfway through the process. Let stand 3 minutes. Sprinkle with salt and white pepper before serving.

Nutty Sweet Potatoes

YIELD: 4 SERVINGS

4 sweet potatoes (or yams)
6 tablespoons butter or margarine
4 tablespoons sherry
½ cup orange juice
¼ teaspoon nutmeg

1 cup chopped pecans
Salt and pepper
1 tablespoon brown sugar
½ teaspoon cinnamon

Choose potatoes of uniform size and shape. Scrub them well and pierce them twice through with a long fork or skewer. Place in a circle on paper toweling and bake 16 to 18 minutes. Test them by inserting a fork.

Remove from the oven and let stand 5 minutes. Peel the potatoes and cut them into an electric mixing bowl.

Beat the potatoes with the butter, sherry, orange juice and nutmeg until smooth. Stir in the pecans and season to taste with salt and pepper.

Place the mixture into an oven-serving dish. Sprinkle with a mixture of the brown sugar and cinnamon. Microwave 4 minutes uncovered.

If the dish is prepared in advance and refrigerated, allow 10 minutes for reheating and keep the dish covered.

Cabbage in Caraway Sour Cream

YIELD: 4 SERVINGS

4 cups shredded cabbage

2 tablespoons butter or margarine

½ teaspoon salt

1 cup commercial sour cream

½ teaspoon caraway seeds

1/8 teaspoon white pepper

1 tablespoon chopped parsley

Combine the cabbage, butter or margarine, salt and sour cream in a deep 1½-quart casserole. Cover and microwave for 6 minutes, stirring well halfway through the process.

Before serving, stir in the caraway seeds, pepper and parsley and taste to be sure the cabbage is sufficiently salted.

Red Cabbage Casserole

YIELD: 4 TO 6 SERVINGS

6 cups shredded red cabbage

1 tablespoon butter or margarine

3 slices bacon, diced

½ cup chopped onion

1 large apple

2 tablespoons red wine vinegar

2 tablespoons honey

½ teaspoon salt

*¼ teaspoon freshly ground black
   pepper*

Shred the cabbage and put it in a large bowl of cold water for 5 minutes.

Heat the butter and diced bacon in a deep 2- or 3-quart casserole for 1½ minutes.

Stir in the onion and microwave for 1 minute.

Core the apple and cut it into eighths without peeling.

Add the apple and the drained cabbage (with whatever water clings to it) to the casserole. Add the vinegar, honey, salt and pepper and stir well.

Cover and microwave 7 minutes, stirring twice during the process. Taste for salt before serving since the saltiness in bacon varies.

Zucchini in Sour Cream

YIELD: 4 SERVINGS

6 small zucchini

3 tablespoons butter or margarine

½ cup chopped onion

2 tablespoons chopped parsley

½ pint commercial sour cream

Salt and pepper

Wash the zucchini and slice in ½-inch pieces.

Heat the butter or margarine in a deep casserole (1½ quarts) for 40 seconds.

Stir in the onion and parsley and microwave 1 minute. Stir and cook 1 minute longer.

Add the zucchini and stir until all the pieces are coated with the butter. Cover with wax paper and microwave 6 minutes, turning the dish every 2 minutes.

Stir in the sour cream and season with salt and pepper. Microwave uncovered for 2 minutes or until well heated.

Baked Potatoes

The microwave oven is the perfect stove for the working man
or woman who longs for a baked potato but can't get home
an hour before dinner time. A good supply of uniform
sized (7- to 8-ounce) Idaho potatoes is all that is necessary.

Wash the required number of potatoes carefully and prick each potato through twice with a long fork or a skewer. Place the potatoes in the oven. If there are several potatoes, place them in a circle but do not put anything in the center of the circle. There should be breathing space of an inch between the potatoes. Allow 5 minutes for 1 potato, 8 minutes for 2, 10 minutes for 3 and 12 minutes for 4. Let the potatoes stand 5 minutes after cooking to allow for even distribution of heat.

Savoury Baked Potatoes

YIELD: 4 SERVINGS

4 (7-8 ounce) Idaho potatoes
2 tablespoons butter or margarine
2 tablespoons chopped chives
4 tablespoons chopped mushrooms
½ cup commercial sour cream

4 tablespoons whole wheat bread
  crumbs
1 teaspoon poultry seasoning
Salt and pepper
Paprika

Prepare the potatoes for baking as in the preceding recipe.

Bake the potatoes and remove them from the oven for their 5 minutes of standing.

Microwave the butter for 40 seconds in a shallow Pyrex dish. Stir in the chives and mushrooms and microwave 2 minutes, stirring once halfway through the process.

Cut the potatoes in half and scoop out the insides into a bowl; mash with a fork, stirring in the mushroom mixture, the sour cream, bread crumbs and poultry seasoning. Mix well, seasoning to taste, and stuff the shells with the mixture.

Just before serving: Sprinkle the tops with the paprika. Place the potato halves in a large circle on paper towels, leaving breathing space between. Microwave 4 to 5 minutes uncovered.

French Green Peas

YIELD: 4 SERVINGS

*French green peas are peas cooked with lettuce, which supplies
the necessary liquid. They are deliciously different.*

2 pounds fresh-picked peas
2 tablespoons chopped chives
1 tablespoon chopped parsley
3 tablespoons butter or margarine

1 teaspoon sugar
1 small bay leaf
4-5 large lettuce leaves

Shell the peas and place them in an oven-serving dish.

Sprinkle with the chopped herbs and dot with butter.

Sprinkle with the sugar and top with the bay leaf.

Wash the lettuce leaves. Do not dry them but tear them in large pieces and place them on top of the peas.

Cover with waxed paper and microwave 7 minutes, stirring twice during the process, after 4 minutes and after 6 minutes.

Before serving, remove the bay leaf and season to taste with salt and pepper.

Corn on the Cob

YIELD: 4 SERVINGS

*There are some who claim that the vegetable to be preferred
above all others is fresh corn on the cob cooked in a
microwave oven. It deserves total attention,
so plan to serve it as a separate course.*

*8-12 ears of corn (depending on
    appetite)*

*Melted butter
Salt and pepper*

Discard the outer husks. Carefully lay back the inner pale green husks and remove the corn silk. Spread each ear with melted butter and sprinkle with salt and pepper. Encase the ears in the husks, fastening the ends with a small rubber band. This may be done in advance.

Just before serving, place 4 ears of corn on a glass dish. Microwave 4 minutes. Turn each ear over and give the dish a quarter turn. Cook 4 minutes longer.

Cook another 4 ears while enjoying the first set. Extra butter, salt and pepper should be on the table. Each person will "shuck" his own corn. Leaving the husks on keeps them piping hot.

Stuffed Tomatoes

YIELD: 4 SERVINGS

4 large ripe tomatoes

½ cup safflower, corn or peanut oil

½ cup chopped onion

2 tablespoons chopped parsley

½ cup soft whole wheat bread crumbs

¾ cup cooked brown rice

2 tablespoons chopped walnuts

Salt and pepper

Cut out the stem end of each tomato and hollow it out, reserving the pulp in a bowl. Leave a half-inch shell. Turn the tomatoes upside down on a rack to drain.

Heat the oil in an ovenproof pie plate for 2 minutes. Stir in the onion and parsley. Microwave 1 minute. Stir and cook 1 minute longer.

Add the onion mixture, bread crumbs, rice and walnuts to the tomato pulp.

Mix thoroughly and season to taste with salt and pepper.

Fill the tomatoes with the mixture and place in a circle on the pie plate. Cook uncovered for 4 minutes, turning the plate once during the process.

Corn Stuffed Green Peppers

YIELD: 4 SERVINGS

These peppers can be prepared in advance and given their final cooking just before serving. If chilled, allow 2 more minutes for cooking.

4 green peppers

1½ cups fresh corn kernels

2 tablespoons cream

4 tablespoons butter or margarine

4 tablespoons chopped scallions
(green onions)

2 tablespoons chopped parsley

1 cup cooked brown rice

Salt and pepper

½ cup grated Cheddar cheese

Cut off the top quarter of the peppers and carefully remove the fibers and seeds. Place the peppers an inch apart in an oven-serving dish. Cover with wax paper and microwave for 4 minutes, turning the dish once.

Dice the tops rather coarsely.

Scrape the corn from freshly picked ears (if available), using the dull side of the knife.

As soon as the peppers are cooked, remove from the oven and cook the corn with the cream in a small ovenproof bowl for 5 minutes, stirring once halfway through the cooking time.

Meanwhile heat the butter in a small skillet and cook the chopped scallions, using some of the green part, for 3 minutes over gentle heat. Stir in the parsley and cooked rice and mix well. Combine with the diced pepper and the corn. Season to taste with salt and pepper.

Remove any water from the peppers and stuff with the corn mixture. Microwave 12 minutes, turning the dish every 4 minutes. Sprinkle with cheese and cook 30 seconds or until the cheese melts.

Mustard Glazed Carrots

YIELD: 6 SERVINGS

4 cups sliced carrots
4 tablespoons butter or margarine
4 tablespoons water
4 tablespoons brown sugar

1 teaspoon dry mustard
½ teaspoon salt
1/8 teaspoon white pepper

Scrub the carrots but do not peel unless the carrots are very old.

Place the carrots in a deep (1½-quart) casserole, with the butter or margarine and water. Cover and microwave 8 minutes, stirring twice during the process. Drain off any excess liquid.

Combine the sugar, mustard, salt and pepper and sprinkle over the carrots. Microwave 5 minutes longer, stirring once. Let stand 2 to 3 minutes before serving.

Apple Nut Acorn Squash

YIELD: 2 SERVINGS

1 acorn squash (approximately 20 ounces)
2 apples
1 tablespoon water
2 tablespoons butter or margarine
1 tablespoon honey

¼ teaspoon salt
1/8 teaspoon pepper
1 teaspoon vanilla extract
½ teaspoon cinnamon
2 tablespoons chopped cashews

Wash the squash well and pierce it in several places with a long skewer or fork. Place in an ovenproof dish and microwave 10 minutes, turning the squash over once during the process. Remove from the oven and let stand 3 to 4 minutes.

Core, quarter and peel the apples. Place in an ovenproof bowl with 1 tablespoon of water. Cover with wax paper and microwave for 4 minutes, stirring once halfway through the cooking.

Remove the apples with a slotted spoon to a blender or mixer.

Add the butter, honey, salt, pepper, vanilla and cinnamon and spin until smooth. Stir in the nuts.

Halve the squash and remove the seeds and fibers. Fill the cavities with the apple mixture and place the squash halves on an oven-serving dish. Microwave for 3 minutes uncovered.

Parslied Parsnips

YIELD: 2 TO 4 SERVINGS

4 parsnips
3 tablespoons butter or margarine
2 shallots, chopped fine, or
   1 tablespoon chopped onion

2 tablespoons chopped parsley
Salt and white pepper

Choose parsnips of uniform size. Trim and peel them and cut them lengthwise into quarters. Place them in a 1½-quart casserole with 4 tablespoons of water. Cover and microwave for 4 minutes. Give the dish a quarter turn and cook 5 minutes longer. Remove from the oven and let stand 5 minutes.

Heat the butter or margarine in an oven-serving dish for 40 seconds. Add the shallots or onions and the parsley. Microwave 2 minutes, stirring once during the process.

Spread the butter mixture evenly on the bottom of the dish and place the parsnips in a single layer. Microwave 2 minutes. Carefully turn the quarters over and cook 2 minutes longer. A little freshly chopped parsley sprinkled over the top will enhance the presentation.

Baked Onions and Nuts

YIELD: 4 OR 5 SERVINGS

This is a delicious accompaniment to meat or game.

24 small white onions
¾ cup chopped dry roasted cashews
¼ cup butter
¼ cup commercial sour cream

1 tablespoon honey
½ teaspoon salt
¼ teaspoon nutmeg
Paprika

Peel the onions.

Chop the cashews coarsely.

Heat the butter in an oven-serving dish for 40 seconds.

Stir in the onions so that they are well coated. Cover and microwave for 6 minutes.

Combine the sour cream, honey, salt and nutmeg and when well mixed pour over the onions. Dust with paprika. Cook uncovered for 2 minutes, giving the dish a quarter turn halfway through the process.

Brussels Sprouts au Gratin

YIELD: 4 TO 6 SERVINGS

1 pound (1 quart) Brussels sprouts　　　*1 cup grated Cheddar cheese*
Salt and pepper　　　　　　　　　　　*2 tablespoons butter or margarine*
2 slices whole wheat bread

Choose small, compact, bright green sprouts. Trim off any wilted leaves and make a cross in the bottom of each one with a sharp pointed knife. Soak in salted water for 15 minutes and drain.

Place in a 1½-quart casserole with 4 tablespoons of water. Cover with wax paper and microwave for 8 minutes, giving the casserole a quarter turn halfway through the process. Let stand 3 minutes.

Toast the bread well but do not burn. Crumble it and mix with the grated cheese.

Drain the sprouts. Pat the surface dry with paper toweling and sprinkle with salt and pepper. Cover with the crumb mixture and dot with butter.

Microwave 2 minutes or until the cheese is melted.

Brussels Sprouts and Cashews

YIELD: 4 SERVINGS

1 pound Brussels sprouts　　　　　　*¼ teaspoon freshly ground black*
1 tablespoon water　　　　　　　　　　* pepper*
2 tablespoons butter or margarine　　*1 cup cashews*
½ teaspoon salt

Jean François Millet
THE GLEANERS

Place the sprouts in a 1½-quart casserole. Add 1 tablespoon of water, cover and microwave for 4 minutes. Give the dish a quarter turn and cook 4 minutes longer. Test to be sure the sprouts are cooked but just tender.

Stir in the butter or margarine, salt, pepper and cashews. Microwave 2 minutes, stirring halfway through the cooking.

Cover and let stand 5 minutes before serving.

Cauliflower Mornay

YIELD: 4 SERVINGS

1½ pounds cauliflower
3 tablespoons butter or margarine
2 tablespoons flour
¾ teaspoon salt
¼ teaspoon white pepper
1 cup milk

¾ cup grated Cheddar cheese
2 tablespoons pulverized wheat bran
  cereal
2 tablespoons dry whole wheat bread
  crumbs
8 thin pimiento strips

Remove the leaves and hard core from a cauliflower. If there are dark spots on the top, cut them off with a small sharp knife.

Place the cauliflower in a deep casserole with 4 tablespoons of water. Cover and microwave 10 minutes. Test for doneness by inserting a fork deep into the center. It should be *just* tender.

While the cauliflower is cooking, make a cheese sauce: In a saucepan heat 2 tablespoons of the butter or margarine. Stir in the flour and cook for 1 minute. Add all the milk, salt and pepper and whisk until smooth and the mixture begins to boil. Add ½ cup of cheese and stir until the cheese melts.

Heat the remaining butter or margarine in a small pan and stir in the cereal and bread crumbs. Cook until the mixture is browned.

Drain off any water from the cauliflower. Cover with the sauce. Sprinkle with the crumb mixture and make a lattice with the pimientos on the top. Microwave 3 minutes, giving it a quarter turn halfway through the cooking. Let stand 3 minutes.

Leeks Vinaigrette

YIELD: 2 SERVINGS

6-8 medium leeks

½ cup hot water

2 tablespoons red wine vinegar

1 teaspoon Dijon mustard

6 tablespoons olive oil

¼ teaspoon salt

1/8 teaspoon black pepper

1 tablespoon chopped parsley

Cut all but 3 inches from the stems of the leeks. Cut the stems in half just down to the white bulb. Spread the stems with your fingers under running water to remove any sand. Cut off the very end and the outer skin of the leek bulb.

Place the leeks in a glass dish and pour over the hot water. Cover the dish and microwave 8 minutes. Let stand for 2 minutes.

Remove the leeks to a small serving platter. Cool completely but do not chill.

Mix the vinegar, oil, mustard, salt and pepper well and just before serving pour over the leeks. Sprinkle with fresh chopped parsley.

Green Beans and Sprouts

YIELD: 4 SERVINGS

1 pound green beans

2 tablespoons butter or oil

2 tablespoons chopped onion

1 cup bean sprouts (see Reference Chapter)

1 tablespoon soy sauce

Cut the beans in 1-inch pieces. Place them in a 1½-quart casserole. Cover and microwave for 6 minutes, stirring every 2 minutes. Remove from the oven and drain.

Heat the butter or oil in an oven-serving dish for 40 seconds. Stir in the chopped onion and microwave for 2 minutes. Stir in the bean sprouts; and when they are well coated with butter, microwave for 2 minutes.

Stir in the beans and cook 2 minutes longer. Remove from the oven and toss with the soy sauce. Serve immediately.

MAKING
LIGHT OF IT

The High-Fiber, Low-Calorie Diet

In those days again, it was lack of food
that drove fainting bodies to death;
now contrariwise it is the abundance
that overwhelms them

—Lucretius

There are many injustices in this world but one of the meanest is the way that some people can eat all they want and never gain an unwanted pound while others seem to gain weight by just looking at the picture of a luscious dessert. We have already established the case for high-fiber foods in challenging the problems caused by poor nutrition and bad digestion, but even the high-fiber diet can be too costly, calorically speaking, for some. There *has* to be a high-fiber low-calorie method of improving our health and reducing our poundage that allows us meals that are neither hard to make nor hard to take. There is—as the week's menu and recipes that follow will demonstrate. Once the method is established you will invent your own recipes, eating most of the foods you are used to but preparing them in a slightly different manner.

Few people will stick to a diet very long if it (a) is expensive, (b) is a bore and (c) requires much work. We contend that this diet avoids all three pitfalls, but the fact remains that to be effective a diet should be pleasant. Thanks to modern technology there are foods on the market to serve as substitutes for calorie-loaded butter, mayonnaise, sugar, eggs, soft drinks and other such enemies of the waistline. No one is going to claim that these substitutes taste just as good as their prototypes or that a French chef is going to endorse them; but when eaten in small quantities they provide a texture that satisfies, a flavor that approximates the real thing. With proper seasoning, they allow the dieter good and satisfying meals.

The importance of bran—the unprocessed bran flakes that are to be found at health food stores and the wheat bran cereals to be found on every grocer's shelf—cannot be overemphasized. The unprocessed bran is unsweetened and it is highest in fiber while the bran cereals have had some sugar and flavorings added to make them more palatable though they still contain enough fiber to maintain a

236

proper digestive balance. Either kind of bran may be used "as is" or pulverized in the blender and then used in recipes.

For the dieter, the qualities of both brans are almost magical. They act as a filler for some dishes, making them seem heartier and more satisfying; they add a flavor that is so subtle as to be unidentifiable, and they act as a thickening agent for low-calorie sauces and soups.

You will be eating only moderate amounts of meats, fish, soups, vegetables, fruits and breads (many prepared with bran) because your appetite will be less. Never eat more than you actually want. Forget what your mother said about cleaning your plate, but be sure that you are getting enough bran. Start with two teaspoonfuls before each meal and increase the amount every day by just a little. Drink water with the bran or soon after taking it. Bran needs liquid to be effective. One delicious way to eat bran is to mix the lightly sweetened bran cereal with a third as much of the unprocessed bran. With skim milk, this makes a very satisfying breakfast. Another easy way to fulfill your three times a day requirement is to mix the unprocessed variety with tomato juice or clear chicken or beef broth. This has the twofold effect of getting your bran and taking the edge off your appetite. The amazing thing about eating bran and whole wheat foods is that you lose the desire for sweets, and white flour products seem pallid and boring.

There are a few tricks to keeping the ever-important bran at hand. Treat yourself to some attractive covered jars that go with the decor of your kitchen and fill them with a several days' supply of the different kinds of bran—unprocessed bran (keep the main source of supply in the refrigerator), wheat bran cereal as it comes from the package and wheat bran cereal pulverized in the blender. You will be using these ingredients every day in food preparation so you will want to keep them handy, and they might as well be decorative. For traveling or just for going to the office, carry a small supply of bran in a new tobacco pouch or cosmetic bag, along with a small plastic spoon, so you can discreetly sprinkle the proper ration in soup or on salad in a restaurant.

Finally, relax and enjoy. If you find yourself in a position where sticking to your diet is an embarrassment forget it, but consciously make up for it at the next meal by increasing your fiber intake and reducing calories.

No one will lose weight if he doesn't want to, but anyone can if he or she will prepare the kind of food prescribed in the following menus.

Here are a few Do's and Don'ts.

1. Do ask your doctor about this diet before you start.

2. Do eat as much fiber as your system will easily digest.

3. Do drink at least eight glasses of liquid a day.

4. Do *eat* your fruit. Don't drink it.

5. Do eat poultry (white meat only and free of skin and fat).

6. Do eat fish at least twice a week.

7. Do take regular daily exercise and try to increase it day by day.

8. Do not eat more than you want. Bran is filling.

9. Reduce consumption of products containing refined white sugar or refined white flour.

10. Do not eat red meat more than twice a week.

11. Do not eat pork products as long as you are trying to lose weight.

12. Do not use much salt and use sea salt, if obtainable.

13. Try to avoid all alcohol—but read the section on cocktail parties at the end of this chapter.

Above all *do* think high-fiber low-calorie until it becomes a tune in your head, so that when you plan a meal or go out to a restaurant you will keep on the right track until you reach your desired weight.

Note: A high-fiber low-calorie diet is, like any other diet, more fun if shared with someone else. In the menus that follow the breakfast portions are for one person, while the lunches and dinners are for two. All the recipes in this chapter are planned for two people but they are easily divisible if you are embarked on a solitary crusade.

Monday

BREAKFAST (EACH SERVING)

½ cup Grapenuts mixed with
2 teaspoons-1 tablespoon unprocessed bran

4 ounces skimmed milk

1 slice whole wheat toast

½ teaspoon diet margarine

1 small whole orange

Coffee or tea (1 tablespoon skim milk and
artificial sweetener if desired)

LUNCH

Club Sandwiches

Carob Banana Ice Milk

DINNER

Beef broth with 1 tablespoon unprocessed bran

Mixed Grill

Cauliflower Gratinee

Strawberry Cheese

Club Sandwiches

4 slices (thin) whole wheat sandwich
  bread
1 tablespoon imitation mayonnaise
½ teaspoon Dijon mustard
Iceberg lettuce

4 tomato slices
Soybean "bacon" bits
2 slices white turkey or chicken meat
Salt and pepper

Lay out the bread slices and spread thinly with the mayonnaise mixed with the mustard.

Tear the lettuce so that you will have several layers together. Flatten them with the palm of your hand so that they will lie flat in the sandwich.

Place stacks of lettuce on each of two pieces of bread. Cover with the tomato slices and sprinkle with "bacon" bits.

Spread with the remaining mayonnaise and cover with the turkey or chicken. Sprinkle with salt and pepper and cover with another stack of lettuce.

Top with the remaining bread slices and press down gently. Cut in half before serving.

Carob Banana Ice Milk

1½ cups skimmed milk
2 tablespoons carob powder
1 medium banana, sliced

6 ice cubes, crushed
2 teaspoons artificial sweetener
  (optional)

Just before serving, put the milk, carob powder, sliced banana and the ice cubes which have been partially crushed into the blender. Save out 2 slices of banana.

Add sweetener if desired.

Spin these ingredients until smooth.

Serve in 2 tall glasses with straws, each garnished with a slice of banana.

Mixed Grill

2 loin lamb chops

2 lamb kidneys

2 tomatoes

*2 tablespoons pulverized wheat bran
    cereal*

2 teaspoons minced onion

1 teaspoon olive oil

8 mushrooms

*1 strip bacon, cooked and chopped
    fine*

1 lemon

2 small bananas

2 teaspoons diet margarine

Salt and pepper

Wipe the chops with paper toweling to remove any possible bone dust. Sprinkle with salt and pepper.

Split the kidneys and remove the filament and fatty hard core. Sprinkle with salt and pepper.

Wash and halve the tomatoes. Sprinkle each half with a mixture of the bran and minced onion. Season with salt and pepper and sprinkle with oil, allowing ¼ teaspoon to each half.

Place all components of the grill on a Teflon baking sheet.

Wash and stem the mushrooms. Dry the caps well and chop the stems. Mix with the chopped bacon and divide between the mushroom caps.

Peel, halve and quarter the bananas and wrap in foil.

Twelve minutes before serving place the bananas on a lower rack in a 375-degree preheated oven. At the same time, turn on the broiler and slip the pan 3 inches below the broiler. Broil 5 minutes. Turn the chops and the kidneys and broil for 3 or 4 minutes longer.

Arrange the chops, kidneys, tomatoes, mushrooms and bananas on a heated platter. Garnish with watercress or parsley and wedges of lemon. Sprinkle with freshly ground black pepper.

Cauliflower Gratinée

1 small head cauliflower   *1 tablespoon grated Parmesan cheese*
1 teaspoon salt   *1 tablespoon diet margarine*
1 teaspoon cider vinegar   *Salt and pepper*

Remove the thick stem and leaves from the cauliflower with a sharp knife. Soak the cauliflower in salted water for 15 minutes to remove any hidden insects.

Put 1½ cups of water in a saucepan. Add the salt and cider vinegar and bring to a boil.

Place the cauliflower in a steaming basket in the saucepan. Cover and steam for 12 to 14 minutes or just until tender. Do not overcook. Drain and cut the head in half.

Put the cauliflower halves in a shallow oven-serving dish. Sprinkle with salt and pepper, sprinkle with cheese and dot with the margarine.

Brown under the broiler while arranging the mixed grill.

Strawberry Cheese

½ pint cottage cheese   *1 tablespoon artificial sweetener*
4 tablespoons yogurt   *½ pint fresh strawberries*
1/8 teaspoon salt

Beat the cheese in a blender or electric beater bowl until smooth. Place it in a strainer lined with cheesecloth and suspend over a bowl. Let stand in the refrigerator for several hours until all the whey has dripped through.

Mix the cheese with the yogurt, salt and artificial sweetener. Spoon into 2 dessert glasses and garnish with fresh strawberries.

Tuesday

BREAKFAST (EACH SERVING)

1 cup hot Wheatena mixed with
2 teaspoons-1 tablespoon unprocessed bran and 6 raisins

4 ounces skim milk

Artificial sweetener (optional)

Coffee or tea

LUNCH

Danish Open Face Sardine Sandwich

Green Salad with Cottage Cheese Dressing

Fresh blueberries with artificial brown sugar and yogurt

DINNER

Chicken broth with 1 tablespoon unprocessed bran

Poached Fish with Caper Sauce

Chinese Green Beans and Sprouts

Dried Fruit Sundae

Danish Openface Sardine Sandwiches

1 can sardines (4 large sardines)
2 ½-inch slices of whole wheat bread
Mustard
2 teaspoons imitation mayonnaise

2 teaspoons chopped parsley
2 teaspoons chopped chives
1 hard-cooked egg

Remove the sardines to paper toweling and wipe off all excess oil.

Spread the bread first with mustard and then with mayonnaise (½ teaspoon to each slice).

Mix together the chopped herbs and sprinkle most of them over the slices of bread.

Place the sardines on the bread so as to form a "V" and fill in the center with overlapping slices of hard-cooked egg.

Garnish with the remaining mayonnaise and herbs.

Green Salad with Cottage Cheese Dressing

4 cups salad greens (escarole, garden
  lettuce, spinach leaves, watercress,
  etc.)

DRESSING:
½ cup low-fat cottage cheese
4 tablespoons plain yogurt

2 tablespoons wheat bran cereal
2 teaspoons cider vinegar
½ teaspoon artificial sweetener
  (optional)
2 tablespoons minced chives
2 tablespoons chopped celery
Salt and pepper

Wash the salad greens. Tear them into bite-size pieces. Dry thoroughly and chill.

Spin the cottage cheese with the yogurt, bran, sweetener and vinegar in a blender. Pour into a bowl and stir in the chives and celery. Season to taste with salt and pepper.

Serve the salad in salad bowls and top with the dressing.

Poached Fish with Caper Sauce

2 fillets (1/3-½ pound each) of white
   fish (sole, haddock, scrod or
   halibut)
½ carrot, sliced
1 tablespoon chopped onion
½ bay leaf
1/8 teaspoon thyme
½ teaspoon salt
1/8 teaspoon white pepper

3 cups water

SAUCE:
2 tablespoons imitation mayonnaise
2 teaspoons minced green onions
   (scallions)
½ teaspoon anchovy paste (optional)
1½ teaspoons coarsely chopped capers
¾ teaspoon lemon juice

Choose fillets of equal weight and thickness.

Put the vegetables, herbs and seasoning in the water and bring to a boil. Simmer 10 minutes.

Add the fish and poach 5 to 10 minutes, according to the thickness of the fish.

Test for doneness by pricking with a fork. If the fish flakes easily, remove with a slotted spatula to paper toweling to drain thoroughly.

Meanwhile heat the mayonnaise, onions, anchovy paste and capers in the top of a small double boiler over simmering water, stirring until warm (not hot).

Serve the fish on a heated platter. Coat with the sauce and serve with wedges of lemon.

Chinese Green Beans and Sprouts

½ pound garden-fresh green beans or
   1 box frozen green beans
1 tablespoon safflower or peanut oil
1 clove garlic, sliced

1 cup bean sprouts (fresh or canned)
½ cup chicken broth
1 tablespoon tamari (soy sauce)
2 tablespoons wheat bran cereal

If using the fresh beans, wash them well and snap them into 1-inch pieces. Boil in salted water for 2 minutes. Drain and rinse in cold water. Shake to dry.

If you are using the frozen variety, thaw and drain dry.

Heat the oil and garlic in a small wok or skillet. When the oil is smoking hot, remove the garlic with a slotted spoon and add the beans and chicken broth. Cook 3 minutes. Add the sprouts and tamari and continue to cook for 5 minutes, stirring constantly.

Remove from the stove and stir in the bran. Serve very hot.

Dried Fruit Sundae

1 cup pot cheese
4 tablespoons plain yogurt
2 teaspoons artificial sweetener
  (optional)

1 dried peach
1 dried pineapple slice
½ teaspoon vanilla extract
1 teaspoon sliced almonds

Spin the pot cheese and the yogurt in the blender and pour into a small bowl.

Add the sweetener if desired, the vanilla and the peach and pineapple cut into small pieces. Save a few pieces for garnish.

Spoon into dessert glasses. Chill thoroughly and garnish with bits of fruit and a few sliced almonds.

Wednesday

BREAKFAST (EACH SERVING)

1 cup Hot Spiced Tomato Broth with
2 teaspoons-1 tablespoon unprocessed bran

1 poached egg on unbuttered whole wheat toast

½ cantaloupe

Coffee or tea

LUNCHEON

Luncheon Shrimp Salad

2 bran muffins (see page 54)

Chilled pineapple slices

DINNER

Artichokes with Sweet and Sour Salad Dressing

Rosemary Broiled Chicken

Brown Bran Rice

Glazed Turnips

Raspberry Parfait

Hot Spiced Tomato Broth

1½ pints V-8 juice
1 tablespoon diet margarine
2 tablespoons pulverized wheat bran
   cereal or unprocessed bran

2 teaspoons artificial sweetener
   (optional)
2 tablespoons yogurt

Heat the V-8 juice. Add the margarine and bran. (If using the bran cereal, further sweetening will not be necessary.) Stir until the mixture reaches the boiling point.

Remove from the heat and stir in the yogurt. Serve very hot in soup plates.

Luncheon Shrimp Salad

20 medium-size shrimp
2 tomatoes
Lettuce leaves
Vege-Sal

DRESSING:
½ cup cottage cheese

2 tablespoons chopped green onions
   (scallions)
4 teaspoons apple cider vinegar
1 tablespoon chopped parsley
½ teaspoon artificial sweetener
   (optional)
2 tablespoons pulverized unprocessed
   bran

Use freshly cooked and cleaned shrimp or the canned variety.

Wash the tomatoes and cut them into wedges without cutting the bottom. Spread like a flower and place on lettuce leaves which have been sprinkled with Vege-Sal or other seasoned salt.

Fill the center of the tomatoes with the shrimp. Chill in the refrigerator.

Spin the cottage cheese in the blender until smooth. Stir in the remaining ingredients and pour the dressing over the salad.

Artichokes with Sweet and Sour Salad Dressing

2 large artichokes

DRESSING:
4 tablespoons apple cider vinegar

½ teaspoon Dijon mustard
½ teaspoon salt
1 teaspoon artificial sweetener
Freshly ground black pepper

Choose large fresh artichokes. Cut off the stems evenly so that the artichokes will be steady on the plates. Cut off the top third and snip off the spiny ends of the remaining leaves with scissors. If you want to be very elegant, carefully spread the leaves apart until the choke is revealed. Twist out the choke with your fingers and reform the artichoke.

Place the artichokes in a steamer or on a trivet in a saucepan with 2 inches of water, a teaspoon of salt and a tablespoon of vinegar. Cover and steam 35 to 45 minutes or until an outer leaf is easily torn from the artichoke.

Meanwhile mix the ingredients for the dressing, adding as much pepper as suits your taste. Place in a small bowl.

To serve: Drain the artichoke thoroughly, turning it upside down and squeezing out the liquid. Place upright on the edge of a plate. Elevate one side of the plate using a spoon or knife. Pour a little sauce on the side of the plate nearest the eater and dip the tips of the artichoke leaves in the dressing before scraping the inside of the leaf with your teeth. The pot at the end of the rainbow is the artichoke bottom which is eaten with fork and knife and a fresh supply of dressing.

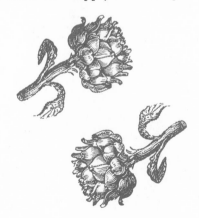

Rosemary Broiled Chicken

2 chicken breasts   *Salt*
1 lemon   *Freshly ground black pepper*
½ teaspoon rosemary leaves *Paprika*

Place the chicken breasts on a rack in a shallow broiling pan, skin side down. Sprinkle with the juice of a half lemon, the rosemary leaves and a little salt and pepper. Let stand for 30 to 60 minutes.

Preheat the broiler.

Broil the chicken, allowing 10 to 12 minutes on each side, depending on the size of the breasts.

Using a sharp knife, remove the skin from the chicken breasts. Sprinkle with salt, black pepper and paprika. Put back under the broiler for a few moments to brown. Sprinkle with the juice of the remaining half lemon and serve very hot.

Brown Bran Rice

1 tablespoon safflower, corn or   *6 tablespoons brown rice*
  peanut oil   *1¼ cups well-seasoned chicken broth*
2 tablespoons minced onion   *4 tablespoons unprocessed bran*
1 tablespoon chopped parsley

Heat the oil in a small skillet. Add the onion and parsley and cook 1 minute.

Add the rice and stir until thoroughly coated.

Add the chicken broth, bring to a boil and cover tightly. Reduce the heat and simmer 25 minutes.

Stir in the bran and cook for 5 minutes or until the rice is just tender.

Glazed Turnips

½ pound white turnips
2 cups chicken broth
1 teaspoon diet margarine

Salt and pepper
1 teaspoon artificial sweetener
Paprika

Slice the turnips ¼ inch thick.

Bring the chicken broth to a boil and add the turnips. Boil 5 minutes with the cover on. Remove the cover and cook over moderately high heat until most of the liquid has disappeared.

Add the margarine, salt and pepper and sweetener and continue cooking until the turnips have a glazed surface and all the moisture has disappeared.

Dust with a little paprika before serving.

Raspberry Parfait

½ cup nondairy whipped topping
4 tablespoons yogurt
1 teaspoon fresh lemon juice

½ pint raspberries
Artificial sweetener (optional)

Force half the raspberries through a strainer, using the back of a spoon.

Combine the raspberry juice with the lemon juice and half of the non-dairy topping. Mix with the yogurt.

Spoon 1 tablespoon of the mixture into the bottom of each of 2 parfait glasses.

Top with half the remaining raspberries. Sprinkle with sweetener if desired.

Repeat the process and finish with 2 tablespoons of the nondairy whipped topping garnished with a perfect raspberry.

Serve very cold.

Thursday

BREAKFAST (EACH SERVING)

½ grapefruit

1 cup hot Ralston mixed with
2 teaspoons-1 tablespoon unprocessed bran

4 ounces skimmed milk

Coffee or tea

LUNCHEON

Individual Tomato Aspics

Open Face Muenster Cheese Sandwiches

Cinnamon Applesauce Dessert

DINNER

Cucumber Boats

Tarragon Lamb Steaks

Minted Carrots

Orange Delight

Individual Tomato Aspics

1 cup V-8 juice
2 tablespoons pulverized unprocessed
  bran
1½ teaspoons gelatin
1 tablespoon water
2 artichoke hearts

1 tablespoon low-fat cottage cheese
2 teaspoons chopped chives
Imitation mayonnaise
Lettuce leaves
Chopped parsley or tarragon leaves

Heat the juice. Dissolve the gelatin in the water and add it and the bran to the juice. Stir 1 minute.

Fill 2 individual 6-ounce molds or custard cups 1/3 full with the hot mixture and place in the refrigerator until firm.

Drain the artichoke hearts well. Spread the leaves slightly and fill with the combination of cottage cheese and chives bound together with a teaspoon of the mayonnaise.

Reform the hearts and place them upside down in the molds. Fill the containers with the remaining juice. Refrigerate until very firm.

Unmold the aspics on lettuce leaves. Garnish with a teaspoon of mayonnaise and a sprinkling of parsley or tarragon leaves.

Open Face Muenster Cheese Sandwiches

2 slices whole wheat bread
Dijon mustard

4 thin onion rings
2 1-ounce slices Muenster cheese

Toast the bread on one side only.

Place on a baking sheet, toasted side down, and spread with the mustard.

Cover with the onion rings and a slice of cheese.

Place under the broiler and cook until the cheese is melted. Cut each piece into 4 squares and serve with the aspics.

Cinnamon Applesauce Dessert

4 apples
2/3 cup water
¼ teaspoon grated lemon rind

2 tablespoons low-fat cottage cheese
¾ teaspoon cinnamon
Artificial sweetener

Wash the apples well and cut into pieces without peeling or coring them.

Put in a saucepan with the water and bring to a boil. Add the lemon rind and simmer until very soft.

Force the apples through a food mill or strainer and sweeten with about 1 tablespoon of artificial sweetener. Spoon the sauce into 2 dessert glasses.

Season each tablespoon of cottage cheese with ¼ teaspoon cinnamon and 1 teaspoon of sweetener. Fashion into balls.

Bury the cottage cheese balls in the applesauce and dust with a little more cinnamon. Serve very cold.

Cucumber Boats

1 medium-size cucumber
2 tablespoons water-packed tuna
1 teaspoon anchovy paste
1 tablespoon minced green onion

1 tablespoon imitation mayonnaise
½ cup low-fat cottage cheese
Salt and white pepper

Scrub the cucumber but do not peel it unless it is tough or has been waxed.

Cut the cucumber in half lengthwise, scooping out the seeds with a spoon and extending the cavity almost to the ends. Sprinkle the cavity with salt and white pepper.

Work the tuna fish and anchovy paste with the back of a fork in a small bowl until blended. Add 2 teaspoons of the minced onion, the mayonnaise and the cottage cheese. Mix well.

Fill the cucumber halves with the mixture and sprinkle with the remaining green onions. Serve on small salad plates lined with lettuce leaves.

Tarragon Lamb Steaks

2 lamb steaks (4-5 ounces each)*   ½ teaspoon lemon juice
3 tablespoons imitation mayonnaise   1/8 teaspoon salt
2 teaspoons chopped tarragon   Freshly ground black pepper
¼ teaspoon Dijon-type mustard

Place the lamb steaks, which should be at room temperature, on a rack in an open broiling pan. Sprinkle with unseasoned meat tenderizer and let stand 20 minutes.

In a small bowl combine the mayonnaise with the tarragon, mustard, lemon juice, salt and a little freshly ground black pepper. Set aside.

Preheat the broiler.

Set the pan 2 inches from the broiling unit and broil 3 to 5 minutes on each side, depending on preference. Some people like lamb rare (a la francaise)—others well cooked (a l'anglaise).

Transfer the steaks to a small heated platter and spread with the tarragon sauce. Serve immediately.

*When you buy a leg of lamb for a dinner party ask the butcher to saw off two ¾-inch steaks from the butt end. These may be wrapped and frozen for later use.

Minted Carrots

1½ cups sliced carrots   1 teaspoon artificial sweetener
1 cup chicken broth   (optional)
1 tablespoon diet margarine   ½ teaspoon chopped fresh mint
½ teaspoon lemon juice   Salt and white pepper

Scrub the carrots well but do not peel. Cut the carrots into ¼-inch slices.

Heat the chicken broth in a small saucepan and add the carrots.

Cover and cook over moderately high heat for 12 minutes.

Remove the cover and cook until the carrots are almost dry and just tender. Add the margarine, sweetener if desired, lemon juice and chopped mint. (Use half the amount of dried mint if fresh mint is not available.) Season with salt and pepper.

Orange Delight

2 navel oranges
2 maraschino cherries
2 teaspoons unsweetened shredded
   coconut

½ teaspoon lemon juice
2 teaspoons artificial sweetener
   (optional)
2 mint leaves

Slice the very tip off the bottom of the orange so that it will sit gracefully on a plate.

Using a very sharp small knife, notch out the top as you would for making a jack-o'-lantern for Halloween. Set the top aside.

Hollow out the fruit by running a knife around the edge and scooping out the fruit with a teaspoon. Cut the fruit fiber and flesh into pieces into a bowl so that none of the juice is lost. Combine with the cherries cut into small pieces and the coconut.

Add the lemon juice and the artificial sweetener if desired.

Fill the oranges with the mixture. Replace the cover, inserting a mint leaf at a jaunty angle on one side. Chill well before serving.

Friday

BREAKFAST (EACH SERVING)

6 ounces tomato juice with 1 tablespoon unprocessed bran

Breakfast Cheese Dreams

Coffee or tea

LUNCH

Escarole Chicken Soup Parmesan

2 slices whole wheat toast

2 Carob Chip Cookies (see page 208)

Coffee

DINNER

Baked Stuffed Mushrooms

Hungarian Goulash with 2 dumplings (see page 96)

Poppy Seed Cabbage

Broiled Grapefruit

Breakfast Cheese Dreams

1 large Whole Wheat Pita Bread
*   pouch (see page 34)*
4 tablespoons grated Swiss cheese

1 tablespoon minced onion
2 teaspoons soybean "bacon" bits

Preheat the broiler.

Trim the edges of the pouch with scissors and lay the two halves on a baking sheet.

Cover with the grated cheese and the onions. Sprinkle with the "bacon" bits.

Broil until the cheese melts. Cut each half into quarters and serve immediately.

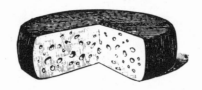

Chicken Escarole Soup

1 tablespoon diet margarine
2 tablespoons minced onion
1 head escarole (or other garden
*   lettuce)*
1 quart chicken broth

1 teaspoon salt
¼ teaspoon white pepper
4 tablespoons pulverized wheat bran
*   cereal or unprocessed bran flakes*
2 tablespoons Parmesan cheese

Heat the margarine in a 2-quart saucepan.

Add the onion and cook for 2 minutes without letting it brown.

Add the escarole, which has been washed and torn into pieces.

Cover and steam for 5 minutes or until the lettuce is wilted.

Add the chicken broth, salt and pepper (unless the broth is already highly seasoned). Cover and simmer 30 minutes.

Stir in the bran and simmer 5 minutes longer.

Ladle the soup into heated soup plates and sprinkle with Parmesan cheese.

Baked Stuffed Mushrooms

8 large mushrooms

2 teaspoons chopped parsley

2 teaspoons chopped chives

1 small clove garlic, minced

2 tablespoons pulverized wheat bran
   cereal or unprocessed bran

4 tablespoons chicken broth

½ teaspoon salt

¼ teaspoon freshly ground black
   pepper

8 medium shrimp

2 tablespoons grated Parmesan
   cheese

1 tablespoon diet margarine

½ lemon

Choose mushrooms of uniform size. Remove the stems. Wash stems and caps briefly and pat dry with paper toweling. Arrange the caps in 2 lightly oiled individual baking-serving dishes.

Chop the mushroom stems quite fine and combine them in a bowl with the parsley, chives, garlic and the bran softened in the chicken broth. Season with salt and pepper and mix well.

Put half the mixture in the mushroom caps. Top with a shrimp and cover with the rest of the mixture. Sprinkle with Parmesan and dot with a little margarine. Sprinkle with the lemon juice.

Just before serving, bake 15 minutes at 350 degrees F. Serve hot.

Poppy Seed Cabbage

½ pound cabbage
1 cup chicken broth
4 tablespoons yogurt
4 tablespoons pulverized wheat bran
   cereal

1 teaspoon poppy seeds
Salt and freshly ground black
   pepper

Shred the cabbage coarsely.

Heat the chicken broth to the boiling point. Add the cabbage. Cover and steam for 10 minutes. Remove the cover and cook until almost all the liquid has disappeared. Stir to prevent scorching.

Remove from the heat and stir in the yogurt, bran, poppy seeds and salt and pepper to taste. Serve very hot.

Broiled Grapefruit

1 medium to small grapefruit
2 teaspoons maple sugar

1 teaspoon diet margarine
2 maraschino cherries (optional)

Preheat the broiler.

Cut the grapefruit in two and cut around the outside and along the natural sections for easier eating.

Place the grapefruit in a baking pan.

Spread each one with a teaspoon of maple sugar and dot with the margarine.

Place under the preheated broiler and cook just until the sugar melts.

Topping with a maraschino cherry will only increase the caloric count by 18, so indulge yourself if you wish.

Saturday

BREAKFAST (EACH SERVING)

½ cup All-Bran or Bran Buds
mixed with 2 teaspoons unprocessed bran

½ sliced peach

4 ounces skimmed milk

Artificial sweetener (optional)

Coffee or tea

LUNCHEON

Diet Gazpacho

Hot Crab Meat Sandwich

Coffee Banana Jelly

DINNER

Watercress Salad

Chicken Oriental with Stuffed Tomatoes

Braised Celery

Cantaloupe Bowls

Diet Gazpacho

4 tablespoons pulverized wheat bran
   cereal or unprocessed bran flakes
1 cup cold water
1 cucumber
1 onion
1 clove garlic
½ green pepper

1 tablespoon corn or safflower oil
1 tablespoon red wine vinegar
1 pint tomato juice
½ teaspoon salt
1/8 teaspoon paprika
1/8 teaspoon black pepper
1 slice whole wheat bread

Put the bran in the blender and cover with cold water while preparing the vegetables.

Peel the cucumber. Dice a third of it and set aside; put the rest, cut in chunks, in the blender. Peel the onion and garlic, cut them in pieces, and put them in the blender. Dice a tablespoonful of the green pepper and set aside; put the rest, cut in chunks, in the blender. Add the oil, vinegar, tomato juice and seasonings. Spin the blender until the soup is smooth. Chill in the refrigerator.

Serve the soup in large soup plates, garnished with the diced cucumber, green pepper and croutons made from the whole wheat bread, toasted.

Hot Crab Meat Sandwich

2 slices whole wheat bread
½ pint crab meat flakes, fresh or
   canned
2 tablespoons imitation mayonnaise

½ teaspoon lemon juice
Salt and pepper
Parmesan cheese

Toast the bread very lightly on one side. Place on a baking sheet. Dry the crab between two pieces of paper toweling. Mix with the mayonnaise and lemon juice. Spread the untoasted side of the bread with the mixture and sprinkle with salt, white pepper and Parmesan.

Heat under the broiler until the crab mixture starts to bubble and the surface is lightly browned. This is best eaten with fork and knife.

Coffee Banana Jelly

1½ cups black coffee
2 teaspoons artificial sweetener
2 teaspoons sherry
1 package plain gelatin

1 small banana, sliced
2 teaspoons nondairy whipped
  topping

Heat the coffee and add the sweetener and the sherry previously combined with the gelatin and ¼ cup of water. Stir over heat until the gelatin is dissolved.

Slice ½ of the banana into each of two 8-ounce custard cups or decorative individual molds.

Fill with the coffee mixture. Cool and then put into the refrigerator to set.

Unmold onto dessert plates and garnish with the topping.

Watercress Salad

½ bunch watercress
2 small beets, sliced thin
1 onion, sliced thin

DRESSING:
1 tablespoon safflower or corn oil

2 teaspoons cider vinegar
2 anchovy fillets, cut fine
¼ teaspoon salt
Freshly ground black pepper
2 tablespoons pulverized wheat bran
  cereal or unprocessed bran

Wash the watercress well, discarding any wilted leaves and tough roots. If the stems are long, cut them into pieces. Place in a bowl.

Cover with the beet slices and onion rings.

Combine the oil, vinegar, anchovies, salt and black pepper according to taste.

Just before serving toss the salad with the dressing. Add the bran and toss for another minute.

Chicken Oriental

Cold sliced chicken (white
　only, no skin)
2 tablespoons imitation mayonnaise

2 tablespoons minced scallions
　or green onions
1½ teaspoons soy sauce

Cold cooked chicken in the refrigerator can be the dieter's best friend; it is a good source of protein that is relatively low in calories, and the flavor goes well with almost everything. When serving only the white meat, allow half the breast per person; it can be baked, roasted or poached in a small quantity of seasoned broth.

Before serving, make a sauce by combining the imitation mayonnaise, minced scallions and soy sauce. Use a sharp knife to slice the meat across the grain. Serve the chicken slices with the sauce, flanked by the Mushroom Stuffed Tomatoes.

Mushroom Stuffed Tomatoes

2 medium-size tomatoes
½ pound mushrooms
1 tablespoon diet margarine
1 tablespoon minced shallots

2 tablespoons pulverized wheat bran
　cereal or unprocessed bran flakes
1/8 teaspoon mace
Salt and pepper

Wash the tomatoes and hollow out a hole from the stem end large enough to hold the stuffing. Turn the tomatoes upside down on a rack and let drain while preparing the filling.

Wash the mushrooms. Dry and chop rather coarsely.

Heat the margarine in a small skillet and sauté the shallots for 1 minute without browning. Add the mushrooms and stir until coated with the margarine. When the mushrooms have exuded their juice stir in the bran and stir until the mixture is thickened and almost dry. Season with mace and salt and pepper to taste.

Turn the tomatoes and place in a small baking dish and sprinkle the interior lightly with salt and pepper. Fill the tomatoes with the mushroom mixture and bake 10 minutes at 350 degrees F.

George Henry Hall
RASPBERRIES IN A GAUNTLET

Braised Celery

1 bunch celery

1 cup chicken broth

*1 heaping tablespoon pulverized wheat
  bran cereal or unprocessed bran
  flakes*

1 tablespoon diet margarine

*1 teaspoon artificial sweetener
  (optional)*

Salt and pepper

Trim the tops off the celery, leaving 4 to 5 inches of stalks. Cut the celery into quarters and wash very carefully.

Bring a shallow pan of salted water to a full boil and parboil the celery for 5 minutes. Drain.

Place the celery quarters in a shallow heatproof serving dish. Add the chicken broth mixed with the bran, the margarine and the sweetener if desired.

Cover tightly and simmer 20 minutes over moderate heat. Remove the cover and continue cooking until the liquid has almost entirely disappeared. Sprinkle lightly with salt and pepper.

Cantaloupe Bowls

1 cantaloupe

1 small orange

1 cup fresh raspberries or strawberries

1 peach

Take care to choose very ripe fruit so that extra sweetening is not really necessary.

Cut the cantaloupe in half and cut off a tiny piece from the bottom of each half so that the "bowls" will sit well on a plate.

Remove the seeds from the cantaloupe and scoop out enough of the flesh with a small melon ball cutter to make room for the rest of the fruit.

Combine the scooped-out melon with small sections of orange, the berries and thin peach slices, mixing gently. Taste for sweetness and add artificial sweetener if desired. Fill the cantaloupe halves.

Serve on dessert plates lined with large grape leaves and top each with a mint leaf. Serve cool but not cold if the full flavor of the fruit is to be appreciated.

Sunday

BREAKFAST (EACH SERVING)

½ cup applesauce mixed with 1 tablespoon unprocessed bran

Broiled Finnan Haddie

1 slice whole wheat toast or 1 boiled potato

Coffee or tea

SUNDAY DINNER

Oysters with French Shallot Sauce

Braised Veal Chops

Zucchini Provencale

Whole wheat French bread

Baked Banana Tortola

SUNDAY SUPPER (OR LUNCH)

Asparagus Soup

Fruit Nut Salad

Broiled Finnan Haddie

½ pound finnan haddie in 2 pieces
1½ cups skimmed milk

2 teaspoons diet margarine
Black pepper

Place the finnan haddie (smoked dried haddock) in a shallow dish. Cover with milk and let soak 1 hour. Cover and bake 30 minutes at 300 degrees F.

Drain off all the milk and spread with the margarine.

Place under a preheated broiler and broil for 3 minutes.

Sprinkle generously with black pepper.

Oysters with French Shallot Sauce

If oysters are unavailable or not beloved, substitute sliced cucumbers, using the same sauce.

12-24 oysters

SAUCE:
3 shallots, minced

¼ cup red wine vinegar
¼ teaspoon coarsely ground black
* pepper*

Oysters served on the half shell should be thoroughly washed and chilled before opening. One-half teaspoon of the sauce is placed on the oyster before eating.

If oysters in the shell are not available, shucked or canned oysters should be chilled and served in 2 stemmed sherbet glasses with the sauce poured over.

Braised Veal Chops

2 thick veal chops (1½ inches thick)

2 tablespoons minced celery

3 tablespoons chopped onion

1 clove garlic, minced (optional)

1 carrot, diced

2 cups chicken broth

2 tablespoons pulverized wheat bran
  cereal or unprocessed bran

1 tablespoon chopped parsley

Preheat the oven to 300 degrees F.

   Sprinkle a Teflon-lined skillet with salt and heat the pan thoroughly.

   Brown the chops on both sides. Set aside.

   Prepare the vegetables and cook them 5 minutes in ½ cup chicken broth in a small saucepan.

   Spread the vegetables in the bottom of a lightly buttered casserole.

   Place the chops on the vegetables and add the remaining broth.

   Sprinkle with salt and pepper. Cover and bake 40 minutes.

   Remove the chops to a heated platter. Pour the vegetables and the liquid into the saucepan and add the bran. Stir until the mixture boils. Pour over the chops and sprinkle with chopped parsley.

Zucchini Provençale

1 medium-size onion, sliced thin

1 large clove garlic, sliced

2 medium zucchini, sliced ½ inch
  thick

2 tomatoes, washed and sliced

1½ cups chicken broth

½ bay leaf

½ teaspoon oregano

2 tablespoons pulverized wheat bran
  cereal or unprocessed bran flakes

1 tablespoon olive oil

Salt and pepper

Prepare the vegetables and put them in a saucepan with the chicken broth, bay leaf and oregano.

Cover and simmer 10 minutes. Remove the cover and continue cooking until the liquid is reduced by half.

Add the bran and olive oil. Cook until the mixture thickens slightly and season to taste with salt and pepper.

Baked Banana Tortola

2 ripe bananas

Salt

1/3 cup dry white wine

½ teaspoon butter

1/8 teaspoon mace, cinnamon and cloves

2 teaspoons coconut (optional)

Peel and slice the bananas and put them in a small Teflon-lined skillet. Sprinkle lightly with salt. Add the wine.

Cover and simmer 10 minutes.

Remove the cover and dot the bananas with butter and sprinkle with the spices.

Cover and cook 5 minutes longer. Serve warm sprinkled with coconut if desired.

Asparagus Soup

1 bunch asparagus, cooked or frozen

1 pint chicken broth

2 tablespoons pulverized wheat bran cereal or unprocessed bran flakes

2-4 tablespoons yogurt

Salt and white pepper

Combine the cooked or thawed asparagus with the chicken broth and bran in a blender. Save out a few tips for garnish. Blend until smooth.

Heat the soup to the boiling point and season to taste with salt and pepper.

Stir in the yogurt and pour into heated soup cups, garnishing with the reserved asparagus tips.

Fruit Nut Salad

This must be considered a dessert.

1 cup diced apples
1 small banana, sliced
1 small orange, sectioned
6 cashews, coarsely chopped
Vitamin C

DRESSING:
½ cup cottage cheese
1 tablespoon pulverized wheat bran
  cereal
¼ cup water
1 teaspoon lemon juice
2 teaspoons artificial sweetener

Wash, core but do not pare the apples. Cut in small pieces.

Combine with the sliced banana and sectioned orange and mix with 1/8 teaspoon powdered vitamin C. Cover and store in the refrigerator.

Combine the bran with the water and lemon juice and sweetener.

Blend with the cottage cheese until smooth.

Serve the fruit on lettuce leaves and top with the dressing. Sprinkle with the cashews.

A Diet Cocktail Party

Since cocktail parties are a way of life for an ever-increasing number of people, it's better to face the problem for dieters. The thoughtful host or hostess will always supply nonalcoholic drinks for nondrinkers and provide decorative and low-calorie snacks and canapes along with the usual calorie-high nibbles. For the guest who just cannot resist a martini, a bourbon or a Scotch, there are tricks to the trade. Limit yourself to one drink. Don't get too far from the ice supply. Constant replenishing with ice can make one drink last all evening. No one said it was as good as the usual method but it works. Below are a few look-alikes—drinks that cause no comment— and a few canapes that are pretty to look at and pleasant to eat.

Drinks

CALF SHOTS
Pour canned bouillon over ice into an old-fashioned glass. Season with ½ teaspoon of lemon juice. (Don't use consommé; the resulting gelatin becomes unmanageable.)

SEA JUICE
Pour bottled clam juice over ice and garnish with a twist of lemon peel.

NOT-SO-BLOODY MARYS
Pour 4 ounces of tomato juice over rocks. Add ½ teaspoon Worcestershire, 2 or 3 drops of hot sauce and 1/8 teaspoon garlic powder. Garnish with thin strips of cucumber.

Edibles

PINEAPPLE STICKS
Using an apple corer, dig out the pineapple sticks by following the sections of the pineapple. A ripe pineapple needs no sugar.

MELON PICKS

Cut small squares of cantaloupe. Wrap them in small pieces of paper-thin dried beef. Spear with a toothpick and serve very cold.

ARTICHOKE BITS

Cut canned artichoke bottoms into small squares. Sprinkle with both seasoned salt (Vege-Sal) and garlic salt. Serve with toothpicks around 1 whole artichoke (to be cooked and eaten later).

APPLES AND CHEESE

Using the kind of apple sectioner that removes the core and cuts an apple in 8 pieces, divide an apple on a wooden serving tray. Discard the core but leave the apple in the sectioner. Surround the edge of the platter with thin slices of Muenster or Swiss cheese. Have a bowl of bright red apples nearby because the guests will continue to "core" for themselves with great pleasure.

VEGETABLE DIP

Combine 1 cup of chopped fresh spinach, ½ cup chopped green onions (scallions), 1 clove minced garlic, 1 tablespoon of soy sauce, ½ cup of imitation mayonnaise and 1 cup of cottage cheese in a blender and spin just until mixed. Place in a bowl and surround with cucumber sticks, celery sticks, carrot sticks, raw cauliflower and broccoli florets and radishes.

HONEYDEW PARMEGIANO

Cut honeydew melon into small balls with a ½-inch melon cutter. Roll in Parmesan cheese and spear with a toothpick. Stick into a grapefruit and surround with fresh mint.

MUSHROOMS

Choose medium to small mushrooms. Wash them carefully and dry well. Trim off the stem ends. Dip each mushroom into a lemon juice solution (1 teaspoon of lemon juice to a quarter cup water). Serve stem side up around a small bowl of seasoned salt or Vege-Sal.

THE FINAL RECKONING

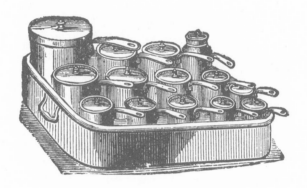

A Reference Chapter

Basic White Sauce

YIELD: 2 CUPS

4 tablespoons butter or margarine   *2 cups milk*
4 tablespoons whole wheat flour   *Salt and pepper*

Heat the butter or margarine in a small, heavy saucepan. Stir in the flour and cook 2 minutes over moderate heat, stirring with a fork or whisking until smoothly blended.

Add half the milk and stir vigorously with a whisk while the mixture comes to a boil. When it is smooth, add the remaining milk and continue to cook and stir until the sauce thickens. Season to taste with salt and pepper.

Halve or double the ingredients to make a smaller or a larger quantity. White sauce may be stored in a covered container in the refrigerator for several days, or in the freezer for months. If it separates after freezing, spin it in a blender or whisk vigorously until smooth again.

Cheese Sauce

YIELD: ABOUT 3 CUPS

2 cups white sauce   *¼ teaspoon paprika*
2 cups grated Cheddar cheese

Make the white sauce. When it is smooth, reduce the heat and stir in the grated cheese and paprika. Stir until the cheese melts.

Mock Tartar Sauce

YIELD: 1 SCANT CUP

½ cup white sauce

¼ cup mayonnaise

1 tablespoon minced onion

1 tablespoon minced green pepper

1 tablespoon minced sweet pickle

2 teaspoons lemon juice or vinegar

Combine the white sauce and the mayonnaise and blend well. Stir in the other ingredients and store, covered, in the refrigerator until serving time.

Tomato Sauce

YIELD: ABOUT 1 QUART

2 tablespoons butter

2 tablespoons olive oil

½ cup chopped onion

1 large clove garlic, minced

1 large (20-ounce) can plum tomatoes

1 6-ounce can tomato paste

½ cup red wine

1 cup water

1 teaspoon salt

½ teaspoon sugar

¼ teaspoon black pepper

2 teaspoons chopped fresh basil or

   ½ teaspoon dried basil

½ teaspoon oregano

Heat the butter and oil and sauté the onion and garlic just until soft. Add the remaining ingredients and whisk over high heat until the mixture comes to a boil. Reduce the heat and cook gently for 30 minutes, stirring frequently.

Mushroom Sauce

YIELD: ABOUT 2 1/3 CUPS

Butter or margarine
2 tablespoons finely chopped onion
3 tablespoons whole wheat flour
1½ cups beef stock or canned bouillon
2 tablespoons Madeira or sherry

½ pound mushrooms
1 teaspoon lemon juice
1/8 teaspoon nutmeg
Salt and pepper

Heat 3 tablespoons of the butter or margarine in a saucepan. Add the onion and cook until lightly browned. Remove the onion with a slotted spoon and discard. Add the flour and, stirring slowly, let the mixture brown. Add the stock or bouillon and wine. Stir until smooth. Reduce the heat to low and simmer, covered, for 20 minutes.

Meanwhile clean and slice the mushrooms lenghwise and sauté them in 3 tablespoons of butter or margarine until almost dry. Add the lemon juice and nutmeg and combine with the sauce for the last few minutes of cooking. Season to taste with salt and pepper.

Blended Cashew Gravy

YIELD: ABOUT 2 CUPS

2 tablespoons arrowroot flour or
  cornstarch
2 cups water
½ cup chopped cashew nuts

½ teaspoon salt
2 tablespoons onion powder
2 tablespoons tamari (soy sauce)
2 tablespoons vegetable oil

In a saucepan combine the arrowroot flour or cornstarch and the water. Stir until dissolved. Add the other ingredients and cook, stirring continually, until the mixture thickens.

Serve cashew gravy with meatless main dishes such as Vegetarian Meat Loaf and Oat Burgers, or on cooked brown rice.

Whole Wheat Sausage Stuffing

YIELD: ABOUT 4½ CUPS OF STUFFING

½ pound lean bulk sausage
½ cup chopped green pepper
½ cup chopped onion
1 cup chicken broth
1 teaspoon salt

½ teaspoon sage
½ teaspoon crushed rosemary
½ teaspoon thyme
½ teaspoon pepper
4 cups whole wheat bread crumbs

Place the sausage in a large skillet and cook it over moderate heat, stirring frequently, until browned. Do not overcook.

Add the green pepper and onions and continue cooking, stirring frequently, until the vegetables are just tender.

Stir in the chicken broth and the seasonings and bring to a boil. Remove from the heat.

Add the bread crumbs to the hot liquid and stir just until all moisture is absorbed. Cover and let stand 5 minutes.

Serve in Baked Acorn Squash or use as a stuffing for poultry (turkey, capon or roasting chicken).

Corn Bread Stuffing

YIELD: 3 TO 4 CUPS OF STUFFING

Old-fashioned corn bread,
  broken into crumbs
½ cup finely chopped onion
½ cup finely chopped celery
½ cup melted butter, margarine or
  bacon drippings

1 cup soft whole wheat bread crumbs
1 teaspoon salt
¼ teaspoon white pepper
½ teaspoon poultry seasoning
¼-½ cup hot water

Make the corn bread unless you have some left over. You will need 2 to 3 cups of crumbs, depending on how the stuffing is to be used.

    Sauté the onion and celery in the hot shortening until the celery is almost tender.

    Add the corn bread, bread crumbs and seasonings and toss lightly to mix.

    Sprinkle the hot water over the top. If you prefer a dry stuffing, add ¼ cup. Increase the amount of water for a more moist dressing. Toss until blended.

    Taste for seasoning and use as directed.

Savory Mint Stuffing

YIELD: ABOUT 3½ CUPS OF STUFFING

3 cups day-old whole wheat bread cubes
3 tablespoons butter or margarine
1 cup sliced mushrooms
4 tablespoons chopped onion
4 tablespoons diced celery
2 tablespoons chopped parsley
½ cup chicken stock or broth

¾ teaspoon garlic salt
¼ teaspoon rosemary leaves
¼ teaspoon thyme
¼ teaspoon crushed mint leaves
1/8 teaspoon freshly ground black
  pepper

Place the bread cubes in a mixing bowl.

Heat the butter and sauté the mushrooms, onion, celery and parsley until the onions are tender.

Add the chicken stock and seasonings and, when well blended, pour over the bread cubes. Toss until well moistened.

Use as a stuffing or bake in an ovenproof serving dish about 30 minutes at 350 degrees F. and serve as a side dish with roast lamb.

Savory Bran Dressing

YIELD: ABOUT 4½ CUPS

¼ cup butter or margarine
¼ cup finely chopped celery
¼ cup finely chopped onion
1 tablespoon chopped parsley
½ cup water
½ teaspoon poultry seasoning

1 can condensed cream of mushroom
   soup or 1¼ cups homemade
   mushroom sauce
1 egg, beaten
1 cup wheat bran cereal
4 cups dry bread cubes

Melt the butter or margarine in a large saucepan. Add the celery and onion and cook over moderate heat, stirring frequently, until the vegetables are almost tender. Remove from the heat.

Add the water, parsley, poultry seasoning, soup or sauce and the egg. Stir until blended.

Add the bran cereal and bread cubes and toss lightly until the cereal and bread cubes are evenly moistened. Use as stuffing for poultry or spread in an oiled 8-inch by 8-inch pan and bake for 30 minutes at 375 degrees F.

Cream Cheese-Honey Frosting

YIELD: FROSTING FOR 1 LARGE CAKE

4 ounces cream cheese, softened
2 tablespoons milk
½ cup honey

1 teaspoon vanilla extract
2½-3 cups nonfat dry milk powder
Dash of salt

Combine the cream cheese, milk, honey and vanilla. Beat until smooth.

Beat in the dry milk powder and salt.

Variation: For chocolate-flavored frosting, beat in 1 to 2 tablespoons carob powder.

Cream Cheese-Maple Frosting

YIELD: FROSTING FOR 1 LARGE CAKE

8 ounces cream cheese, softened
2 tablespoons milk
½ cup soft butter or margarine

1 teaspoon vanilla extract
3 tablespoons maple syrup
1 cup nonfat dry milk powder

Combine the cream cheese, milk, butter or margarine, vanilla extract and maple syrup. Beat until smooth.

Beat in the dry milk powder.

Ingredient Information

Alfalfa. A legume rich in vitamin K, calcium and other vitamins and minerals. The leaves, seeds and sprouts are edible.

Arrowroot flour. An unrefined product that is a good source of minerals. It may be used in place of cornstarch for thickening soups, sauces and gravies.

Baking powder. Rumford brand, a phosphate-based baking powder, is preferred by some to the double acting or tartrate-type products. Also available: a low-sodium baking powder.

Barley. One of the oldest of the cereal grains, now grown mostly for use in brewing beer. The milled or "pearled" barley found in supermarkets has little nutritional value. Look for natural brown barley (hulled but not polished) which is available at some health food stores. Serve it as a hot cereal, or as a substitute for rice or potatoes.

Barley malt. A natural sweetener made from barley.

Bran. The fiber-rich outer layers of the wheat kernel. Buy unprocessed or miller's bran at health food stores, or the packaged wheat bran cereals available at all supermarkets (they contain some sugar, salt and flavorings, added for palatability). Add bran or bran cereals to ground meat dishes, salads or baked goods as desired to increase the fiber content of these foods.

Brewer's yeast. A food supplement rich in the B vitamins, phosphorus and other minerals, not to be confused with the yeast ordinarily used as a leavening agent in baking. Add 1 teaspoon to 1 tablespoon of brewer's yeast to any soup or bread recipe, as desired. Also called nutritional yeast. One tablespoon per day is recommended as a diet supplement.

Buckwheat. A cereal grain not closely related to wheat, buckwheat is tolerated well by people who are allergic to wheat. Whole or cracked buckwheat is sold under the names buckwheat groats or kasha; serve it as a cooked cereal or as a substitute for rice or potatoes. Buckwheat flour may be used in muffins, waffles, pancakes and dumplings.

Bulgur. Wheat that has been processed by steaming, drying and cracking, so as to cook more quickly than ordinary wheat. Serve cooked bulgur as a hot breakfast cereal, or as a substitute for rice or pasta, or use as a meat extender (use up to 1¼ cups of dry bulgur with 1 pound of ground meat, adding 1 cup additional liquid, which the bulgur will absorb as it cooks).

Carob flour, powder or chips. A natural sweetener made from the dried fruit of the St. Johnsbread tree, carob has a flavor similar to chocolate. Carob products are tolerated well by many persons allergic to chocolate, and they do not contain the stimulant caffeine that is in chocolate. Carob is also a good source of the B vitamins.

Chick-peas (garbanzos). A legume that is a good source of protein. Available dried or cooked and canned among the ethnic foods at supermarkets, or at Italian or Spanish groceries.

Coconut. A natural sweetener that is also a good source of fiber. Grated fresh coconut is preferred, but when it is not available use unsweetened grated or flaked coconut.

Cornmeal. Stone-ground yellow cornmeal packaged without preservatives is available at many supermarkets as well as health food stores. Keep it in the refrigerator or freezer, to avoid spoilage.

Date sugar. A natural sweetener made from dried and finely ground dates. Serve it with cereals, or use it as you would use brown sugar. Buy it at health food stores.

Dulse. Dried seaweed, dark red color, dulse is rich in iodine and other minerals found in the sea. Buy it at health food stores or at Oriental groceries.

Familia. A granola-like cereal mixture containing dried fruits and nuts.

Flaked rice, rye and wheat. Grains that have been steamed and rolled flat, similar to rolled oats. Use the flakes "as is," toast them and add to granola mixes, or cook and serve as hot cereal.

Flax seeds and sprouts. Flax seed meal and flax seeds for sprouting may be purchased at health food stores. Like other seeds, a good quick-energy food containing protein, vitamins and minerals.

Flour. Stone-ground whole grain flours (100 percent extraction—meaning the flour contains all parts of the grain) are preferred for most purposes; they are available at some supermarkets as well as health food stores. Wheat flour is the only kind that contains much of the gluten which forms the structure of bread by becoming smooth and stretchy when kneaded, so rye flour, cornmeal and other flours are combined with some wheat flour when used to make bread. Store whole-grain flours in the refrigerator or freezer, as they spoil more quickly than refined white flour. When a lighter-textured product is required, or for making pie pastry, use a combination of whole wheat and unbleached white flour or the whole wheat pastry flour available at health food shops.

Honey. A highly concentrated natural sweetener, honey varies in flavor, texture and color depending on the kinds of flowers from which the bees gathered nectar. Mild flavored honey is most suitable for table use or for use in baking. Substitute ½ to 2/3 cup of honey for 1 cup sugar, and reduce slightly the amount of liquid called for in the recipe. Since baked goods made with honey brown quickly, you may wish to bake at a slightly lower temperature.

Kelp. Dried seaweed that may be used as a salt substitute and a nutritional supplement, kelp may be purchased in powdered form at health food stores. It is one of the best natural sources of iodine, and it is also a good source of the B-complex and other vitamins.

Lentils. Dried lentils, whole or split, may be purchased at most supermarkets. Like dried peas and beans, they are legumes useful as low-cost sources of protein. Use them in soups, salads and in vegetarian main dishes.

Millet. The traditional cereal grain of Africa, millet has a pleasantly mild flavor and is a good source of fiber. Buy the grains hulled, whole or cracked, from health food stores. Serve as a hot breakfast cereal or as a substitute for rice or pasta, or sprout the seeds.

Miso. A fermented paste made of soybeans and barley, miso is a good source of protein, potassium, phosphorus and other minerals. Use it in soups or as a thickener in sauces. It is available along with cheeses in some supermarkets and at Oriental groceries.

Molasses. A liquid sweetener derived from sugar cane or sugar beets, molasses contains varying amounts of trace minerals and vitamins. One disadvantage is the distinctive, sometimes strong, flavor that makes molasses unsuitable for some uses. The light-colored and sorghum varieties are mildest. Blackstrap molasses has the strongest flavor; it is also the richest source of vitamins and minerals. Use unsulfured molasses as a sweetener on cereals, pancakes and waffles, or in recipes as a substitute for an equal quantity of sugar. As a nutritional supplement, 1 tablespoon of blackstrap molasses daily is suggested.

Mung beans. Excellent for sprouting. Buy the seeds at health food stores and Oriental groceries.

Nuts. Nuts are a rich source of unsaturated fats, protein, the B complex vitamins, vitamin E, trace minerals and fiber. Naturally sweet, nuts can serve as a substitute for candy and snack foods. Buy raw fresh nuts when available. Store shelled nuts in the refrigerator, as the oils they contain make them subject to rapid spoilage.

Oats. Whole oats (sometimes called oat groats), steel-cut or cracked oats and oat flour may be purchased at health food stores, while oatmeal (rolled oats) is to be found in every supermarket. Use rolled oats as a casserole topping or an extender for ground meat mixtures, or serve it as a breakfast cereal. The slow-cooking variety is preferred for most uses. Serve cooked whole grain oats as a hot breakfast cereal, or as a substitute for rice or potatoes.

Oils. Preferred for cooking uses are the vegetable oils highest in unsaturated fats: safflower, corn, sunflower, soybean, sesame and olive oils. They should be cold-pressed, as heat in processing destroys some vitamins. Avoid coconut and cottonseed oils which are likely to be higher in saturated fats, also hydrogenated shortenings and lard.

Pastas. Spaghetti, macaroni and noodles made from whole wheat flour are nutritionally superior to those made from white flour. Also available: spinach noodles.

Peanuts and peanut butter. Like the other legume seeds, peanuts are a good low-cost source of protein, iron and the B vitamins. Buy fresh raw peanuts when available. Buy peanut butter that is unhydrogenated and without additives at health food stores, or make your own from freshly ground peanuts.

Peas. Fresh green peas are the immature seed of this legume. The mature dried seed is available whole or split at most supermarkets; use it in soups and in vegetarian main dishes. Like beans and lentils, a good low-cost source of protein and minerals.

Pumpkin seeds. Like other seeds, a quick-energy food good for snacking. Pumpkin and squash seeds are rich in protein, the B vitamins and vitamins A, D and E along with some minerals. For extra nutrition, add pumpkin seeds to salads, casseroles or cookies.

Rice. Brown, unpolished rice which retains the outer layer of bran is richer in fiber, protein, trace minerals and vitamin E than milled white rice, so it is preferred for all uses. Because of the bran layer, brown rice requires more water for cooking and a longer cooking time (2½ cups liquid to 1 cup of rice, simmer 45 to 55 minutes). Compared to white rice, the brown is less light and fluffy; it has a firmer texture and a pleasant nut-like flavor. Due to natural oils in the bran layer, brown rice won't keep on the shelf as long as white rice; store it in the refrigerator.

Salt. Sea salt made by evaporating seawater is a good source of iodine and several of the trace minerals; buy it at health food stores, or buy iodized salt. Many people consume too much salt, causing a mineral imbalance in the body that can contribute to numerous health problems. Vege-Sal, Spike, tamari or soy sauce, garlic, kelp and fresh herbs can replace all or part of the salt you normally use to season foods, to reduce the family's salt consumption.

Sesame seeds and sprouts. Buy the unhulled, unpolished seeds when available; they are a source of fiber as well as protein, vitamins and minerals. Add sesame seeds to snack mixes, casseroles and baked goods. Sesame seed sprouts are an excellent source of vitamin C. Buy at health food and specialty shops. Also available: sesame seed meal and sesame seed paste (tahini) similar to peanut butter.

Soybeans and sprouts. A nutritious legume native to Asia, the soybean is now widely cultivated in the United States but mostly for industrial purposes or as livestock feed. Health food stores sell the seeds, excellent for sprouting, and also soy (soya) flour which is rich in protein, soy milk and soy grits. To add extra nutrition to baked goods, replace 1 or 2 tablespoons of each cup of wheat flour with soy flour. Miso, tofu and tamari are products of fermented soybean origin available at Oriental food shops.

Spike. A mixture of dried vegetables, used for seasoning.

Sprouts. When seeds sprout and begin to grow the starches they contain are rapidly converted into natural sugars, vitamins, proteins and enzymes. For example, the dry soybean seed contains no vitamin C at all, while the sprouted soybean, when eaten raw in salads or sandwiches, is a good source of vitamin C. Sprouts are an excellent source of vitamins A, D, E and the B complex vitamins, as well as C, and the minerals calcium, magnesium, phosphorus and potassium. They are easy to grow—no elaborate equipment is required—and very economical, since a few seeds swell into a much larger quantity of sprouts. Use sprouts raw in salads and sandwiches or add them to cooked dishes. They can also be toasted and salted like nuts. The flavors and textures vary, so try several different kinds to learn which you prefer. (See How to Sprout Seeds.)

Sugar. A quick energy food, sugar occurs naturally but in varying quantities in all foods derived from plants, including all fruits and vegetables. Most of the sugar produced commercially for industrial uses and for use in foods is derived from sugar cane or sugar beets, but many other plants are also sources of sugar. Corn syrup is made from corn; maple syrup and maple sugar from the sap of the maple tree. Sugar made from grapes has some special uses.

Sunflower seeds. Available hulled or unhulled at health food stores, sunflower seeds are an excellent source of protein. Other products include flour (sunflower seed meal) and oil. Sprouted sunflower seeds are an excellent source of vitamin C. Use the seeds in snack mixes, the sprouts in salads and sandwiches.

Tahini. A butterlike paste made of sesame seeds. Buy it at health food stores.

Tamari. A superior variety of soy sauce, made of naturally aged and fermented soybeans and wheat without additives. Buy at health food stores and Oriental groceries.

Tofu. Also called beancurd or soybean cheese, tofu is rich in usable protein and the minerals calcium and phosphorus. It is available at health food stores or Oriental groceries. Use it in soups, salad dressings and in vegetarian main dishes.

Vegetable stock or broth. Vegetable stock is the liquid the wise cook saves when cooking vegetables and stores in a covered jar in the refrigerator. Additional stock can be made from vegetable trimmings—pea pods, carrot skins, bean ends, parsley stems and onion tops—cooked in lightly salted water to cover. Simmer for 30 minutes, then strain and store in the refrigerator. Use vegetable stock to add nutrition and flavor when making soups and sauces.

Vinegar. Apple cider vinegar is preferred over distilled vinegar; it is a natural acid containing valuable minerals and it has a better flavor.

Wheat. When whole grains of wheat are sold for human consumption they are usually called wheat berries. They are excellent for sprouting. Also available at health food stores: cracked wheat and bulgur. Serve as a hot breakfast cereal or as a substitute for rice or pasta.

Wheat germ. The embryo within the wheat kernel, the part from which a new plant can grow. Rich in vitamins, fat and other nutrients, it is removed and discarded in the milling of refined white flour. Fresh, raw wheat germ is preferred; it can be purchased at health food stores and at some supermarkets. Store it in the refrigerator, as the natural oils it contains make it subject to spoilage. Toasted and sweetened wheat germ which is more expensive may be purchased at supermarkets. Sprinkle wheat germ on ready-to-eat cereals, salads, meat dishes or desserts.

Yeast. Bakers bulk dry yeast which may be purchased at health food shops is preferred, as it contains no additives or preservatives. One tablespoon of the bulk yeast is equal to one envelope of the packaged kind.

Yogurt. The beneficial bacteria contained in yogurt make it a natural antibiotic as well as a food supplement rich in the B complex vitamins, vitamins A and D and protein. It is a milk product, fermented by a mixture of bacteria and yeast. Homemade yogurt is preferred, as much of that produced commercially contains artificial preservatives. One tablespoon per day is suggested as a diet supplement.

How to Cook Grains and Pasta

To cook 1 cup of white rice, wheat berries, cracked wheat, bulgur, barley or oats you will need 2 cups of liquid (water or broth). To cook 1 cup of brown rice, millet or buckwheat you will need 3 cups of liquid. Wash the grains in cold water before cooking. Bring the proper amount of liquid to a boil. Stir in the grains. Return to a boil, cover and simmer gently until the liquid is absorbed and the grains are tender. Cooking time will vary from 20 minutes for bulgur or white rice to 45 or 50 minutes for brown rice or millet. Add salt if desired.

To cook pasta (macaroni, noodles, spaghetti, etc.) bring a large kettle of salted water to a full rolling boil. Add the pasta gradually so that the water never stops boiling. Continue to boil until the pasta is just tender but not mushy (5 or 6 minutes for white flour products, 8 to 10 minutes for whole wheat). When cooking a large quantity of pasta add 1 tablespoon vegetable oil to the water to prevent sticking.

How to Sprout Seeds

A *Saturday Evening Post* reader suggests this somewhat unorthodox but very easy method that works beautifully for her. She writes:

"I use a plastic container that is about 6 inches high and 6 inches across and holds 10 cups of liquid. With an ice pick I punch 3 or 4 holes on one side of it, about 1 inch up from the bottom, for the water to drain through. I put anywhere from ½ cup to 2 cups of seeds into it (mung beans, lentils, sunflower seeds, etc.) and then fill it with water and set it on the edge of my sink to drain. I usually do this 2 or 3 times a day. In about 3 or 4 days the seeds sprout and are ready to eat. Then I drain them and refrigerate them. If I rinse them thoroughly every 2 or 3 days, to prevent the growth of bacteria, they keep very well in the refrigerator."

Almost any whole, untreated seeds may be sprouted. Some suggestions:

Alfalfa seeds sprout in 3 or 4 days and are ready to eat when 1 to 2 inches long.

Lentils sprout in about 3 days and are ready to eat when ½ to 1 inch long.

Mung beans sprout in 2 or 3 days and are ready to eat when 2 to 3 inches long.

Soybeans sprout in about 3 days and are ready to eat when ½ to ¾ inch long.

Wheat and most other grains sprout in 2 days and should be eaten when the sprout is the length of the seed.

Sunflower seeds sprout in 2 days and should be eaten when ¼ inch long.

Garbanzos (chickpeas) sprout in 3 days and should be eaten when 1 inch long.

Begin by washing the seeds or beans well and discarding any that float. Soak the seeds overnight in a generous quantity of warm water. In the morning, drain off the water but do not discard it, as it will contain nutrients. Use it for vegetable stock, or use it to water your house plants. Place the seeds or beans in the sprouting container where they will be moist, warm and dark but not without ventilation. If the sink-edge plastic container method doesn't work well, try one of the following containers: (1) A clean, unglazed clay flowerpot that has been soaked in water. Plug the hole loosely, set it in a shallow pan of water and cover with a saucer. (2) A wire strainer (for small seeds) or a colander (for beans). To rinse, hold container under the tap. At other times keep the container covered with a clean, moist cloth so the seeds don't dry out.

FOODS THAT ARE SOURCES OF FIBER

Quantities listed are the calories of food energy and the grams of crude fiber in one 100-gram serving of the edible portion.

	Calories	FIBER Grams		Calories	FIBER Grams
Almonds	598	2.6	Cashew nuts	561	1.4
Apples, unpeeled	58	1.0	Cauliflower	27	1.0
Apples, peeled	54	.6	Celery	17	.6
Apricots	51	.6	Cherries	58	.1
Apricots, dried	332	3.8	Chestnuts	194	1.1
Artichokes	24	2.4	Chives	28	1.1
Asparagus	20	.7	Coconut	346	.5
Avocado	167	1.6	Collards	45	1.2
Banana	85	.5	Corn, sweet	83	.7
Barley, pearled	349	.5	Corn cereals		
Beans, dry, cooked	118	1.5	Flakes	386	.7
Beans, green or snap	32	1.0	Puffed	399	.4
Beans, mung, sprouted	35	.7	Corn bread	207	.5
Beets	32	.8	Crackers		
Beet greens	18	1.1	Saltines	433	.4
Black-eyed peas	108	1.8	Graham	384	1.1
Blackberries	58	4.1	Whole wheat	403	2.4
Blueberries	62	1.5	Rye, whole grain	342	2.2
Boysenberries	36	1.9	Cranberries	46	1.4
Bran (see Wheat bran)			Cucumbers	15	.6
Bran cereals (see Wheat			Currants	54	2.4
bran cereals)			Dandelion greens	33	1.3
Brazil nuts	654	3.1	Dates	274	2.3
Bread			Eggplant	19	.9
Boston brown	211	.7	Elderberries	72	7.0
Cracked wheat	263	.5	Endive (escarole)	20	.9
Raisin	262	.9	Farina	271	.4
Rye	243	.4	Figs, fresh	80	1.2
Pumpernickel	246	1.1	Figs, dried	274	5.6
White	219	.2	Filberts (hazelnuts)	634	3.0
Whole wheat	243	1.6	Gooseberries	39	1.9
Broccoli	26	1.5	Grapefruit	41	.2
Brussels sprouts	36	1.6	Grapes	69	.6
Bulgur, cooked	168	.8	Grits (hominy), cooked	51	.1
Cabbage	24	.8	Guavas	62	5.6
Cantaloupe	30	.3	Hickory nuts	673	1.9
Carrots	42	1.0	Kale	38	1.3

| | | FIBER | | | FIBER |
	Calories	*Grams*		*Calories*	*Grams*
Kohlrabi	24	1.0	Peppers, green	22	1.4
Kumquats	65	3.7	Persimmons	127	1.5
Leeks	52	1.3	Pimiento, canned	27	.6
Lentils, cooked	106	1.2	Pineapple, fresh	52	.4
Lettuce	13	.5	Pineapple, canned	59	.3
Loganberries	62	3.0	Pistachio nuts	594	1.9
Macadamia nuts	691	2.5	Plums	66	.4
Macaroni, cooked	111	.1	Pomegranate pulp	63	.2
Mangos	66	.9	Popcorn	386	2.2
Millet, cooked	327	3.2	Potatoes, baked in skins	93	.6
Miso (fermented soybeans)	171	2.3	Potatoes, boiled	65	.4
Muffins, bran	261	1.8	Prunes, dried	255	1.6
Muffins, corn	288	.5	Prunes, cooked	119	.8
Mushrooms	28	.8	Pumpkin	33	1.3
Mustard greens	31	.9	Pumpkin seeds	553	1.9
Nectarines	64	.4	Radishes	17	.7
Noodles, cooked	125	.1	Raisins	289	.9
Oat cereals			Raspberries, black	73	5.1
Shredded	379	1.8	Raspberries, red	57	3.0
Puffed	379	1.1	Rhubarb	16	.7
Flakes (with soy)	379	.9	Rice, brown, cooked	119	.3
Oatmeal (rolled oats)			Rice, white, cooked	109	.1
Dry	390	1.2	Rice cereals		
Cooked	55	.2	Flakes	390	.6
Okra	36	1.0	Puffed	399	.6
Olives	116	1.3	Rolls and buns		
Onions, mature	38	.6	White	298	.1
Onions, green (scallions)	36	1.0	With raisins	275	.9
Oranges	49	.5	Whole wheat	257	1.6
Orange juice	45	.1	Rutabagas	35	1.1
Parsley	44	1.4	Sesame seed	582	2.4
Parsnips	66	2.0	Soybeans, cooked	118	1.4
Peaches, fresh	38	.6	Soybeans, sprouted	46	.8
Peaches, canned	58	.4	Spinach	26	.6
Peaches, dried	340	4.0	Squash, summer	19	.6
Peanuts	582	2.7	Squash, winter	50	1.4
Peanut butter	581	1.9	Strawberries	37	1.3
Pears, unpeeled	61	1.4	Sunflower seeds	560	3.8
Pears, canned	32	.7	Sweet potatoes	141	.9
Peas, green	71	2.0	Swiss chard	18	.7
Peas, dry split, cooked	115	.4	Tangerines	46	.5
Pecans	687	2.3	Tomatoes	22	.5

	Calories	FIBER Grams		Calories	FIBER Grams
Turnips	23	.9	Wheat cereals		
Waffles, white flour	279	.1	Hot wheat cereal	65	.2
Walnuts, black	628	1.7	Puffed	363	2.0
Walnuts, English	651	2.1	Shredded	354	2.3
Watercress	19	.7	Wheat and barley		
Watermelon	26	.3	flakes	392	1.8
Wheat bran, unprocessed	213	9.1	Wheat and malted		
Wheat bran cereals			barley granules	391	1.5
All-Bran, Bran Buds	240	7.8	Wheat germ	363	2.5
40% bran flakes	303	3.6	Wild rice	353	1.0
Raisin bran flakes	287	3.0	Zucchini	19	.6

FOODS THAT ARE NOT SOURCES OF FIBER

The foods listed below contain only a trace of fiber (less than .1 gram per 100-gram serving) or no fiber at all.

Meats and poultry	Beverages (except for unstrained lemonade
Fish and shellfish	and orange juice which may contain .1
Dairy products (including cheese)	gram fiber)
Eggs	Sugar and syrups
	Oils and shortenings

Index

Recipes marked "low calorie" serve two persons. For the other recipes see the number of servings indicated where the recipe appears in the book.